GROOVIN'

HORSES, HOPES & SLIPPERY SLOPES

RICH ISRAEL

Sandra Jonas Publishing
Boulder, CO

Sandra Jonas Publishing
PO Box 20892
Boulder, CO 80308
www.sandrajonaspublishing.com

Printed in the United States of America

Book and cover design by Sandra Jonas

Publisher's Cataloguing-in-Publication Data

Names: Israel, Rich.
Title: Groovin' : horses, hopes, and slippery slopes / Rich Israel.
Other titles: Grooving.
Description: Boulder, CO : Sandra Jonas Publishing House, 2017.
Series: The Hippie Adventurer Series.
Identifiers: LCCN 2016954857 | ISBN 9780997487138
Subjects: LCSH: Israel, Rich—Travel—United States. | Hippies—United
    States—Biography. | LCGFT: Autobiographies.
Classification: LCC CT275.I87 | DDC 305.568 — dc23
LC record available at http://lccn.loc.gov/2016954857

PHOTOGRAPHY CREDITS

Adobe Stock/skarin, 1; Adobe Stock/wojciech nowak, 2; Adobe Stock/
tanyadzu, 29; WPClipart, 67; Adobe Stock/jugrozyan, 93; Adobe Stock/
Adrian Niederhäuser, 133; Adobe Stock/Sascha Burkard, 134; Adobe
Stock/miloskontra, 193; Adobe Stock/lolabean, 194; CanStockPhoto/dra-
ganmilenkovic, 287; remaining photographs courtesy of Rich Israel.

In memory of
Jackie Pyka, Ron Tilson, and Jeannie Zazzi,
who live on in these pages

Contents

Author's Note

The 1960s was a time like no other. A time when strong-willed youth, prompted by mind-expanding chemicals, ventured off the straight, hard asphalt of society's mandated route. They searched for softer and more colorful definitions of what it means to be accepted, successful, prosperous, normal, sane, and worthwhile.

Strong visionaries along with the disillusioned walked away and dropped out of the status quo that the social order ambitiously preserved. These adventurers, willing to take youthful rebellion to its limits, earned the label of "flower children," and only the true children of that era know the magic of that time. This is the journey of one young man.

I have been retelling stories about my escapades for nearly fifty years, and was inspired to write them down when I became a father. I wanted my daughter to know more about the fabric that created the person I am—and to transport readers into this special time in our history.

In the late '60s, my moral compass was right on point. My love for adventure propelled me, and my passion and appreciation for life inspired me. In fact, I use the person I was during that time as a mentor—to remind myself of my own potential as a human being.

Prepare yourself for an honest if sometimes youthful portrayal of my actions, thoughts, feelings, strengths, and inadequacies. I don't hide anything. Growing up was never one of my aspirations.

Some of what you read may seem hard to believe. But the experiences and events I describe are true. They have not been construed or embellished. It is said, "If you remember the '60s, you weren't there." (Unless, of course, you're lucky enough to have flashbacks.) Still, I have been blessed with a good memory of the events from that period. For me, it was a time like no other.

In the course of writing this book, I contacted old friends who shared my experiences, and we compared notes. Many of those fine people appear in these pages, though their names have been changed to protect their privacy. And our conversations are fictitious to the extent that exact dialogue is impossible to recollect. But all the pets' names are real.

These stories are my personal treasures, preserved deep within my mind and heart. I have always loved to share valuable thoughts and feelings, whether a beautiful experience or a good tale. I hope you find as much enjoyment in reading about my adventures as I've had in living, remembering, and writing about them.

Though I expose much of the wildness of that time, my intention is not to promote the use of drugs or promiscuous behavior. The risks have increased over the past decades, due to stronger drugs, more dangerous consequences from unprotected sex, and the fact that younger children are experimenting with both.

Nevertheless, these ingredients, along with events like the Civil Rights Movement and the Vietnam War, acted as catalysts to inspire a sizable and positive shift in the evolution of our society. They fueled the hippie phenomenon, which in the '60s began as a brotherhood of love, compassion, rebellion, and the motivation to experience life's essence. This shift in consciousness influenced and is continuing to influence the course of history itself.

PART 1

School Daze:
Getting a *Higher* Education

*One had to cram all this stuff into one's mind for the
examinations, whether one liked it or not . . . It is, in fact,
nothing short of a miracle that the modern methods of instruction have not yet entirely strangled the holy curiosity of
inquiry; for this delicate little plant, aside from stimulation,
stands mainly in need of freedom. Without this
it goes to wrack and ruin without fail.*
—Albert Einstein

1.

Blood, Sweat, and Fears
March 1967

As I faced the danger before me, a battle raged within. A battle between *Oh shit! Oh shit! Oh shit!* and *Man, don't sweat it. You can do this.* The ferocity of my brutal opponents terrified me, but I was determined to push past the fear.

The cold night air nipped at my ears. Stuffed into my funky blue down jacket, I could hardly bend my arms, having layered every shirt and sweater I'd brought. Damn, I must have looked like the Michelin Man.

One foot in front of the other, I told myself, peering into the darkness. Yet my feet seemed caked in lead.

Grisly pictures of bloody victims flashed in my mind. My chest constricted. My heart pounded. Every cell was on high alert. I was no match for what could lie ahead.

Just keep going forward.

Touching the outside pocket of my jeans, I checked for my pocketknife. Still there. Not much of a defense against an opponent with the strength of ten men armed with weapons that could shred a human. *Stop thinking like that.* Even so, it would be like taking on a Sherman tank with a BB gun.

How did the day end up like this? Spring break at the University of California, Davis, had prompted my buddy Rod and me, hungry for adventure, to hitchhike to Yosemite to visit Hal, who worked at the park. When we arrived at his living quarters, we found him with his friends Jeff and Sarah in a fifteen-foot-square, wood-framed canvas tent. The five of us sat huddled together, knee to knee, on two of the four cots, under the light of a single bulb. A crackly version of "Puff the Magic Dragon" played on the radio.

Leaning forward, elbows propped on his thighs, Hal curled both ends of his well-manicured handlebar mustache with his fingers. I had met him the year before, when he was a sophomore and I was a junior. His mustache had impressed the hell out of me, inspiring me to cultivate one of my own.

Sarah, her silky-blonde hair cascading down her shoulders, took out a small red-and-gold tin box full of sugar cubes. She passed it to Hal and then Jeff, who each took one, rolled it with admiration in their fingers, and tossed it into their mouths.

Sporting a silly grin, Hal cocked his head at us. "Acid, guys?"

"Hmm . . ." Rod raised his eyebrows and flashed me a crooked smile.

"What the hell!" was all I could say, and we joined the party.

The world of hallucinogens was new to me, though I had smoked pot for over a year, thanks to Hal, who had helped me score my first weed, packaged in a small Diamond matchbox.

I didn't notice the acid initially, but an hour or two later, the odd sensations became too intense to deny. The inside of the tent, drab upon my arrival, exploded with sharp, vivid colors, like a scene out of *Fantasia*. I could hear a noise beyond the songs on the radio, something between a faint tone and soft breeze undulating in my head. The sound increased and decreased with a will of its own, as if someone were playing with the volume dial on my ethereal radio:

Whoosh . . . Buzzzz . . . Zing . . . Whirrrr

When Sarah removed her wig and became a brunette with a pixie cut, Rod jumped up and shouted, "Jeez Louise! Did I really see that?"

He paced back and forth over the scrap of floor space not occupied by bunks, his arms flailing the way they did when he was excited, like a marionette handled by someone with the jerks. Then he fell back in a slump on one of the beds, wildly shaking his mop of curly hair. We all laughed hard and long, clutching our sides. I thought my ribs would crack.

Later in the evening, when I wandered into the bathhouse to take a leak, it felt like I was there for hours, but who could tell? My concept of time had vanished. Hallucinations were coming on strong. When I looked in the mirror, instead of my familiar mustached face and shaggy dark hair, a stream of freaky images morphed before my eyes, one after the other.

I swear I could see right through my skin to every one of my blood vessels, veins, and capillaries, and all the blood cells flowing through them. Then each muscle in my face appeared, as if I were reading some physiology book. Next, the bones of my face became distinct— my skull, my jawbone with all my teeth, every filling visible. A kaleidoscope of facial tissues and colors swam in the mirror, like a child's finger painting.

Sometimes my features would turn into different characters, personalities, and creatures, from frightening to inviting, from grotesque to beautiful. It was difficult to watch—but I couldn't tear myself away, gripping the sink in disbelief. Was this for real?

That's when my mind switched to bears. Every story I'd heard about Yosemite as a child had a bear mauling in it. "Beware of the bears!" "Don't feed the bears!" The bloody stories. The thought of being someone's dinner sent shivers down my spine. Bears? Why so much fear about bears? Had it always been there, and I just wasn't aware of it?

I was a rational person and often looked at my feelings in a therapeutic way, weighing what was fact and disregarding irrational emotions and reactions. Even in my far-from-normal state, a soft voice told me my fears were foolish. Standing in the bathhouse, I decided to confront this nagging dread and walk off into the woods.

I approached the halfway mark across the immense clearing, an empty dirt parking lot that separated the tiny tent city from the deep woods. The light from a single, tall wooden lamppost mingled with the faint night mist, bathing the area in an eerie glow. My nose was numb and moist from the chilly air, and though I hated the restriction of heavy clothing, I was grateful for its warmth.

No bear in his right mind would break hibernation and come out when it was this cold. Feeling emboldened, I moved forward, placing each step lightly, but the dirt and gravel scrunched under my feet, shattering the silence. *Shhhhh!* I sounded like a moose stomping through a field of cornflakes.

It must have been near midnight, but there was no way I'd take my eyes off the darkness to check my watch. An image popped into my mind of a guy I heard about who had hid food under his pillow while camping in bear country. . . I shook it off and moved ahead, all thoughts about time forgotten.

Behind me, perhaps forty to fifty feet, were the tent and Hal's '52 Willys Jeep station wagon backed up to the entrance. Along with the far-off music from Hal's radio, I could hear the occasional steel clang of something being thrown on the metal tailgate as the guys loaded the car for the trip down the mountain in the morning.

It had taken me forever to get as far as I had. And with each excruciating step, my heart drummed harder.

By now the edge of the dense woods was ten yards in front of me.
You can still turn back . . .
No! Stop it!
The battle within me continued, the two voices shouting in my head. Shouted? Could thoughts have volume?

I saw the dark outlines of the trees.
Why the hell are you doing this? Go back!
Shut up! Don't be silly.
Still two voices? Who would win?

Whoosh . . . Buzzzz . . . Zing . . . Whirrrr

I flashed back to when I was five years old and about to have my tonsils removed. The nurse placed an ether mask over my face and said, "Take a deep breath." Programmed to please, I inhaled the vapors, and that's when the nightmares began. I remembered running down a narrow path with deep drop-offs raging with violent flames on both sides. Beyond the flames was only darkness. And all the while, I was being chased by a large, ferocious bear.

One more step. All that spelled safety was behind me. I gulped and turned for a last look at the tent and Hal's Jeep silhouetted in a hazy glow. How comforting they both felt, and yet so far away. Then something caught my eye. Two men in park ranger uniforms were heading toward the vehicle.

I leaped the last step into the woods and observed from a place of concealment. The rangers marched to the tent as Hal and Jeff came out to meet them, Hal standing at least a foot taller than Jeff.

The rangers' sharp tone pierced the quiet. I couldn't make out their words, but I picked up enough from all the arm waving and finger pointing. Though it was doing no harm, the Jeep was in an area not designated for parking and had to be moved.

Watching Hal climb into the driver's seat, I felt a strange shift in my body and looked down to see that I had transformed into a deer, a huge buck to be precise, heavy antlers weighing on my head. My movements became quick and cautious as I peered at the scene from between two young oaks, adjusting my neck to observe every detail. I shriveled my moist black nose to pick up the human scent, but the chill and the distance made it impossible.

Adrenaline raced through my veins, causing my tail to twitch and my legs to tremble as they prepared for flight. I moved with stealth, careful not to brush my antlers against the foliage and give myself away.

What was once a place of refuge was now an unfriendly threat. Instead, I felt secure in the comfort of the woods. Nothing in the darkness behind me felt sinister anymore. Any fear of bears in Yosemite had disappeared.

This was my real home, where I belonged. How could I have distrusted the domain of nature?

We are nature. There is no separation.

My head tilted to the right at the sound of gravel snapping and crumbling under the Jeep's tires as it rolled toward the parking area.

2.

What, Me Worry?

March 1967

The following morning, Hal's Jeep rambled noisily down the mountain highway, heading back to Davis. Hal sat in the driver's seat, Jeff at shotgun, and Rod behind the two guys, his head hunched over between them. I use the word "seat" loosely. Hal had installed a hot engine in the thing, a 1961 Chevy V-8, but cared little about seating. He reclined in an old wooden lawn chair with arm rests, the legs removed, and both Jeff and Rod joggled around on upside-down wood-and-metal milk crates, anchoring their crude furniture with the weight of their bodies.

My dad, a highway engineer for the state of California and a fanatic about seat belts, would have pissed his pants.

In the back, I stretched out on a thin gray mattress—the kind I imagined on every military, prison, and asylum bunk in the nation (though prior experience for me was limited to Boy Scout camp). An inch thick, probably stuffed with cotton, it felt wonderfully comfortable to my weary body, even though it rested on the steel-ribbed bed of the Jeep.

My head was fuzzy, and the world seemed distant. It was as though my brain had swollen and pressed against the inside of my skull—no doubt the product of overworked synapses coupled with lack of sleep.

I stared as if in a dream at the paisley design on the material lining the Jeep's ceiling. The night before, when I was ripped, the dimly lit pale-green canvas ceiling and walls of the tent had broken out in a paisley design. Now I understood why my stoner friends loved paisleys.

As I lay with my head over the Jeep's rear axle, I marveled at the near-deafening racket: an awkward symphony of vehicular sounds mixed with music from Hal's makeshift tape deck.

I picked out various sources: a loose license plate clanged, the chains on the tail gate jangled, the under-inflated tires on the asphalt groaned, the wrenches in Hal's metal toolbox jiggled, the unlatched back-window hatch flopped, and the two out-of-sync rusty hinges squeaked—all of that coupled with the overpowering rattling of the tin-can shell of the Jeep and the whooshing of air through the open windows.

And somehow, mysteriously, Ravi's loud, melodious sitar playing at the front of the Jeep drew the confusion of sounds into a marvelous, twisted harmony. Every pothole we hit bounced me along with the sounds of the toolbox and tailgate—like crashing cymbals at the end of a drumroll.

The voices and laughter of my friends occasionally broke through when their banter rose in volume. But the deafening chorus kept lulling me away from their conversation, back into my own thoughts. I treasured the solitude.

I hadn't always been this mellow. As the coddled child of a Jewish mother, I fretted about most things. Jewish mothers often have a high-strung worry gene they desperately try to pass on to their offspring. For many years my mother's attempts succeeded, especially in pressure situations. When I took a test, worry would paralyze me, greatly hampering my ability to answer questions.

But all that changed my senior year in high school—in Mr. Flimberg's physics class.

If you projected a life-sized shadow of a bowling pin onto a wall, you'd see a perfect silhouette of Mr. Flimberg. The poor man spent his youth carrying mortar for bricklayers, and his shoulders never developed properly. The bigger tragedy was that if a real bowling pin had taught that physics class, it would have been more fun. Flimberg managed to take boring to a new, impressive level, making his class as exciting as watching snails race uphill. Of course, my lack of interest in the subject didn't help.

I probably should have felt more sympathy for the unfortunate fellow, but at age seventeen, I focused more on my own excessive boredom. Still, as they say, God works in mysterious ways.

A couple of months before graduation, in the spring of 1963, my mind was doing its usual crazy thing during a physics quiz. I was worrying and thinking, worrying and thinking, when out of nowhere, a thought exploded in my head: *Why worry?*

A river of thoughts always rages through our brains. But once in a long while, a special idea gets lodged in an understanding neuron and takes hold. My consciousness shifted. *Why worry? . . . Why worry?*

It's so simple. Worrying has absolutely no effect on the outcome of any situation. If we worry and the undesired result actually happens, the worrying didn't prevent it. And if the undesired result doesn't happen, we wasted all that time making ourselves miserable for nothing.

The only thing that worrying offers is agony and discomfort while we wait for the normal unfolding of our lives. We each have the choice to engage in this preoccupation or abandon it.

How beautiful. We can go from A to B with or without fretting. And "without" is much more pleasant.

I realized this on more than just an intellectual level. Thanks in part to Mr. Flimberg, I had the sort of deep, gut-level epiphany that rewires our belief system so we no longer think or behave in the same way. I soon found that worry had clouded my judgment, and without it, I could see more clearly than ever before.

From then on, I became a mellow, slow-moving, relaxed fellow. Without the interference of fearing the outcome of my actions, the qualities of compassion, honesty, gratitude, and respect could emerge. No longer anxious about what others might think, say, or do, I was free to observe them as they really were. Their masks melted away, and their true feelings became apparent. And I saw that most people were simply looking for love, acceptance, and safety.

As a result, my love for others and for having fun grew, and my thirst for experiencing life intensified. Though some occasions called for legitimate concern, worry was something I rarely bothered with.

In the end, my mom failed in her mission—and that was a good thing.

I smiled. Bears were off that worry list now as well.

Alfred E. Neuman's face popped into my head—the freckled-faced poster boy for *Mad Magazine*, with his unkempt hair and foolish, gap-toothed grin, who always said, "What, me worry?" I shared the same realization with one of the lesser minds of the time. Was it possible that his silly smirk really hid the musings of a sage? I could have felt embarrassed to find I had something in common with goofy old Alfred, but guess what? It didn't worry me at all.

3.

Chasing Love
March 1967

A pothole jostled me out of my daydream, nearly sending me airborne, but my body was too rag-doll loose to register any complaints. I was aware again of the racket and the distant voices of my friends. Rod went on about someone he had met, but only snippets reached me through the noise: ". . . groovy chick . . . zoology class . . . hotter than . . . believe me . . . not shy . . ."

I couldn't wrap my head around getting back to studying. I had no great love for academics, nor did I aspire to greatness. College was merely an opportunity to be on my own. I was smart enough to do the work and sensible enough to know that grades held the ticket out of my parent's house—and out of the draft.

I settled back into a warm, thick soup of love, leftover from the previous night. Acid had shown me another flavor of that delicious dish. Wasn't it this feeling of love I was always chasing? Hell, in second grade, I chased Nancy Pascal into the girl's bathroom to kiss her. I smiled at the memory of sitting on a green schoolyard bench where Mrs. Haslow had grounded and reprimanded me. I'd felt humiliated, not because I had run after Nancy or kissed her, but because I was being punished for loving someone.

I bloomed late. Throughout my childhood and adolescence, I was short and chubby. Then during my senior year of high school, I shot up almost seven inches without gaining a pound. Finally, I felt eligible to score with the ladies.

When I entered college, I hit the ground running, casting my virginity to the wind. I wanted to know everything about women: what made them tick, how they felt, what they really meant beyond their words, why they were so damn intriguing. And I learned that you could glean much useful information by listening, observing, and showing a sincere interest. Perhaps I was getting an education after all.

Rod shouted from the front of the Jeep, "Hey Rich, you okay back there?"

I resented the interruption, but quickly came to my senses and appreciated my friend's concern. Barely opening my eyes, I flashed him the universal symbol for okay by making a circle with my thumb and index finger. "I'm groovy, man."

"Cool. Just checking."

I closed my eyes again and thought about the new girl Rod had mentioned. He reminded me of how much more energy I used to put into pursuing women and dating than I did now.

As recently as a couple of years back, most girls were still terrified of compromising their reputations, and for good reason. If a girl was considered "easy," people would gossip, and she would be branded a slut or a whore. What a burden, since young women seemed equipped with plenty of sensitivity, passion, and desire.

It was tricky for girls, and even trickier for guys if they wanted to get to first base. During my sophomore year, the university helped us connect with the opposite sex by providing free and frequent on-campus dances, featuring live bands. My three roommates and I would arrive at the events, search the crowd for compatible women, and dance our hearts out for the next few hours.

When the campus affair wound down, we would ask our dancing partners if they wanted to go to another party. Since people who love to dance usually like to party, our invitations were seldom turned down. All eight of us would arrive at the festivities, which were located in . . . our apartment. Who said a party had to be large?

We had gotten everything ready in advance: apartment cleaned, snacks laid out, and plenty of alcohol purchased. My record player held four stacked long-playing 33s: when one record finished, the arm would lift up out of the way, the next one would fall on the turntable, and the arm would swing back to play the new record.

I had stacked the discs strategically. To get everyone in the party-ing mood, Dave Brubeck came first. That gave us a while to drink and chat. Next up was Ray Charles to get everyone dancing. Number three, Andy Williams, slowed down the dancing and put us in a warm, fuzzy, amorous mood. I'd top it off with Andre Previn, whose soft, dreamy music was custom-made for romance. (I should thank the Columbia Record Club, who pestered me month after month with the perfect selection of mailed 33s.)

It was all a game designed to get close to our dates while protecting their reputations. Even the slightest hint she had "done it" could lead to a young woman's demise, so we had to maintain proper etiquette. Admittedly, this sounds calculated. But I prided myself on being a genuine, caring romantic, operating under a laid-back "I don't give a damn" attitude and powered by a testosterone-fueled drive aimed at anything in a skirt.

Vivid scenes from that restricted time flickered through my foggy brain. I recalled an intimate evening with one sweet girl whose image was sharp even if her name escaped me. Her long, silky hair, angelic face, and delicate body invoked a mild shudder in my heart.

In those days, merely talking about sex in mixed company had been considered taboo. But now, in my senior year, things were chang-ing, thank God. Drugs and the "free love" movement were helping everyone let go of the old rules about sex. People were becoming less inhibited and more tolerant and sensitive. When they turned on, they usually behaved with greater awareness, making the usual games silly and unappealing.

Just then, the Jeep bounced, jerked, and came to a stop. Someone turned off Ravi's music as well. I sat up and looked out the window upon a hillside filled with lush grass and hundreds of bright yellow-orange California poppies glistening in the sunlight. Who could resist their *Wizard of Oz* enchantment? We climbed out of the vehicle and made our way up the gentle slope.

Careful not to crush the delicate flowers, we each found an open space and settled into a cushion of tall grass. Yellow cabbage butter-flies and a variety of wild bees moved from one dazzling poppy to the next. The four of us lay there, talking to the clouds.

After a while, we fell silent and soaked in the sun's warmth. The air had a moist, earthy smell, and the gentle breeze caressed me as I listened to the buzzing insects. The subtle love I bathed in, despite my exhaustion and mushy brain, felt as sweet as the love I had for the women I'd pursued. This love for everything that existed was perhaps what I had always been chasing after.

My mind was empty, and my heart was full. It felt good to be alive.

4.

Grist House
March 1967

Later that evening, I sat alone in my small pea-green room at Grist House, located on a quiet corner of Third and University, just a few steps from the Davis campus. Still reflecting on my acid trip the night before, I basked in an afterglow, every cell in my body smiling.

Rod was the one who told me about this room after he moved to Grist House. He and I had met last spring in a beekeeping class. I'd signed up for a couple of easy credits, and to my surprise, it changed my enthusiasm for school. I hadn't become an ardent scholar, but the class intrigued me.

I majored in biological sciences because I liked animals and life in its natural state. But after several semesters, the closest I had gotten to anything living was a dead frog. That was, until I took Beekeeping 101. I was right in there with millions of dynamic, buzzing organisms. That's right, bugs.

Rod and I hit it off from the start. A fun-loving former marine, he had a smirky smile and a hearty laugh that filled the room. We ended up being next-room neighbors in Grist House, where we became the best of friends, as well as pot-smoking buddies.

Mrs. Grist (hence "Grist House"), a tiny, hunched-over, gray-haired matriarch in her late sixties, had converted the upstairs of her old home into six small rooms for male students, along with a large communal bathroom. We had our own entrance from a narrow stairway that led up into a wide hallway, where a refrigerator, pay phone, and radiator had been installed. All the wood-paneled walls were painted pea-green, and a thick coat of army gray covered the wood floor.

Mrs. Grist's face looked like it would crack off in a stiff wind. The cantankerous old woman had two things to share with us: a long list of rules and a short sense of humor. But it didn't worry us. We'd rarely catch sight of her unless the rent was due, so she didn't cramp our style.

The rooms came fully furnished with a bed, table, chair, and small dresser. I also owned an old standing lamp with a frayed beige shade, and a delightfully comfortable ruby-red easy chair, where I spent a lot of time either studying or staring out the window at the back of the bookstore across the alley. On this evening, one night post-acid, I looked out to watch dusk racing toward darkness.

I had added a few things to the room's décor: an old wooden steamer trunk and a record player. On the wall hung a red-white-and-blue bumper sticker that read "FUCK COMMUNISM," the ultimate uptight generation mind-fuck.

In the corner, a birdcage on a stand housed my green-feathered parakeet friend, Opium Greenfields. He seemed pleased to have me back, judging from his incessant chirping. Even though I always left his door wide open, he seldom ventured out of his cage.

The night before had not been my first run-in with LSD. For that, I can credit Mason Dundridge, a research assistant and my coworker in the bacteriology department. A notorious bohemian with a scraggly gray-and-black beard, he once told me, "I sent a letter to the president. I wrote, 'President Johnson's war in Vietnam makes Americans barf.' The next thing I knew helicopters were buzzing my apartment, and a couple of FBI agents knocked at the door."

"Shit, Mason. What happened?"

"They told me I was threatening the president, and if enough people barfed on him, he could drown!"

One day at work, my boss called me into his office. He held a small brown-glass bottle filled with some lab chemical, the bottom half wrapped in paper.

"This needs to be returned. Take this to Mr. Jeffery at the campus shipping office right away. He knows what to do with it."

I didn't think twice about his instructions. As the chief gofer and odd-job specialist for the department, I was used to some strange assignments. At least once a month, I had to go out to a barn where they kept three cows with big rubber stoppers in their sides, surrounded by a rubber ring that had somehow been sutured into their bodies. My job was to pull the stopper out of the side of the cow and then stick a handmade copper-and-rubber eyedropper the length of my arm through the hole and suck out stomach fluid. I'd squirt several droppers-full into a glass container and take it back to the lab.

The stench of this stuff was so nasty it burned my nostrils. Breathing through my mouth didn't keep me from retching—I had to stop breathing altogether. I would joke that if some of the disgusting juice dripped on my hand, I wouldn't hesitate to rub it on a fresh cow paddy to get it off.

The following day I ran into Mason. "Rich, I was looking for you. Do you know that bottle you took to shipping? It contained D-lysergic acid. I ordered it for a bacteriology experiment. There was enough in that bottle for 10,000 hits." He shook his head. "A hell of a lot of acid trips got away yesterday."

Sadly, Mason got away as well. A few days later, he was dismissed from the university.

When it came to pot smoking, I learned to restrict it to weekends. Rod and I had once taken a few puffs and attempted to study for a test. It didn't work out. (There's a reason they call it "dope.") So I decided to study hard during the week and play hard on the weekends.

Opium flew from his cage, took a few loops around the room, and landed on my shoulder. He shuffled over and gently nibbled on my earlobe, chirping a sonata of happy, high-pitched sounds. It was good to be home.

As time went on, my LSD adventure in Yosemite faded. I focused less on bears and more on girls. For a while, I went out with Brandi, a ripe, bosomy blonde with Sophia Loren eyes, the kind of dark eyes that draw you in and leave your heart feeling like a bowl of warm honey.

We liked to smoke a joint in the evening and walk through the empty streets to a small local playground, where we'd swing on the swings. Trying to touch the sky with our feet, we would talk about our dreams and how to make the world a better place. Then we'd go back to her small apartment and make love for hours.

The morning after one of those memorable nights, Brandi drove me back to my place. As we approached Grist House, I watched a jet-black cat ambling toward us down the sidewalk. Something was sticking out of his mouth—a familiar green wing.

"Quick—stop the car! Stop the car!" I shouted.

Before she reached the cat and before the car came to a stop, I threw the door open and leaped out, hitting the ground at a full run toward my target. The feline was so startled he dropped his jaw, along with my friend Opium, who took flight to an elm tree directly across from Grist House. I approached the bird, careful not to startle him. To my astonishment, he acted as if nothing unusual had taken place. In fact, it looked like he was enjoying his adventure.

After parking the car, Brandi joined me. "Keep an eye on him!" I yelled over my shoulder, running like a caffeinated cheetah across the street, down the walk, and up the stairs to my room. I grabbed my butterfly net from where it stood in a corner and raced back. My feathered buddy was still there, and I climbed the tree.

Jockeying the net into place, I needed just a few . . . more . . . seconds, when I glimpsed movement out of the corner of my eye. Turning, I saw a fat robin fly by—and my good friend Opium followed. Within seconds, he'd disappeared over the rooftops.

My heart sank. "Damn."

I placed his cage on the roof of Grist House with the door still clamped open in the hopes he might return. I sat next to the cage for a while, wishing for a glimpse of my friend. But I never saw the tiny guy again. From that day on, my little green room was never the same.

5.

Blowing the Mind
April 1967

One warm spring day, I sat on my bed chatting with a young woman named Kathleen, whom I'd met a few hours before at the campus coffee shop. Her walk home took her past Grist House, so I'd invited her up to see my place.

A pretty young thing with coppery shoulder-length hair, she had sparkling green eyes and a delicious Southern accent. Her full lips and perky breasts had my blood racing with possibilities, but then, unaware of my pot proclivities, she blurted out, "I don't like people who smoke marijuana because they are dirty and don't take baths."

On that cue, we heard a clanking outside my room.

I opened the door partway to investigate. When I stuck my bare foot into the hall (I never wore shoes on warm days), the top of it turned white. Rod stared up at me from the floor, a container of white powder in his hand. His bloodshot eyes told me right away he was stoned.

"Yikes!" He scurried back into his room on all fours and slammed the door.

From her position on the bed, Kathleen couldn't see any of this. I brushed off my foot and ankle, pulled my leg back in, and nonchalantly closed the door. "Just my neighbor," I said.

After she left, I knocked on Rod's door. His eyes darted every which way, and his bush of curly hair looked wilder than a windblown tumbleweed.

"Man! I got really wasted, and I thought I saw a cockroach." He shuddered, uncharacteristic of this former soldier. "I decided to throw some pesticide powder around my room, just in case. Then I thought I'd better squirt a little bit under your door too." His eyes got huge. "When I reached your room, the biggest roach I ever saw came running out. Shit! I threw powder at it and split for cover. Man, it totally blew my mind."

Laughing, I understood his distaste for these insects. In our entomology classes, we had learned about their disease-carrying capabilities—how their oily bodies were a magnet for bacteria and how they could crawl through dog crap and then through your silverware drawer. That information alone would have been enough to build a major prejudice against roaches—but Rod and I had also taken the same insect physiology course.

On the first day of class, the professor said, "Since we will be dissecting roaches, we might as well get used to handling them." He reached into a glass terrarium and pulled out a large hissing Madagascar roach. We were instructed to pass this beast from hand to hand until everyone in the class had held it for a minute.

Now a Madagascar roach is the Godzilla of the species. The one our professor had selected must have been close to three inches long. When you held it in your hand, it had so much power in one of its spiny legs, it could push away your finger. And you'd have to hurry to regain control with that finger before it started to push another and then another with its many legs. If this weren't hideous enough, the greasy monster would vibrate violently and make loud hissing sounds by forcing air through holes along the sides of its body.

Once exposed to this nightmarish experience, you would never forget how really awful roaches are—especially when you had to cut up its smaller, but still disgusting, cousins in class on a regular basis.

Lucky for us, Grist House seemed free of roaches. And when Rod figured out that the monster roach coming out of my door had only been a human foot—namely, mine—he let out a howl.

He and I shared a love of getting our minds blown. There was something about that blank stare on a person's face when you were able to derail their mental progression.

Getting your mind blown is a special gift—a moment when the world stands still, when true freedom exists. That's why I've always found it so refreshing to be open to new and unusual experiences.

In time, others stopped by Grist House on Friday evenings to shoot the breeze with Rod and me. Sooner or later, we'd grab a lid of grass hidden in the ivy vines outside the bathroom window, roll a joint, and pass it around. Buzzed, Rod and I, along with a few friends, would pull out our Blues Harp harmonicas and improvise, filling the room with raucous music.

When "the munchies" took over, someone would suggest, "Let's go down to Baskin-Robbins and get a German chocolate cake ice cream cone." Before we knew it, we'd be marching down the street, four or five or six of us, all chanting over and over again, "We're going down to Baskin-Robbins to get a German chocolate cake ice cream cone." We didn't give a damn if anyone thought we were nuts. A few times, others joined our parade.

6.

Va-r-o-o-o-o-m!
April–May 1967

Soon after spring break, I bought my first motorcycle, a 650 BSA with a metallic, candy-apple-red gas tank and lots of chrome.

Hal came by to check it out. Standing tall and sturdy like a Viking warrior in the bright sun, his long reddish-brown hair tucked behind his ears, he studied the bike. "You've got some badass wheels here, Rich."

He folded his towering frame onto the seat and grabbed the high-riser handlebars. "Let me give you some advice." He had already owned several street and dirt bikes. "If you steer with your butt, not your bars, you'll have more control. And remember to keep the right amount of pressure in the tires and apply equal pressure to the front and back brakes."

He dropped his hands and sat back. "Oh yeah, and one more thing. This is good. An old man once told me, 'Never fear anything, but always be careful.'"

"Deep. I like that." His words stayed with me, becoming a guiding principle in my life.

We put the bike in Hal's Jeep and drove to a meadow near the creek. As we unloaded the bike, he asked, "Can I give it a test spin?"

"Sure."

After driving around the area for a few minutes, he pointed to a low mound of dirt. "Do you mind if I jump over it?"

"Go for it."

He made a wide loop and headed toward the jump at a good clip.

He flew over the mound, and when he hit the ground, the right handle-bar crimped, and the bike collapsed.

I ran over and helped him up. "Are you okay?"

"Yeah, I think so." He picked some dry grass out of his hair. "The handlebar folded in half."

"Wow, you really could have been hurt."

We examined the high-risers and found they were made of flimsy aluminum.

"These are bicycle handlebars," Hal said, shaking his head. "Can you believe it? They look fancy, but they have no strength."

"Shit, man, I'm glad you're okay."

The accident was a blessing. It was only a matter of time before the handlebars busted. And it could have happened while I was screaming down the freeway—damn, I would have been roadkill.

It didn't take long to get the ape hangers replaced with standard motorcycle handlebars. Now I didn't have to reach over my head to find the grips.

One evening the following week, I took my friend Bonnie for a bike ride through a new part of town, where roads had recently been installed. As the gorgeous sunset faded behind us, she leaned toward me. "Have you heard the new Mamas and Papas song 'Dedicated to the One I Love'"?

Nodding, I opened my mouth to elaborate, when my headlight revealed we'd soon run out of road. Just a few feet ahead of us at the end of slick, sandy asphalt were two-foot-tall blocks of concrete.

Bonnie screamed.

"Oh shit!" I hit the brakes, but the bike skid in the loose gravel.

No way could I avoid a collision. And that meant pain—a whole lot of it. Yet somehow the next thing I remember, I was on the ground, flat on my face, unharmed, the bike on its side revving at high speed.

I jumped up and ran to Bonnie, turning off the bike on the way. "Are you okay?"

"My shoulder hurts, but otherwise I'm fine." We walked to her house, where I fetched her car and drove her to the medical center. She had a small fracture in her collarbone, but she was a good sport about it. Thank God it hadn't been more serious.

Fortunately, I had my VW Bug for transportation, because my bike was in the repair shop for several weeks. In the meantime, I improvised a motorcycle diversion using items I had lying around. That Friday night, once we were all stoned, Rod helped me demonstrate my creation.

He sat on my steamer trunk in the middle of the room and put on the goggles I had fashioned from two large highway reflectors I'd gotten a while back from my dad. Prying off the backings, I made glasses out of them with several rubber bands. One side was red and the other was white, producing a multifaceted kaleidoscopic effect.

Then I placed two beer bottles on their sides under Rod's feet and the damaged high-riser handlebars in his hands. While an electric fan blew air in his face and an album on the record player produced go-cart sounds, two other friends lifted the trunk by the handles at each end and produced a gentle, rolling motion.

"Out of sight, man!"

The psychedelic motorcycle ride "Riding the Harley Trunk" became a popular pastime at Grist House.

Shortly after my BSA was repaired, Hal dropped by with his buddy Russ, a lighthearted, down-home art student with a full black beard and receding hairline.

Sitting on my bed, Hal took a hit off a joint and passed it to me. "Hey," he said, blowing out the smoke, "there's this Marlon Brando movie *The Wild One* playing at a bar downtown. Brando's motorcycle gang takes over a small California town where they raise hell with the locals. It's based on a true story, when the Hell's Angels took over Hollister. That's a little mountain town near Gilroy, south of San Jose."

"Sounds like a blast. Count me in!" I said.

Russ tugged on his beard. "Groovy. Me too," he said, his voice slow and deep.

Though the movie didn't inspire us to take over a town, it did nudge us in the direction of hell-raising and bike riding that night.

Hal was between bikes, but I had my BSA, now with stylish Triumph front forks instead of the ones I had destroyed. Russ had a Yamaha 500. Hal sat behind me, and we took off toward the outskirts of town.

We should have gotten a clue about rethinking our plans when we stopped at the first traffic light. Hal put his feet down to stretch his long legs, and as soon as the light turned green, I zipped off, unaware I no longer had a passenger. I heard shouts and turned to see his silhouette in the headlights, arms waving, as he ran after me. I nearly fell off my bike laughing.

Hal now reseated behind me, we made it out of town and flew through the countryside, letting the wind whip through our hair, our earlobes trailing behind. When we passed a sign that read "LIBERTY ISLAND—12 MILES," Hal shouted over the roar of the engine, "We've got to make it to Liberty Island. Like Steve McQueen in *The Great Escape*." I played along with his fantasy, racing down the road as the white line flicked by.

At some point, I switched with Hal so he could drive. Russ was in the lead when the road curved sharply to the left. Because Russ's bike was smaller than mine, he could navigate the curve at a faster speed.

"We can't make it," Hal shouted. "Hold on!"

My heart leaped into my throat as we took to the air, cleared a ditch, and came down with a jolt and a wobble, making a bumpy landing in a plowed field. Somehow, Hal kept the bike upright and under control and finally brought it to a stop.

He didn't move, his hands still clutching the handlebars. "Wow, can you fucking believe that? We rode it out."

"Damn." I exhaled with relief.

We were examining the bike for damage when Russ returned and called out, barely visible from the road, "What's up?"

Still filled with adrenaline, I joked, "Oh we thought we'd jump some ditches. It was great! You ought to try it."

Hal and I went back to inspecting my bike, making sure we didn't miss anything in the dim light. Then we heard the shifting of gears.

We turned to see a lone headlight coming from the direction we had just traveled. "Russ, no! No! No!" We both yelled as the headlamp sped toward us.

When we pulled the bike off him, Russ muttered, "Shit, man. How'd you do that?"

My "I was only kidding" didn't provide much comfort. We must have had a guardian angel because, except for his pride, Russ wasn't hurt, nor his bike damaged. And neither was my BSA.

Back in the driver's seat, I resumed our ride to Liberty Island—that was, until an unusually bumpy railroad track sent Hal airborne. After taking out my taillight on the way down—as well as the seat of his jeans on the sandy asphalt—we reconsidered our adventure.

What was it that Will Rogers said? "Good judgment comes from experience, and a lot of that comes from bad judgment." We decided to head back before someone got killed. Quite satisfied with ourselves, we arrived back in Davis, lucky as hell to all be in one piece.

PART 2

Summer of the Flower Children

Hitchhikers, children of the wind,
Floating on the breeze of friendly strangers,
Some a bit odd to my way of thinking . . .
But all kind enough to take the time to stop
And carry me along for a while.
—Rich Israel, 1967

7.

Don't Bug Me

June 1967

Classes ended, but graduation wouldn't take place for me until the end of the fall semester. I needed more credits because I had wasted my first year as an engineering major, a misguided attempt to follow in my dad's footsteps. It didn't take long for me to discover that a steady diet of math, physics, and chemistry was like eating stale, unsalted crackers—a dry, unfulfilling experience. I hated it, and my grades suffered.

My love for nature drew me to the biological sciences, but the dean told me I couldn't transfer until my grade-point average improved significantly.

"You might as well give up trying to resurrect your grades, Rich," he said, his arms crossed. "That's practically impossible at this point."

Gee, thanks for the encouragement.

The rebel in me wanted to prove him wrong. By the end of the next semester, I had become a biological science major.

I couldn't break free of school for the summer until I completed a mandatory five-week insect-collecting course at the University of California, Blodgett Forest, located about thirty miles northwest of Placerville.

I shared this time with eleven serious entomology students and an even more serious Professor Max Miller, who, I had to admit, taught me a lot about finding insects. "Attune your attention to all levels of the forest—in the air, on the ground, under rocks, bark, or leaves. When you're around lakes, streams, and puddles, notice what's in, on, and above the water. And dead animals provide a treasure trove of amazing insect populations." All helpful tips, but the thought of picking bugs off dead animals took some getting used to.

Every day we would take short trips as a group to different ecosystems or wander on our own personal safaris near camp. Armed with butterfly nets and a series of "kill jars" filled with wax and cyanide crystals, we hunted for a full spectrum of the insect population. In the evenings, we identified and mounted the specimens on pins and labeled them with their family and species names, along with the location where they had been captured.

It was an entomological Auschwitz. But considering that most insects spend just days to a few weeks as adults, we weren't shortening their lives by much. Besides, you couldn't find a more beautiful place than the Sierra forest to hang out.

After a month of insect annihilation, I got antsy, so to speak, eager to begin my cross-country journey. My latest plan was to hitchhike my way east to the world's fair in Montreal. Along the way, I would stop to visit Hal and his friend Pete, who had summer jobs near Aspen, Colorado.

First I had to complete a ten-page paper due a few days before the end of the course. Since my interests tended toward insect behavior, Professor Miller told me to write about the robber fly, the subject of an extended study he'd made during graduate school. He would loan me his paper, he said, to give me some background for the assignment.

Before knuckling down to work, I ventured off by myself into the woods for some downtime and found a secluded spot next to a small stream with a smooth boulder, perfect for resting my butt. I pulled out a joint, until then safely concealed in my toilet kit, and lit up—the only time I got stoned those five weeks.

Feeling a good buzz, I was soon enjoying the warmth of the sun, the murmur of the mountain stream, and the strong scent of pine. When I glanced down, I happened to notice a big, fat jet-black robber fly sitting on a stone, a little below and to my right. He faced the water, and as long as I sat still, he didn't seem to mind sharing his space with me.

From a previous class, I knew that robber flies can catch insects in midair and that their bite instantly paralyzes their prey. One overzealous entomologist had enticed a robber fly to bite him on his fingertip. According to the story, the fly's potent venom kept his whole arm numb for weeks.

As I observed the black insect, I saw a dragonfly zip along the stream. The robber fly took off after the dragonfly, made a quick circle, and within seconds returned to his position on the rock. Hmm. He probably decided he didn't want to tangle with someone ten times his size. Good thinking! When another large insect zipped by in the other direction, the little bugger repeated the same maneuver.

Would he fly at anything that moved? I picked up a pebble and placed it like a marble between my middle finger and thumb. After taking aim, I flicked it past the robber fly. Sure enough, he flew toward it and then zoomed back to his post. I tried it a few more times, and when my aim was true, I got similar results.

Being aware that streams and roads are natural flight paths for insects, I wandered over to a nearby dirt logging road and came across several robber flies sitting on rocks or logs, all facing in the direction of the road. Satisfied I had enough material for my paper, I went back to my boulder by the creek and soaked up the afternoon sunshine.

Though I had brought along my net and hunting supplies, I didn't want to kill anything, so I took the afternoon off from stalking insects. My mind wandered to the little beings in our kill jars. Did they suffer? Caring about my actions, especially in my hypersensitive state, I wanted to be a better judge of what happened. Just then, a good-sized fly of the family Sarcophagidae landed on my boulder.

Now this Sarcophagid, also known as a flesh fly, had to be the ugliest, most detestable-looking member of the species. Resembling a housefly, it had red eyes and drab shades of gray and black on its hairy body and a pinkish-red, puke-colored stub of a butt. These common flies have a nasty reputation, so I didn't hesitate to catch this one and place it in my kill jar. The fly crumpled up, kicked a little, and in less than ten seconds lay dead. It was still painful to watch.

Ready for a change of scenery, I returned to camp. Through the window into the lab, I saw five of my classmates busy mounting their insect specimens. They all looked much too earnest, so I decided to lighten things up.

Stepping into the room, I shouted, "You won't believe what I found!" I hurried over to a nearby table and fumbled through my pack for the kill jar. Always excited about the prospect of viewing a rare specimen, everybody jumped up to see what great insect treasure I had to share.

"What is it?"

"What did you find?"

I ignored their inquiries and continued searching through my pack, stalling until everyone had made it to my corner of the lab. Finally, I pulled out the kill jar but made sure my hand surrounded it to conceal its contents, building suspense like a magician at a children's party.

Eager faces surrounded me. I bent over the table, and they all pressed in close. Then I dumped out the single dead fly. "Voilà."

One guy turned to me, his lip curled in a sneer. "A Sarcophagid? Is that all?"

"It's just a Sarcophagid!" a girl said, rolling her eyes.

Everyone stood there staring at the ugly dead fly as I walked out the door, giggling to myself.

That evening I completed the rough draft of my paper. Based on my impromptu research, I highlighted three observations: robber flies align themselves to the natural flight paths of insects (roads, paths, and streams), propel themselves in the direction of anything moving by rapidly, and get close enough to the target to determine if it is suitable prey.

The next morning, I looked over Professor Miller's behavioral thesis for the first time. To my surprise, following six months of study, he had come up with the same three conclusions I had realized in thirty minutes of marijuana-induced observation. Handing in the assignment, I told him, "I know you might not believe me, but I didn't read your thesis until after I had written my paper."

We had to stay an extra day to receive our grades, so I celebrated with a motorcycle ride through a few mountain towns. Floating along a narrow highway, I whistled the tune to "Strawberry Fields Forever," in great spirits, itching to get my hitchhiking adventure underway. On the long gravel drive into Bloggett, I tipped my butt left and right, allowing the bike to sashay down a ridge in the middle.

Nothing could destroy my euphoria—not even the news that Professor Miller didn't believe me, evidenced by the D he gave me on my paper.

When you operate from a place of honesty and tell someone the truth, but that person doesn't believe you, it feels like a punch in the gut. A hollow space forms below your heart, a mixture of anger and hurt, insult and disappointment. But I shook it off. I'd learned that if you tap into your strength and confidence, the feeling soon dissipates, followed by the understanding that someone missed the opportunity to know the truth.

The low grade itself didn't faze me. It wasn't the first and no doubt wouldn't be the last. What sucked was there's nothing that wounds an honest man more than being considered a liar!

8.

Thumbs Up
July 1967

Back in Sacramento, I stashed my car and bike at my folks' place. It was the first time they knew I had a motorcycle. My dad, a softhearted, quiet man, said, "Well, now I don't have to worry about you going to Vietnam. It's safer than riding that thing."

I spent a sweet last night with Brandi, and she drove me to a highway on-ramp the next morning.

"I wish I could be like you," she said, reaching over and putting her hand on my thigh.

"What do you mean?"

"When you say you're going to do something, you do it. I wish I could."

"Brandi, there's no reason you can't do it too. Just figure out what you want and do it. You can't go wrong if you follow your heart."

Duffel bag over my shoulder, I stuck my thumb out, and after several rides and hours, I made it to Greg and Jeanette's place in Reno. In my sophomore year, I had roomed with the always dapper Greg, a fan of button-down shirts and close-cropped hair. Jeanette and I went to the same high school, though we didn't become close friends until we met up again in college.

Tall and thin with long hair the color of chocolate milk and a mischievous Katharine Hepburn smile, Jeanette charmed everyone with her combination of playfulness and worldly cynicism. We could confide about things as personal as how horny we were. Once, when I'd suggested we help each other remedy this, she said, "Richard, a good friend is better than a good fuck."

Put like that, I found it hard to argue with her, not that it would have done any good. I introduced Greg to Jeanette back then, and a year later—on what they called a whim—the two of them got married at the courthouse.

Intrigued by my trip, Greg decided to drive me as far as Aspen. Before we left, he took me downtown to the casinos, my maiden voyage into the world of gambling. All the blinking lights joggled my eyes. Stretched across the strip, a large neon sign read "RENO, THE BIGGEST LITTLE CITY IN THE WORLD."

The Nevada Club bristled with electricity, the air alive with flashing lights, mirrors, bells, and the mingling of patrons and casino workers. Just stepping into the place quickened my pulse.

I bought a roll of dimes, thinking I'd play some slots, but as we wandered past a roulette table surrounded by a crowd, a sign caught my eye: "10 CENT MINIMUM." Watching the action, I noticed a heavy olive-skinned man in a green suit, who continuously stacked dollar chips on and around red 5: five chips on red 5, five chips each on all four sides of red 5, and an extra pile of ten chips on the red field. He repeated this six or seven times, despite scoring only two small wins when black 8 and red 34 came up. Giving up, he left the table with his few remaining chips.

I felt the urge to duplicate the man's bets. The ball was thrown, and I rushed to stack my dimes, placing them as he had done with his chips. Greg grabbed my arm. "You need to purchase chips," he whispered.

I ignored him. Just as I finished stacking the last dime, putting my extras on the red field, the ball started to slow down. It bounced a few times this way and that and eventually stopped on red 5.

Hot dog!

The young man working the roulette table replaced my dimes with chips and pushed several large stacks toward me. I scooped them up, handing some to Greg because I couldn't carry them all. "Where do we take these for cash?" I asked him. He pointed to a cashier booth. "This should get us to Aspen," I said in a cocky voice.

The total came to over fifty-five dollars, enough to cover Greg's gas in both directions—as well as a much-needed lube job.

On our way to Aspen, we listened to one song over and over: Scott McKenzie's "San Francisco (Be Sure to Wear Some Flowers in Your Hair)," the favorite of Wolfman Jack's right then. The radio blaring and windows rolled down, we sang along, louder and louder, never tiring of it.

Near noon on Friday, we found Hal and Pete not far outside Aspen, framing a building at a soon-to-be ski resort called Snowmass. It was a happy reunion, but they had to work, so we took off for their cabin.

Easy to find, the nineteenth-century, stone-walled structure had one room with two bunks, a tall dresser, and a wood cook stove. A wide rope swing with a wood seat hung from a rafter in the middle. I couldn't help but smile at the high-flying love seat. Stepping out the front door, we entered a large meadow and came across a lightly tread path leading to a gentle stream. All around us, mountain peaks rose sharply, penetrating a cloudless sky. Bushed from the long drive, we fell asleep among the wild flowers in the shin-deep grass.

Saturday morning dawned bright. After a breakfast of eggs and hash browns, courtesy of Hal, and a joint, courtesy of Pete, we took off for a swim in the creek. The tall, lanky Pete led the way, his short blond hair hidden beneath his ever-present cowboy hat. Behind me, Hal and Greg carried a worn wood-and-metal milk crate containing a six-volt car battery, a tape deck, and some tapes. The crude contraption played the familiar Ravi Shankar tape, bringing back memories of tripping in Yosemite.

At one point along the path, my two friends hoisted the funky music box onto their shoulders, directly behind my head. There I was, walking in nature with heavenly music surrounding me. I told my buddies, "Maybe someday someone will invent a way to carry music with you wherever you go. Wouldn't that be cool?"

Greg left for home around noon, and I went to town with Hal to run some errands before we wandered over to a place called Woody's, where I fell in love with a culinary delight known as tomato beer. Never a fan of tomato juice by itself, I discovered that a shot of tomato juice in a beer took the bitter edge off. The combination went down like silk sliding across a baby's cheek.

Pete met us at Woody's, and after another beer and a game of hand shuffleboard, we went to the Red Onion restaurant for dinner. Julie, a bosomy young waitress with rosy cheeks, knew Hal, and I could tell from her eyes (and the free dessert) that she had a thing for him. She told us that the restaurant was looking for a busboy, so I talked to the manager and was hired on the spot. I would start the next evening.

When Julie's shift ended, she and her friend Maggie joined us, and we all piled into Hal's Jeep and took off for a place called Redstone Hot Springs. Maggie passed around a few joints while Grace Slick of Jefferson Airplane belted out "White Rabbit" on Hal's tape deck.

> *One pill makes you larger*
> *And one pill makes you small*
> *And the ones that mother gives you*
> *Don't do anything at all*

Nearly an hour later, Hal pulled off the winding mountain highway onto a dirt shoulder across from towering red cliffs, their tops barely visible in the moonlight. We followed an incline down toward the Crystal River and crowded into a pint-sized galvanized-steel hut—the acrid smell of sulfur assaulted my nostrils. A wide rectangular trough ran the length of the concrete floor, and wisps of steam rose to the ceiling.

We stripped down and eased ourselves into the scalding mineral water, shallow enough for us to sit and still keep our heads above the surface. Already relaxed from the pot, I experienced a whole new level of lethargy from the melting effect of the heat on my muscles.

Before long, sweat was pouring down my face. Hal and Julie climbed out of the water, and Hal motioned for me to follow. We stepped out into the cold mountain air and walked gingerly across jagged rocks to the edge of the river.

Hal turned to me. "Jump in the stream to cool off, and then go back in the hot springs." Without hesitation, he waded out into the shallow river, lay down on his back, and rolled over a few times to douse his entire body. Julie did the same with a few "ohs" and "ouches." Her chilled breasts jiggled like two laughing frog eyes in the silvery moonlight.

Taking my time would only make it more painful, so I jumped in after them. "Oh shit!" The icy water runoff from the snowpack shocked my body and sent an intense rush to my brain. After rolling over several times, I darted back to the shack and the inviting warmth of the springs. We repeated this ritual a couple more times that evening, and by the last plunge, I hardly felt a jolt. I figured the cold had paralyzed my sensory receptors.

After a final soak in the springs, Hal said, "I'm driving, so I'll hit the river one more time." At that point, most of us were cooked, drying by the side of the trough. We dressed as if in a trance and headed for the Jeep.

Invigorated yet totally relaxed, I scrunched down in my seat and listened to the Paul Butterfield Blues Band as we wound our way back to Aspen. Now a believer in the magic of hot springs, I felt right in tune with their song "Mellow Down Easy."

9.

Love-In
July 1967

The next day, Hal, Pete, and I went to a love-in at a small Aspen park. Scanning the crowd, I saw mostly longhairs, along with a scattering of conventional folks. True to its name, a lot of love and joy filled the air. An acoustic folk band played music from the gazebo in the center of the park, and a handful of flower children danced close by.

Reverend Pike, the guest speaker and a popular war protestor, addressed the crowd. Well-dressed in a charcoal suit and starched minister's collar, a touch of white in his black hair, he talked about the injustices of the Vietnam War.

"Listen, people," he shouted, stabbing the air with his index finger. "The military establishment continues to slaughter innocent civilians and send our sons and brothers to their death. We need to stand up and demand to be heard!" His deep, charismatic voice reverberated throughout the transfixed audience.

"And we can do that right now," he said. "Secretary of Defense Robert McNamara lives near here. What do you say we walk over there and let him know how we feel about his war?"

All of us yelled out our support, and before I knew it, we were marching down the street—a colorful menagerie of forty, parading through Aspen. Pike and another man carried peace posters.

Wherever I went, the hip community welcomed me as family, most of them willing to share their friendship—as well as a place to stay or whatever else they had to offer. The message of love spread fast. Timothy Leary, the Pied Piper of acid and getting high, said, "Turn on, tune in, and drop out." As more and more people did, they opened their hearts and realized that love, play, and human beings mattered more than money, prejudice, and accomplishment. Turning on had created a platform and sensitivity that bound our subculture together, bringing much-needed hope.

When we arrived at McNamara's house, no one was home. One girl placed a circle of wildflowers on the secretary of defense's welcome mat. Another added three flowers at angles, turning it into a peace sign, while the rest of us put flowers on windowsills, doorknobs, and anywhere else that begged for a bloom. We left a peace poster leaning against the door.

Could a little love from the flower children have some effect on him?

A few days later, while sitting at my favorite Aspen street corner, I met two fellows from Kansas City looking for a place to camp for the night. I told them they could bed down by the creek in front of our cabin. Hal and Pete wouldn't mind. The cluster of cabins had been abandoned, so we had no landlord to deal with.

The next morning, I sat by the creek swapping stories with Bill and Andy. "A couple of months ago," Andy said in a lazy drawl, "we went to a love-in at a park back home, and three bands were there." Solid in body and face, he wore his brown hair cut close to the scalp except in the front where it kept flopping across his forehead and into his eyes.

"It didn't turn out too good, though," Bill said, his short, wavy Brylcreemed hair sparkling in the sunlight. With his thumb, he smoothed one side of his bushy black mustache, perched on his upper lip like a woolly bear caterpillar.

"Yep," Andy said. "It was fun until some thugs came along and started trouble. I had to bust my guitar over one guy's head. That pretty much ended the thing."

It sounded like the Midwest lagged behind California on the hip evolutionary scale.

Before they left, Bill scribbled down an address and directions to his place in Kansas City. "If you're hitching through KC on your way to Montreal and need a place to crash, you can stay with us."

"Don't be surprised if you find me on your doorstep someday soon," I said.

One evening at the Red Onion, as I unloaded a tray of dirty dishes in the kitchen, a waiter came over to me, a hamburger platter in his hand. "Let me tell you, the guy at table four has been a pain in the ass all night. A miserable drunk. He tipped me a penny earlier, and now he wants another burger."

With his free hand, the waiter took the top bun off the hamburger, hacked up a wad, and spit it on the meat. Smiling, he replaced the bun and left for the dining room.

I winced, reminding myself to always be courteous to a server.

Hermann, the dishwasher, was a frail, skinny little man, his chin and throat covered with white stubble. I pegged him at somewhere around sixty, judging from the fact that white was winning the color war on his scalp. A simple fellow, Hermann worked hard and kept to himself.

One evening, as I headed back to the dining room, I heard the chef shout, "Hermann, quick! Make some toast!"

I returned to the kitchen just as the chef noticed Hermann standing next to two carefully stacked toast skyscrapers adjacent to the four-slice toaster. "What the hell is that?" The chef stormed over to the old man and shook two fingers in his face. "I just wanted two pieces of toast!" Hermann looked down at the floor and said nothing.

Though it was hilarious, I felt sorry for the little guy. He lived in a teeny box of a room above the Onion and was fired a few days later. Apparently, he had plunged an ax into someone's bedroom door upstairs. I guess you could say, "He got the ax for improper use of same."

After a week and a half in Aspen, I was ready to move on. John, a waiter at the Red Onion, was driving to St. Louis, and for some gas money, he agreed to drop me off in Kansas City.

As I said good-bye to my two friends, Hal showed me a way to stow my cash. "Take a razor and make a slit in the inside piece of denim behind your belt. This provides an opening to the inside of the seam. You can slip a few hundred-dollar bills rolled up tight into this space for safekeeping."

I was focusing on stashing my loot when John drove up with a girl in the car. Misty, John's coworker during the winter season, was riding with him to St. Louis. Battling the flu, she slept in the backseat while John and I took turns behind the wheel.

I didn't speak to Misty until the next morning when we stopped for breakfast in Topeka. A short, busty blonde with a cute button nose and a hint of freckles, she was easy on the eyes, even after being sick as a dog and spending fifteen hours sleeping in a car.

"I love skiing," she said, sipping her tea, "so I took a semester off from the University of Michigan and moved to Aspen to work as a ski instructor. When the season ended, I found a waitressing job at a coffee shop. Wish I could have stayed longer, but I need to get back to school early to do some sorority stuff." She'd catch a plane from St. Louis for Ann Arbor.

I told her about my plans to hitch to the world's fair in Montreal. To my surprise, when John dropped me off in Kansas City, she handed me a scrap of paper with her phone number on it. "If your travels take you through Ann Arbor, look me up."

As I unloaded my duffel bag, I glanced at the building where I'd be staying. It was just as Bill had described. The steps led up to the porch of an old Victorian built above a barbershop with a faded red-white-and-blue-striped barber pole. The sign in the window displayed a colorful tub of Butch Wax and read "We specialize in flat tops."

Flat tops? Seriously?

10.

Powerful Funky

July 1967

On a muggy evening close to a week after my arrival in Kansas City, I sat on the battered hardwood floor in the living room, my back against the wall. Five of my newfound friends gathered across from me in the kitchen, a drab space covered with faded, cracked yellow-and-white-checkered linoleum. No cooking or eating went on there as far as I could tell. One cabinet contained an ancient can of peas and carrots, as popular with this crowd as they were with me. It was the only food in the house, except for the few beers stashed in the fridge.

There wasn't much furniture either—only a yellow Formica table with two matching chairs that sat between the kitchen and the living room. An unframed Jefferson Airplane poster was taped unevenly on one wall. Marijuana smoke filled the room.

Bill stood next to one of the chairs in a worn dress shirt and slacks. "The goddamn government doesn't give a shit who they send into the Nam meat chopper. Hell, lots of guys will be running off to Canada." His glasses slid down his nose as he waved his arms with the grace of a symphony conductor. A rusted kitchen faucet provided percussion, leaking a steady drip, drip, drip.

"Right on, Bill." Andy, wearing overalls and brown boots, looked like he just came off the farm. Over the last few days, I noticed he had the peculiar habit of keeping a large wad of gum lodged behind his right ear in wait for another round of chewing. "Someone oughta spike LBJ's coffee with acid, if you ask me."

Leaning against the kitchen counter, an audience of three women shared a joint and listened to Bill and Andy, piping in occasionally. Shirley, Bill's girlfriend, towered over the other two. That night, she wore a long, crumpled blue dress that needed to meet an iron. Though unremarkable looking, she had friendly brown eyes and a genuine smile.

"Hell," she said, "they should make a couple of acid trips mandatory for all politicians."

"I'd vote for that." Tote, Andy's lady, slim and petite, her cheeks covered in freckles, reminded me of Mia Farrow, although Tote's hair was darker. "It'd be a whole different world if some of those old fools would turn on."

Ruth was also there, but Bill, Shirley, Andy, and Tote were the only ones actually living in the house, having rented it for the summer. All five of them attended Missouri Southern State University down in Joplin.

Not to be unkind, but Ruth wasn't the prettiest flower in the garden. Her body was built square like a box, and her mid-length dark-brown hair was box-shaped as well. I couldn't get over how her legs attached to her torso. With most people, the legs come together at an angle at the crotch—not so with Ruth. Her legs approached her body in a parallel fashion, like the legs on a table. I had never seen anything like it. I couldn't stop staring at her crotch, wondering how her legs came together under her mini-skirt.

As I sat there stretched out on the floor, the grass consuming my brain, I remembered a conversation I had with Hal sometime back. "What I like about hitchhiking," he'd said, "is that you're on the outside of life looking in." That's how I felt right then. I could observe human behavior without anyone expecting anything of me.

"Hey, I think I saw a roach slip under the stove this morning," Tote said in her Kansas City drawl, the strongest I'd heard so far.

Ruth wrinkled her face in disgust. "I hate them fuckin' things."

"Yeah, that sucks," Bill said, "but it could be a whole lot worse. Freddie Zarconi lives in a one-room fleabag that's *totally* infested. One day a big roach ran up the wall next to his bed, and Freddie picked up one of his combat boots and smashed it with the heel."

Tote stomped her foot. "Ew! How gross!"

"There's more. The roach's guts splattered against the wall in all directions, inspiring Freddie's artistic sensibilities. He was also pissed at the landlord for not taking care of the roach problem. So the next time he saw a roach on the wall, he grabbed that same boot and smashed it. Now his whole wall is a mural of roach guts." He flashed his toothy smile.

"Stop! Stop! You're making me puke." Ruth put her hands over her ears.

Ignoring her, Andy said, "Wow! That would be something to see. We could give artistic tours. This guy could give Michelangelo a run for his money. Can you imagine the Sistine Chapel lined in bug guts?"

We all fell into a long fit of painful belly laughs. Still giggling, Tote and Ruth ambled over to where I was sitting and plopped down in front of me.

"Why ya hangin' out here all by yourself?" Tote asked. "You okay?"

"Just groovin'."

"This pot's good, ain't it?" she said. "It's better than the wild Missouri stuff we usually have. What do you think of KC?"

"So far I like it. It seems more laid-back than most cities. It's definitely not like California."

"Is California uptight?"

"No. People here move slower, but seem less tolerant about being different."

Ruth scoffed. "In KC, if you're different, they throw you in the crazy house."

"That's for sure," Tote said. "When I was in high school, I didn't act like some of the other kids. I didn't want to be the way my parents expected, so they decided I was crazy. They locked me up in an asylum for six months. Ruth's parents threw her in the nuthouse for even longer."

"Yeah, fourteen months. And only because my dad found out I was sleeping with someone. I tell you, people are backward around here."

"Man, what a bummer," I said. "How did you get out?"

Tote shrugged. "By playing their game."

"Nothing else you can do when you're locked up," Ruth said. "They don't know what to do with people who aren't like them, so they just throw them in those loony houses. I'm sure glad I turned eighteen. My folks can't touch me now."

"That's unbelievable. It sounds like your parents are the loony ones."

They both nodded vigorously.

Andy wanted to show me Kansas City, but first he had to stop at his mother's house to borrow her car. "Hey Mom, this is Rich. He's a hippie from California." I had to chuckle. Nobody had ever called me a hippie before, and I never really thought about being labeled that way.

He drove me to an ancient pool hall where "Minnesota Fats played many a time" and then pointed out a hall where he saw B.B. King play live. Our next stop was the place to get "the best barbecue ribs in the world." We parked across from a raunchy-looking storefront with "Pappy's BBQ" scrawled on the window with black paint. Inside, we sat in one of the three tattered booths. A black couple sat in another booth, both holding a sparerib to their mouths as if they were playing a harmonica duet.

A thin black man with startlingly white hair, wearing a soiled apron and a weary smile, shuffled over to us.

"Two of your rib plates, Pappy," Andy said.

Pappy nodded without saying a word and headed back to the kitchen.

"These are the best ribs you'll ever taste, guaranteed."

"Can't wait. How long you and Tote been together?"

"About a year. She used to be with Ruth. Most of the girls around here are bi."

"Bi?"

"Bisexual. They like girls as much as they like guys. It seems to be a KC thing."

"Everybody's got their own bag. I still can't believe Tote's parents had her locked up in the nuthouse for not being their brand of normal."

"It happens a lot 'round here. Just 'cause kids don't turn out the way parents think they oughta. It's a powerful funky thing."

I loved listening to the melody of Andy's Missouri accent. *Powerful funky.* It was the perfect marriage of two worlds, one Missouri rural and the other hip. You couldn't describe the current stage of the hip movement in Kansas City better. People were starting to "turn on," but long hair was rare. In fact, the only people with long hair I had seen were some guys in a rock group.

Andy was right. Pappy served up the best BBQ I'd likely ever eat.

11.

More for Your Dollar

July 1967

A s the morning rush-hour traffic raced by, I knew I'd miss Kansas City and my new friends. But after ten days, it was time to move on. I kept my thumb high in the air, hoping to snag a ride east. My next stop: Ann Arbor, Michigan. I wanted to see Misty on my way to Montreal.

The night before, my KC buddies had taken me out for Italian food and then for drinks at a club featuring female impersonators. "You gotta see this place," Andy said.

Talk about a strange mix of performers and patrons. I thought I had stepped into a crowded, noisy Fellini movie. As I stood there rooted to the floor, mesmerized by the sights, Bill came over next to me. "Crazy, huh? Have you ever seen anything like it? Too many years of inbreeding have destroyed the gene pool."

Up the road, a couple in an old Ford station wagon pulled over, interrupting my daydream. I grabbed my duffel and jumped in the backseat. James, the driver, a thin twentysomething with a reddish face, desperately needed dental work. A few miles out of the city, he dropped his wife off at her job and offered me a seat up front.

"She's going to divorce me," he said right away. "I don't really know why. Hell, I buy her cigarettes."

You buy her cigarettes? What could I say to that? "Maybe it will work out."

As we drove east on Highway 24, he told me all about the places we passed—stuff only a native would know. "I have this little spread out past Moberly," he said, his face beaming. "I'm fixing up the house so we can move out there. I hate city life—I feel much freer in the country."

After stopping for "some of the best sweet potato pie around," we got back on the road, and he pointed to a lone knoll in the distance. "See that old house up there? A few years back we had a helluva rainstorm and this whole area flooded—except for that hill over yonder. This man and his wife were stranded inside. Crazy as it sounds, all the snakes for miles around went to that piece of land—water moccasins, coral snakes, cottonmouths, you name it—hundreds of them. The couple holed up in the kitchen and stuffed towels under doors and in cracks, but the snakes always found a way in. One of 'em had to stay awake with an ax the whole time. It went on for three days and three nights until someone got out to them with a boat."

"Cripes, glad I wasn't there."

Shortly after noon, James let me off at a highway junction near the turnoff to his place in Moberly. I stood at the top of an on-ramp, pointing my thumb south toward Columbia and Interstate 70. Before long, a fellow pulled up across the street in a green Pontiac station wagon and shouted out his window, "Hey, you wanna earn fifty bucks taking down a carousel? You can ride with us to St. Louis tomorrow morning if you want."

That was something I'd never done before. "Sure!"

I ran to his car and jumped into the passenger seat. Pushing fifty, I'd guess, he had scraggly grayish hair and a jiggly gut, the butt of a cigar hanging from his mouth.

The man drove down the road to a bustling carnival. I followed him to the rides, and he showed me a place under the Tilt-O-Whirl to throw my bag.

"Here's a dollar. Get yourself something to eat over there." He pointed to a small store beyond the carnival. "I gotta leave for a while. See you when I get back."

I accepted the money, and he took off. Of course, he didn't know I had over two hundred dollars on me, most of it hidden in the seam of my pants. I bought a pint of chocolate milk and a packaged slice of peach pie, finishing off my meal with a cigarette while walking back to the carnival grounds.

The man hadn't returned. With nothing to do, I crawled under the Tilt-O-Whirl and lay down in the grass, resting my head on my duffel bag. It was about the noisiest place you could ever find for taking a nap, what with the screeching and clanking of gears and the screaming of people as they spun around wildly above me, but somehow I dozed off.

When I woke up and got my bearings, I crawled out from under the platform to see the carnival man standing close by, as if he were waiting for me.

He narrowed his eyes. "Napping, eh? Come with me."

He led me past a few rides to a concession stand that advertised "Hot Dogs" and "Snow Cones" in huge red letters. Next to the window was a big picture of a red, yellow, and blue smiling clown. As we approached, the pleasant smell of fresh popcorn filled the air. A chubby middle-aged man with thinning hair manned the booth.

The carnival boss pointed his soggy cigar at him. "Hey, Brady, I told you about those cups, you fat fuck! What the hell's the matter with you? I should can your sorry dumb ass!"

I saw fear in Brady's eyes, along with a little hate. He started to open his mouth, but before he could say a word, the boss turned on his heel and headed on in the direction we had been moving.

Jeez. What the hell had the guy done to get reamed out like that?

We walked on to a string of booths. The boss stopped at the first one, where a little man with gray hair was running a pop-the-balloon-with-a-dart-and-win-a-teddy-bear game. There was only a stump where one of the man's arms had been. He probably lost it in one of the giant gears that operated the carnival rides.

The boss got in the old carny's face. "Hey, Stumpy, you set up fifteen minutes late this morning," he said in a sharp, loud tone that could cut cardboard. "I'm so fucking sick of dealing with a freaking mutant. I should throw you out of this goddamn place, you dog-faced idiot."

The little man hung his head in embarrassment.

"Forget about taking a dinner break tonight. Maybe you'll get lucky and grow some brains, you stupid fuck."

What an asshole. This guy was a prick to all his people. Even though he had treated me decently, that didn't make the disrespect he heaped on his employees any more palatable.

He continued to berate the poor chap. When he finished his harassment, he turned around. Reaching into my wallet, I handed him a dollar bill. "I decided I don't want to work for you."

He stood there looking like a dim-witted hound with a fly up his nose as I turned and walked back to where I stashed my duffel. I threw it over my shoulder and headed toward the highway.

Ever since I can remember, I've felt like an observer, a tourist in a foreign land, fascinated by the different ways people behave. I'll never understand why so many of us reject love and choose foolish prejudices and pettiness. Why is it hard for us to see that when we hurt someone, it is at the expense of feeling good about ourselves?

The heat of the afternoon and my duffel bag weighed on me, but I couldn't have felt better about how I'd handled the carnival man. Being principled sometimes exacts a bitter price, but today it sure left me with a good aftertaste.

Two young black kids rode their bikes alongside me for a while, asking questions. We joked together as I walked, and their smiles made me forget my load. Once back at the junction, I didn't have to wait long for a stylish ride. A middle-aged man in a Caddie picked me up, and I was surprised and pleased to find out that both he and his wife had Harleys. We shared biker stories all the way to Columbia, Missouri.

12.

Pray and Beg

July 1967

Finally on Interstate 70, I badly needed a bathroom. The only building in sight was a gas station about an eighth of a mile down the frontage road. Seeing no bushes or other options, I decided to hike there.

As I made my way along the road, a monarch butterfly floated beside me. When it sailed away, I realized that almost everywhere I had stood with my thumb out, I had seen a monarch or two. Their sturdy orange wings made them seem so solid, and it was comforting to have them traveling along with me now.

Arriving at the gas station, I found a small store attached. In the window, a buckskin jacket with two rows of rawhide fringe caught my eye. I'd never seen anything like it outside of a Daniel Boone movie. After first using the bathroom, I tried it on—a perfect fit, as though it had been made for me. Eighteen dollars was steep, but what the hell. I walked out of the shop feeling mighty spiffy in my new threads.

For some time, I'd had a simple wardrobe: blue work shirt, blue jeans, and tall reddish-brown Red Wing boots. I bought the boots when I got my bike, and they were the only shoes I'd worn since. They resembled western boots without all the fancy stitching and pointy shit-kicker toes. In warm weather, I wore cut-off jeans and boots, and if it was hot enough and I wasn't traveling, I'd go barefoot. Granted, I didn't have much variety, but it made shopping for clothes a snap. Now I had a handsome buckskin jacket to add to my attire.

About to head back to the on-ramp, I noticed a young couple driving up to the pump. When I asked if they might be heading toward St. Louis, they hesitated and looked at each other. Figuring I wasn't much of a threat, they agreed to take me as far as they were going.

Both grad students, Joan and Harry were returning to Chicago after visiting Joan's parents in Utah. She wore a white blouse and knee-length skirt, and he a madras button-down shirt and khakis; she studied psychology, and he sociology. Despite their generic, clean-cut appearance, they sparked some stimulating discussions.

Harry went on and on about the military mentality. "A teenager's mind is pliable. These kids are drafted and then brainwashed to the point that they lose their basic human feelings, their morality, especially in combat. They might as well have their hearts surgically removed!"

As dusk set in, they pulled over at a roadside rest stop to pitch their tent.

They invited me to eat dinner with them, a gourmet meal of pears, peanut butter, and potato chips. I contributed some crackers and cheese I had purchased where we met. After wishing them a good night, I laid out my sleeping bag behind some bushes and crawled in. Within minutes, the seesaw sound of scores of crickets lulled me to sleep.

Awakened by the light of dawn, I washed up and shaved in the public bathroom. My friends were still asleep, so I walked to the rest-stop exit to catch a ride. The air was chilly but fresh, and I was grateful for my new jacket. After standing for two lonely hours, Joan and Harry pulled up and carried me past the arch to the eastern side of St. Louis. They dropped me at an exit and drove on to visit some friends.

After several hours, the temperature rising, I had added only six miles to my journey and lost a few minutes off my life—from the cigarettes I smoked to while away the time.

By then I knew all the stages I would go through after being dropped off. First, I'd make a quick evaluation of my surroundings, focusing on practical concerns. Was I in danger of any kind? Where should I stand for the best flow of traffic going in my direction? I looked for a visible spot on the road with plenty of shoulder so drivers could easily see me from a distance and have enough room to stop after driving by and checking me out.

Then the wait would begin, along with a series of emotions. At the beginning, I celebrated my new spot, perhaps recalling my last ride and little snippets of conversation. Filled with confidence, I'd stand there, chest out, my foot on the curb and my thumb held high, anticipating the next segment of my journey. What manner of kind stranger would give me my next ride?

When thirty or forty minutes had passed, I would start getting impatient, pacing back and forth between vehicles, but holding on to a bit of optimism. Give it another twenty minutes or so, and creepy doubts would set in, chipping away at my "What, me worry?" resolve. Was I ever going to get a ride? Wasn't anybody going to stop? Would I still be here after dark? What would I do then?

After two or three hours of standing in a place I never wanted to see again, I'd enter the desperate "pray and beg" stage. As each vehicle approached, I would chant in my mind, *Please . . . please . . . please.* Add another hour and I'd lose every shred of self-respect and fall into stage two of "pray and beg," pleading out loud, "Please. . . please . . . please . . . oh, please!"

Now, waiting at the top of an on-ramp with a pathetic flow of traffic (one car every five, ten, or even fifteen minutes), I had reached the silent stage of pray and beg. Just as I thought I'd become a permanent resident of the St. Louis area, I heard a woman yelling from the bottom of the on-ramp. I turned to see Joan waving wildly out the window of their car. Feeling light with relief, I grabbed my duffel and ran down to meet them. It was a miracle they had spotted me so far above the roadway. No doubt I was the only hitchhiker in history to be picked up by the same driver three times in less than twenty-four hours.

In Effingham, Illinois, our paths finally separated when I asked them to drop me at a huge truck stop in the hopes of finding a trucker heading to Michigan. It took a while, but I managed to catch a ride all the way to Ann Arbor with a kindly Detroit-bound truck driver.

We bounced along like a pair of dice in a leather cup, our voices vibrating when we talked. "Is this tru-u-u-ck always so sha-a-a-ky?" I asked the guy.

"It's the damn trailer-r-r," he said. "I've ha-a-a-d it for six months. It ha-a-a-s special shock absorbers that cushion-n-n the load, but they push every bu-u-u-mp and jerk into the cab. My doctor says it's shaking my-y-y kidneys loose."

I was going only a short distance. How could this guy drive every day in this thing? "Can't you d-o-o-o anything a-a-a-bout it?" I asked, my voice trilling.

"Yeah, get another trailer-r-r. But there's no-o-o way I can do that. It'll take me seven-n-n more years to pa-a-a-y this one off. I'm-m-m stuck with it."

I felt for the guy and at the same time was relieved when he let me off in Ann Arbor late that afternoon. One easy ride took me to the University of Michigan campus, a beautiful place with old brick buildings and lots of grass and trees.

Spotting a pay phone, I called the number Misty had given me two weeks before. Her sorority sister told me she hadn't arrived yet but was expected in a couple of days. What to do now? I found a concrete bench along a walkway and sat in the setting sun, thinking about my next move. Occasionally people walked by, and I spotted a hip girl wearing wire-rimmed glasses and a tie-dye T-shirt.

"Excuse me, do you know if there's a youth hostel around here? I need to find a place to stay for the night."

"Uh . . . I can't think of anything." She looked around as if something might jog her memory. "Wait a second. I know some people who might be able to help you" She pulled a little address book out of her purse and thumbed through it. Then she wrote down an address on a scrap of paper, handed it to me, and gave me directions.

I thanked her, and with nothing to lose, I walked the five blocks to their house. A stocky, attractive young woman answered my knock, her straight black hair fanning out over her shoulders and down her back.

"Hi, my name is Rich, and I came to town to visit somebody, but I found out she won't be here for a few days. A girl I met on campus said you folks might know where I could crash for the night."

She told me her name was Kathy and invited me in. She then introduced me to her roommates, Jill and DJ, and said I could stay on the
couch if I wanted to—without giving it a second thought.

The next morning I went into the kitchen and found no fewer than
eleven large paper shopping bags full of garbage stacked up in one
corner. When I took out the trash, they threatened to keep me there
forever.

13.

A Fair Maiden
July–August 1967

I left my new roommates' phone number with Misty's sorority house, and she called me two days later. Early that afternoon, she picked me up and we drove to the Nichols Arboretum, acres and acres of beautiful trees, shrubs, bushes, and grassy meadows. No one was taking advantage of this urban oasis, so we had the place to ourselves.

Misty had a pretty doll-like face and sweet smile. I loved listening to her. Her voice had a slight vibration to it, like when you hold a single note on a harmonica.

Ann Arbor was going to be just another stop along the way to Montreal. But to my surprise, I was really digging this lady. And she revealed a secret that further endeared her to my heart.

"Guess what?" she said. "When we rode together with John from Aspen, my hair dryer was stuffed with pot." She pulled out a joint and lit it up. "This should be good for some laughs."

I stared at her, grinning. What guts! I never risked carrying dope when I traveled.

We spent that afternoon, as well as the next two, getting stoned and admiring nature in the wonderful arboretum. On the third day, as we sat on a blanket in a haze watching two butterflies tumble over each other with nothing but love on their tiny minds, I talked about leaving soon for Montreal.

"Have you ever been to Canada?" she asked.

"Once, when I was a kid. My folks took my sister and me on a road trip around the country. We detoured into Canada at Niagara Falls and came out in Detroit."

"I'd love to see the world's fair. We can take my car, but I can't be gone too long because rush week for my sorority starts in six days."

"Really? Wow. When would you like to leave?"

"How about tomorrow morning?"

"Perfect. Hey, this will be a blast!"

I'd finally reach my goal and make it to the world's fair—and with this lovely lady for company. You couldn't do better than that!

After a long ten-hour drive, we arrived in Montreal just as dusk fell on the city. I had to wrestle with rush-hour traffic, especially stressful after floating on the highway all day.

We pulled into a gas station to get information about a place to stay, knowing it might be difficult to find something in the crowded city. Although prepared to sleep in the car if necessary, we didn't relish the idea. I studied our map, and as if on cue, a man approached us.

"Are you looking for a place to stay?" he asked with a strong French accent.

"As a matter of fact, we are."

"We have a room set up in our home for guests. It's sixteen US dollars a night. You interested?"

Misty's eyes and mine met in disbelief. "Absolutely," I said.

We followed the man's car to a nearby neighborhood, and his wife showed us to a delightful little room, furnished with a double bed covered with a colorful quilt, an antique dresser, a matching chair, and a pair of bedside tables. Two paintings of European vistas hung above the bed. The adjoining bathroom, scented with lavender, had fresh towels laid out. I paid her for two nights.

After taking turns using the shower, we both slid under the covers. The bed was soft and so was Misty, and even though we were tired from our drive, we took our time making love to keep the moment special.

Limited to only a few days together, we had no time to play dating games. We would be parting company soon and might never see each other again. That made everything simple. Neither of us expected anything or wasted a second on unnecessary questions or petty concerns.

I awoke after a deep sleep to the daylight filtering through the curtains and the romantic sound of French-speaking children playing outside our window. I pulled Misty's warm, smooth body close to mine, and she wrapped her arms around me.

Opening her eyes, she purred. "Morning, mister."

"Morning, sweet lady."

We kissed and kissed and made love again, this time to the musical laughter of children.

Our hearts were still connected as we entered the grounds of the world's fair, hand in hand, and paused to figure out where to go. Looking up from reading a brochure, Misty said, "It says here there are over ninety different pavilions. How are we going to choose?"

I gave her a peck on the cheek. "Nothing to do but start walking."

We wandered everywhere, through halls and exhibits showcasing scientific advancements mankind had achieved or hoped to in the future. Our favorite was AT&T's Picturephone, a device that would allow us to see the person we were talking to.

I laughed. "Dick Tracy, eat your heart out."

"I wonder if we'll live to see something like this in our homes."

"Wouldn't that be neat?"

After many hours and many miles, we headed back to our room, worn out. Standing by the open window, we shed our clothes and shared a few puffs of pot. Our naked bodies, sensitized by the smoke, moved together in a soft, harmonious dance, and we passed another glorious night of lovemaking in that luxurious bed.

As she lay asleep in my arms, her head on my chest, I thought about how wonderful our day had been at the fair, and now this. Did that make her "my fair lady"? Smiling, I knew Misty was the fairest maiden in my heart. I also knew our romantic stay in charming Montreal would be a sweet memory for a long time to come.

I had reached the apex of my journey. Images from my travels flashed through my mind, causing a soft excitement to grow in my chest. I'd soon be heading back home.

14.

California Here I Thumb
August 1967

Opening the passenger door, I felt the sharp chill of the Michigan morning. Misty leaned over and gave me a long, passionate kiss. In a soft, cooing voice, she said, "I'm going to miss you, mister."

I smiled. "It's been real, babe. You have my number if you're ever out west."

She gave me a look that melted my heart. "Careful what you wish for. Happy travels."

As Misty drove away, I once again found myself standing by a highway. I would miss her—we had shared a lot in just a week. I thought about our last evening together, when we'd made love in the backseat of her car. It had been a challenge, me living on a couch and Misty in a sorority house, but we'd made the best of it. I would also miss my three short-term roommates, whom I now considered good friends. But it was time to head west to California.

It took a full day and night and six different rides before I passed St. Louis. For most of the morning, I stood at the junction of Interstate 70 and a country road that led nowhere. The only structure in sight was a distant boarded-up shack with a few obsolete gas pumps beside it.

As usual, I started out bathing in the memory of the last exchange with a friendly driver—in this case, a chubby businessman who had spoken lovingly about his family. But soon he faded from my mind, and after a few hours in the hot sun, my thoughts turned dark.

What if no one stopped? What if I had to walk for miles?

Why had I ever considered such an idiotic undertaking?

Finally, a car pulled over fifty yards down the road—a dirty brown '59 Olds 98. Grabbing my duffel bag, I ran as fast as I could with my load, tossed it in the backseat, and jumped in after it. At that moment, I felt enormous gratitude for the person who had saved me from what I imagined would have been my final resting place, there by the side of that god-forsaken piece of asphalt.

Behind the wheel was a fortyish man in a wrinkled western shirt with a day-old beard and scruffy hair that could use a brush.

"Where you headin'?"

"Back to California, by way of Joplin." My Kansas City friends would be there by now, getting ready for school. Bill had given me an address where I could find them. "Where are you going?"

"I was out drinkin' last night in Louisville, Kentucky, and I felt like takin' a drive. So I got in the car and here I am. Not quite sure where I'll end up. I hear Kansas City's nice. Denver too."

We rode together across Missouri, and after stopping for gas and pie, I drove for about five hours while he slept. He filled his gas hog again and dropped me off short of Kansas City so I could take Highway 69 south to Joplin.

This time, a preacher, probably a Baptist, picked me up. Soon after I got in the car, he asked, "Do you believe in creation or evolution?"

I digested his question for a moment. "Well, you know, there's an awful lot of scientific evidence that supports evolution—if you study the fossil record or you look at how animals evolve even within our lifetime. Fruit flies in lab experiments go through whole generations in just a few days, and they change genetically. Everything points to evolution being a sound theory . . . Of course, it's not for me to say whether evolution is controlled by or in the hands of a higher power."

The good reverend sat there, eyes on the road, not saying anything. Had I thrown a monkey wrench into his proposed sermon? Or had I somehow given him a perspective on the subject he had never considered? Whatever my words had accomplished, I took comfort in the silence that followed.

As I stood again in some Podunk place, three teenagers in an old black pickup flew by, and one of them yelled something as a beer bottle hit the pavement close to my feet. It didn't break, but it would have hurt had it hit its mark. My chest tightened. I kept an eye on the direction they had gone, but happily, the pickup never returned.

My next ride was in a faded brown '54 Ford with two huge beer-in-hand fellows in the front seat and their bulldog named Pete in the back. Hesitant, I climbed into the car and was handed a cold brew. They were friendly, if sauced, and the beer hit the spot. Still, I let out a huge sigh of relief when they let me off in Joplin—especially after they threatened to let Pete drive.

I stopped at a weathered Texaco station with a sign in the window— "CIGARETTES 25 CENTS"—and discovered I was only twelve blocks from my destination. After buying two packs of Marlboros at the dirt-cheap price, I hiked to a faded, little white-and-tan house, where Bill, Shirley, Andy, Tote, and Ruth were just about to leave to get something to eat. We walked to a coffee shop, catching up on the way.

"Hey, Rich," Bill said. "Did you see the hippie article in *Look* magazine?"

"For real?"

"Yeah, a whole spread. They talked about Haight-Ashbury, flower children, a love-in at the park with the Grateful Dead. Some of it was the usual bullshit with a photo of someone shooting up, but a lot of it showed what's really happening. *Look* magazine, man."

That evening they threw a pot party at their pad, and about fifteen people showed up. The grass was so strong I got my mind blown—literally. I saw the top of my head blow off and disintegrate into little sparkly green and gold fragments when it hit the ceiling. The power of the stuff reduced most of the smokers to long fits of laughter and incoherent conversations.

Eventually too stoned to stand, I crashed on the living room floor. I didn't fall asleep, but I had no intention of looking for a better place to rest. Several others sprawled out around me.

Lying a few feet to my left was a woman I'd noticed early on. Taller than most of the guys, with straight jet-black hair, she strapped in her large breasts with one of those pointy-shaped bras that turn tits into torpedoes. I never liked that look—those things could poke your eye out. Sometime during the night we ended up in each other's arms. When I woke up in the morning, she was gone.

A few hours later, after multiple good-byes and enough cups of coffee to function, I had my thumb out again, this time catching a ride that set me down on Route 66 somewhere west of Oklahoma City. I hoped the next ride would take me all the way through the Texas panhandle. It was well known that authorities in the Lone Star State frowned on hitchhikers, especially long-haired ones—and their jails were to be avoided at all costs.

Three guys in a late-model blue Chevy Corvair convertible, the top down, stopped up ahead. The fellow in the back waved his arm for me to come, and I was off running once again.

"Where are you heading?" I asked. *Please, please say New Mexico.*

"California," the driver said.

"Hot damn!"

All my traveling companions were heading to the Golden State. The driver, a young Wall Street trader, tired of New York and the rat race, wanted to return to his roots in San Jose. Beside him was a member of the Gypsy Joker motorcycle gang, en route to Richmond. He'd been picked up south of Chicago, his only luggage a red metal toolbox full of motorcycle tools. Next to me, an army infantryman on leave fresh out of Vietnam, came from somewhere in Ohio and was on his way to visit family in Fresno.

Nonstop talking filled the car. The serviceman talked about battles, bongs, and brothels; the biker, about brawls, bikes, and babes; the trader, about brokers, bonds, and burnout; and I, about thumbing, tripping, and travel. Somewhere outside of Barstow, the radio blared, "Get your kicks on Route 66," and we all sang along to the lyrics.

The time flew by, and before I knew it, I was standing by a highway in the middle of San Jose.

I thought the final eighty miles would be a breeze, but a series of lonely waits and pitiful, short rides added another seven hours to my journey. At last, I climbed the stairs to my cozy pea-green room at Grist House and found a note from Brandi. She had moved to San Francisco, finally doing what she most wanted to do. I'd miss her joyful laugh and warm, curvaceous body, but I felt happy she'd followed her heart.

After a long and most welcome hot shower, I collapsed exhausted in my own bed. A strobe light of memories flickered through my head as I drifted off. I made it. What a trip!

PART 3

I Feel a Draft

Why not go out on a limb?
Isn't that where all the fruit is?
—Frank Scully

Courage is not simply one of the virtues,
but the form of every virtue at its testing point.
—C. S. Lewis

15.

Death Wind
August 1967

"It's a beautiful day for a bike ride," Rod said, looking up at the sky. The day before, he had returned to Davis, hitchhiking back from his parents' house in Billings, Montana.

We sat in the Grist House driveway, he on his Triumph and I on my BSA. Next to me, our buddy Albert had just arrived with his motorcycle, a self-made, hodgepodge of parts painted in primer black, with no brand identification or resemblance to any bike I'd ever seen.

A quiet, gangly fellow, Albert could build and repair practically anything, even tractors. He learned from his father, who restored antique automobiles in a shop behind their home. Now Albert majored in electrical engineering.

As word of his mechanical genius got around, we began to refer to him affectionately as Mr. Wizard, after the science wiz on the TV show *Watch Mr. Wizard*, who performed all kinds of cool experiments to teach kids about chemistry and physics.

The three of us sat in the driveway like three spokes of a wheel, our front tires almost touching, each taking turns talking about the summer.

"You gotta hear this hilarious story," Rod said, his curly blond hair bouncing as his head moved in all directions.

I smiled. I had missed his crazy acrobatics.

"I was standing on some godforsaken road near Rawlings, Wyoming, when these three young guys picked me up in a rusty brown '52 Ford. They told me they'd bought the funky thing for thirty bucks. It was definitely a wreck waiting to happen. That junker topped out at about thirty-five miles an hour.

"As we rolled along the highway, I noticed the fellow riding in the passenger seat. Every so often, he would lean way out the window." Rod stretched his neck and body to the side to demonstrate. "I finally asked him what he was looking at. He turned back and nonchalantly said, 'Front wheel's gonna fall off.'

"I didn't think much of it, and we continued on for a couple of hours with him occasionally hanging out the window. Then he yelled, 'There it goes!' The car tipped to the right with this loud thud and an awful screeching of metal and sparks, and the beast finally came to a stop at the side of the highway. Shit, man, it was a real scene."

"Wild, man," I said.

"But what happened?" Albert asked. "You can't stop there."

Rod shrugged. "Well, we abandoned the car, and there were four of us with our thumbs out. We traveled together all the way to Butte."

Albert bent over to adjust some bike part near his right knee. He looked up, using his finger to smooth the thick, push broom of a mustache he had grown over the summer. "I just got back from a three-week ride through the Sierras on this baby. Circled Lake Tahoe and ended up in Yosemite, camping along the way. I dropped acid at Mono Lake. Man, that's a helluva trippy place. I swear I met some aliens. It freaked me out so much I split." He ran his fingers through his dark, shaggy hair. "Must have driven fifty miles before I could get my head straight again."

Rod nodded. "Damn, I know what you mean, man. Acid can be wicked." Then he launched into a story about the amazing pot he'd scored in Montana.

As I watched his arms slice through the air like knives, a strange heaviness came over me—as though one of those massive red-velvet curtains in the movie theaters had fallen on my life. My heart felt like a hundred-pound brick, squashing any desire to do anything, much less be social.

"Sorry, guys. I really don't feel like taking a ride right now." Getting off my bike, I rolled it across the street into the storage shed and then walked back to the house and up to my room. My friends' voices receded in the distance. For at least two hours, I sat in my rocker, looking out the window but staring at nothing in particular.

For nearly two months, I had enjoyed incredible freedom: no schedules, no responsibilities, no restrictions. It hit me that not only was I going back to school, but I was also nearly finished, and the societal norm and parental pressure dictated it was "time to get a job and settle down for the rest of your life"—a tradition I had no intention of following.

But even more disturbing, I had only one more semester before becoming prime meat for the draft.

I thought about Kevin, his face etched in my memory. I had met him while hanging out with some friends shortly before summer began. On leave from Vietnam, he was just nineteen, yet his eyes seemed old and hard. "There is no way I'm going back," he said in an anxious voice. "I'm heading to Canada in a few days. This war sucks."

I had sensed in him a soft heart surrounded by a hard shell—he might break apart like fine china or erupt like a volcano.

Smoking a cigarette, he turned to me. "So the four of us were speeding down this curvy, narrow, dirt road on our way back to camp after partying in Saigon. We came around this corner and hit this little old man with a cane walking on the side of the road. He flew about thirty feet like a rag doll. The driver didn't even slow down. All he said was, 'One less gook to worry about.'"

My stomach twisted, and I decided on the spot that this wasn't a place I ever wanted to be—not in Vietnam and not with my mind bent into such a heartless place.

That frigid-cold draft. Like one that creeps in through a leaky window on a stormy night. But this draft didn't just chill you to the bone—this one separated your heart from your soul. This draft put M1 rifles in the hands of mild-mannered boys. It forced them to hear whistling bullets and deafening explosions and piercing screams and moans and sobbing. And it forced them to see flames and blood and gristle and torn limbs and death and destruction. Sounds and visions forever embedded in their minds.

This cold wind demanded you take strangers, only boys themselves, into death to save your own skin. This hellishness turned carefree young men into hating, hollow remnants of themselves, full of nightmares and physical, mental, and emotional dysfunction—that is, if they were lucky enough to walk away from the evil storm alive.

The draft was a death wind in every possible way.

The heaviness and darkness transformed my "What, me worry!" into "What the fuck!" My chest felt packed with soggy, wet towels, and I struggled to breathe. How could I return to the lightness that had favored me for so long?

16.

A Very Wrong Turn
August–October 1967

The next day old Mrs. Grist shook up my life even more when she informed Rod and me that she had rented out both our rooms to new tenants starting in September—pretty cold after we had paid rent all summer and were rarely there.

That weekend, I dropped by to see my friend Tammy, who lived with seven other young women in a big Victorian house on 3rd Street. Talking with her and several of her roommates, I mentioned needing a new place to live in less than two weeks. Tammy said their basement was empty, and the other women agreed I was welcome to move in, so we went downstairs to check it out.

I found a bed, a dresser, and a few dusty boxes that some unknown, long-departed housemate had stashed there. The space was more than adequate, and I'd be a fool to give up the opportunity to live with eight women. I drove to Sacramento and picked up my grandfather's large Oriental rug gathering dust in my parent's garage. After some heavy-duty basement cleaning, I added two chairs and my steamer trunk to the furniture that came with the room.

In one of the boxes, I discovered more than a dozen large rectangles of thin, wispy material—the kind used to make sheer curtains—dyed pastel yellow, red, orange, and white. I tacked them to the ceiling above the bed so each one billowed downward like a ship's sail full of wind, creating a canopy bed without posts. The rich colors of the Oriental rug and the diffused light coming through the high basement window gave the bed a storybook look, like something from a sultan's lair—appropriate, what with a virtual harem living above me.

Tammy had a good-sized motorcycle, and another girl had a smaller bike. With my BSA, that made three, and we parked them on an old piece of carpet in a corner of the living room. I built a ramp down one side of the front stairs and another where the walk went off the curb into the street. Riding out the front door, we'd always get double takes from passersby. Life was fun at 3rd Street House.

Except for one thing. The heaviness I'd felt at Grist House moved there with me. It was a constant presence, deep in my chest, although less intense now. I knew it would continue as long as I wrestled with the prospect of war and killing. *Oh, how I missed that laid-back, carefree feeling.*

My housemate Kathy and her boyfriend, Ron, invited me to their afternoon wedding on the east side of Sacramento, and I drove there in my newly acquired red-and-white '59 VW van.

I had only been too happy to trade in my troublesome Bug, vowing to never buy another car shaped like—and the color of—a lemon. After returning from hitchhiking that summer, I'd decided to travel again when school was finished in December, so I chose a vehicle I could easily turn into a home on wheels.

As I passed Kathy in the reception line following the ceremony, she whispered, "We're going to stop off at our apartment on the way to the reception." (Wink, wink, nudge, nudge.)

After sharing a joint with them in their new place, I took off for the reception, soon realizing that the pot was killer strong. Dressed in my usual attire—jeans, denim shirt, rawhide fringed jacket, and Redwing boots—I was way too stoned to hang around so many suits. Normally I didn't think much about my appearance, caring more about comfort and function. But today paranoia crept in.

The only people I knew were the bride and groom—who were obviously otherwise occupied. I started to imagine myself as a life-sized sore thumb in fringed buckskin. Man, that was some powerful shit.

Standing way off to the side, I was approached by a middle-aged couple straight out of the famous painting of the farmer holding a pitchfork next to his wife, serious expressions included. With a mixture of friendly overtures and what I perceived to be an odd fascination with a zoo animal, they tried to carry on a conversation with me. But in my current condition, I failed miserably. Before long they moved on.

Freaking out wasn't normal for me, but on this day I couldn't shake it. Deciding to split, I told my friends I needed to go and was relieved to find myself driving back to Davis.

Interstate 80 didn't go all the way through Sacramento but instead dumped you onto streets, where a confusing series of turns carried you out of the city toward Davis. On one of those streets, I saw a large sign on the side of the road just past an intersection: "I-80 TURN LEFT ONE BLOCK." Not thinking clearly, I immediately turned left and drove one short block, coming to a dead end at a big concrete building with a large sign: "SLOW 5 MPH." The road funneled me down a slight incline that leveled out into an underground parking garage.

I thought I spotted a police car—and another and another and another . . . Oh my God. Was I really seeing dozens of cop cars? Then it hit me like a ten-ton truck—I was at a fucking police station!

My body stiffened, and I swallowed a lump the size of a golf ball. The deafening beat of my heart drowned out the sound of the van's engine echoing off the concrete ceiling. "Oh please, please, don't let anyone come out while I'm here," I whispered, my hands gripping the wheel.

"Okay, keep calm. Stay at five miles an hour so you don't attract attention . . . What do you mean 'attract attention'?" There I was, talking to myself and driving a great big red-and-white hippie van in a freaking buckskin-fringed hippie jacket, bombed out of my mind on pot. Were there any cops around? I didn't see any. Oh shit, man.

I continued slowly (not even five miles an hour) down the single lane, deep into the parking area. It was taking a looooong time. I passed a set of double glass doors to my right, but I didn't turn, afraid to look. Out of my peripheral vision, I saw a brightly lit hallway. Hallway empty. Face straight ahead.

At the end of the building, the lane angled to the left past a string of what must have been twenty bright, shiny, black-and-white police motorcycles, looking pretty as can be—pretty menacing, that is.

My heart slammed against my chest so hard I thought my ribs would break. Be cool, man. Be cool. The muscles in my neck and shoulders had turned to granite.

I rolled along as slowly as I could. What if someone looked out? What if someone came out?

Shit, shit, shit, shit, shit!

Turn left one block. You idiot—what were you thinking? I smacked my forehead with the palm of my hand. That meant you go one block and then turn left, not before. Dumb, dumb, dumb.

I inched along, and after what felt like three weeks and a few days, I finally drove back up the ramp into the sunlight—and emerged from that horror chamber onto the street above. Miraculously, no one had seen me.

But I wasn't safe yet.

I still had to get to the corner and back on the main drag. It was possible a police car would return to the station before I made it.

Finally, I turned the corner, and as I passed the sign "I-80 TURN LEFT ONE BLOCK," I scolded myself again for my stupid mistake. I took a deep breath, maybe the first in a while. It would make a hell of a story, but shit, man. Boy.

What the hell was happening to me? I could usually handle anything. A bum trip on pot? How was that possible? A paranoid fit of freaking out in the police garage was understandable, but at a wedding reception? Was the possibility of going to war getting to me? Had the Flimberg magic worn off?

Back home, my housemate Sherri cracked up when she heard my tale. Then she rubbed the knots out of my rock-hard shoulders and made me some peppermint tea. What can I say? It's so damn good to have a friend around when you need one.

17.

Resistance

October 1967

Two months before school ended, Hal and I sat cross-legged on the carpet in my room listening to music from *The Doors* drifting down from upstairs. He pulled a well-rolled joint from a shirt pocket, flicked his Zippo lighter, and took a long draw. Holding it in, he said in a raspy voice, "A few weeks back, during Stop the Draft Week, over two hundred protesters blocked the entrance to the Oakland Military Induction Center."

Smoke trickled from his mouth as he passed the joint to me. "They arrested forty protesters, including Joan. She's been speaking a lot about civil disobedience and about how this war's never going to end unless we stand up and make some noise about it."

This was one of many conversations I'd had with Hal about the Joan Baez Institute for the Study of Nonviolence. For the past several months, he had lived at the school down in Carmel, and I considered him an expert on the politics of peace.

I took a toke and slowly let it out. "As you know, I graduate in December—and then I'll be fresh fodder for the draft. I'm trying to figure out what the hell to do. I don't think I can kill anybody if they send me to Vietnam. I've never been into fighting with words or fists. Once, in the ninth grade, a bully got off the bus and punched me in the face. I realized right away that hitting him back wouldn't accomplish anything, and it would probably lead to more pain. So after he hit me, I turned around and walked away without a word. I've never really seen any good come from fighting."

"If you don't like to fight and don't see any good coming from fighting or wars, then you're a pacifist," Hal said. "That's the definition."

It made sense. I had just never put a label on it. "When I was a kid, I'd see my parents arguing and want them to stop. I remember thinking if I could make only one wish, I know what it would be. Well, I wasn't a dumb kid, so I'd wish for a million wishes. But if that was against the rules, I would wish that all people could be at peace. So, from what you are saying, I guess I've always been a pacifist."

Hal grinned. "It sure sounds like it."

"Funny thing about that bully who hit me in the face—after I walked away without hitting back, I gained his respect and we actually became friends."

Shortly after my talk with Hal, I applied for conscientious objector status and scheduled a hearing. Three weeks later, I arrived at the Sacramento draft board with a hollow ache in my gut and was asked to sit on a bench in the empty hallway. Twenty long minutes later, a soldier came and told me to follow him. Our footsteps echoed off the highly polished floor as we approached a gray metal door.

The soldier waved me into the room. Straight ahead, behind a worn, wooden table, sat three prehistoric humans—two men and one woman—all in faded, ill-fitting uniforms, a scene Norman Rockwell could have used as inspiration for a *Saturday Evening Post* cover. I estimated their combined age at a figure approaching three hundred.

As I approached, they stared up at me with weary, darting eyes, like turkey vultures evaluating carrion. The thin-faced geezer in the middle chewed on his pencil and looked over some papers. His body might have filled out his uniform decades ago, but now, his skinny, shriveled neck protruded from his collar, making him look like an undernourished ground squirrel.

He pushed his wire-rimmed glasses up his sharp nose and cleared his throat, a strange gargling sound. "Son, are you Richard Israel?"

The room had no other furniture, so I stood before them, my hands by my sides. "Yes."

"You claim you are a conscientious objector." He held up a paper and tapped on it with his pencil. "Why isn't there anything mentioned about it here when you applied for the draft?"

My heart skipped a beat. "Err . . . uh . . . when I registered, I was only fifteen. I didn't have a clue about the world, much less who I was."

"Unfortunately, if you didn't claim it then, you can't claim it now. That's all. You're dismissed, son. Corporal, please show this boy out."

What? I faced the likelihood of taking human blood or spending a few years in Leavenworth Federal Penitentiary, and these old coots couldn't give me two minutes of their time. *Two minutes?*

Speechless, I stared at them, and then turned to follow the young soldier out of the room.

Driving back to Davis, I kept reliving the scene, my body tight with rage. Those heartless bastards didn't give a flying fuck if I rotted in a prison cell. What the hell would I do now? No way was I playing their twisted game—that was for damn certain!

A couple of weeks later, Hal and Russ organized a Davis draft card turn-in on the campus quad, modeled after a recent event in Berkeley. As a crowd gathered on the grass, I found a place to sit near the front, soaking in the warmth of the afternoon sun. At one point, Hal, Russ, and two others approached the mic they had set up.

Hal took the lead and introduced himself. Standing strong and confident, his long hair blowing in the breeze, he commanded attention. Everyone fell silent.

The sun glinted off his brown-rimmed glasses as he held up four small pieces of paper. "We find no other way to express our dissatisfaction with the war in Vietnam," he said, "except through civil disobedience. We are fully aware of the federal law that requires all males eligible for the draft to carry a draft card or face the penalty of prison. Today, the four of us have made the decision to send our draft cards back to the government. We want nothing to do with President Johnson's and the military's brutal war in Vietnam."

Russ and the two other draft resisters took turns at the microphone, each stating their reasons for sending in their cards and severing their relationship with the government, the draft board, and the military.

As I sat there with the rest of the spectators, my blood boiled. Knowing what I needed to do, I gathered my courage and walked up to the mic. "A few weeks ago, I went to the draft board to apply for conscientious objector status. They didn't even give me two minutes of their time—when I could spend two years of my life in Leavenworth Penitentiary. They can have *my* card back too."

Fully aware of the consequences, I would stand up and fight for the right not to fight. Whether I liked it or not, I was now officially associated with the resistance, as well as being a potential felon.

I felt buoyant, as if some weight had been lifted. When Hal and Russ congratulated me, I joked, "Looking back on it, it was probably good that the draft board gave me so little time. Any longer and I guarantee that one of them old geezers would have croaked. Then I'd be left waiting for a replacement."

Even though the bulk of my decision stemmed from my moral beliefs, I also knew that preservation played a small part. This nagged at me. Was I a coward? Then I remembered the courage it took to walk up to that microphone. And I felt proud to stand up for what I knew was right. I had no other option.

The following weekend, I drove to Sacramento to see my parents, planning my usual short visit. Early on in my college career, I learned that I liked spending time with my folks, as long as I kept it to two hours. Beyond that, my sweet mother would revert to her previous programming, unable to shake her habit of over-mothering. I didn't really blame her. After all, she had taught me to tie my shoes and wipe my butt, taking care of me for so many years it was difficult for her to imagine I could do the job myself.

Because I didn't live far away, it was easy for me to drop by and escape again before the initial joviality wore off. By following my two-hour rule, I maintained a pleasant relationship with my folks and enjoyed an occasional home-cooked meal.

When I arrived at my parents' house late that afternoon, my dad was still at work. Sprawled out at the kitchen table, I talked with my mother, trying to sound as casual as possible. "There's something I need to tell you. I've decided to oppose the war, so I sent my draft card back to the government."

Standing opposite me, my mom stiffened, her overprotective maternal instincts aroused. "What? Isn't that against the law?"

"Yeah. But I can't just sit by and do nothing. Somebody has to stand up for what's right. Too many kids are being sent to their deaths."

She gripped the back of a chair. "Rich! Don't you understand you'll ruin your life if you have prison on your record?"

"And getting killed or killing someone in Vietnam won't ruin my life?" I asked. "I can't live with myself if I don't follow what I feel and know is the right thing to do."

She frowned, looking perplexed. "But what do I tell my friends?"

Her friends? "How about that your son has the integrity to stand up for what he believes?"

"But I have always believed my country, right or wrong."

How did that statement come from an intelligent woman like my mother? Even with her quirks, she was smart. "Mom, if it's wrong, it's wrong!"

Luckily I still had the Flimberg place in my brain where I could stash stuff too dangerous to think about. That was where I put the whole prison thing. I'd worry about it when I had to and not before.

Mom slowly began to accept she couldn't change my mind. Her dissatisfaction turned, as it always did, to concern and support. On one of my short visits, she showed me an article she cut from the newspaper. "Rich, it says here that this man in Modesto is ordaining ministers to get them out of the draft."

Much to her dismay, her little Jewish boy was soon on his way to Modesto to become a minister.

An hour and a half later, I arrived at the headquarters of the Universal Life Church, a brick one-story building with a simple wooden cross to the right of the door. I knocked and heard a deep Southern voice say, "Come on in."

When I entered the chilly, fluorescent-lit building, I found the Reverend Kirby Hensley sitting alone at a table behind a beat-up typewriter. A chunky middle-aged man, he wore dark-rimmed glasses too large for his face. A touch of white flickered at his temples. With a cheerful smile, the reverend directed me to sit across from him. "What kin I do for you, young fella?"

"I heard you're ordaining ministers. What's that all about?"

He set his kind eyes on me. "We believe that it's everyone's responsibility to do nothing that infringes on the rights of others and that everyone has the right to religious freedom."

He opened his worn Bible to a marked page and pointed to a passage. "It says here in Romans chapter 2, verse 1 that 'Only God can pass judgment.' It's not up to me to judge who can be a minister. So, son, I'll be glad to ordain you. That will be ten dollars."

I handed him the cash and watched him type up my certificate of ordination. Now a Universal Life Minister, I could legally marry or bury anyone I pleased. As far as the draft was concerned, I wasn't sure if I would ever use the document. But it sure didn't hurt to have an ace up my sleeve.

18.

Climbing the Mountain

November 1967

That fall, I spent a lot of time hanging out at another house, an ancient two-story Victorian over on F Street, where Russ's girlfriend, Marybeth, lived with four other women.

I had first met one of her roommates, Melanie, a year before, during a trip with Hal to the dorm where she lived then. The natural beauty of this petite princess nearly stopped my heart. I couldn't help but stare at her perfectly sculpted face, desperately wanting to reach out and touch her flawless, porcelain skin.

This wasn't a case of falling head over heels in love with someone. When that happened, I usually felt nervous and stumbled over what to say. With Melanie, I experienced sincere awe, like the feeling I'd get seeing a breathtaking sunset—a simple reverence for a miracle of nature.

Spellbound, I blurted out, "You are really pretty!" I'd never said that to anyone before.

Her soft brown eyes widened with surprise. "Well . . . thank you," she said, a slight blush rising to her cheeks. To top it off, unlike many gorgeous women, she accepted her beauty with grace and humility.

One Friday evening, I stopped by the F Street House as Hal came out the door, taking the porch steps two at a time.

"What's up?" I asked.

"I'm heading to a class called Climbing the Mountain given by the Free University. A guy named Tim Putnum is teaching it—I heard that he's really cool. Thought I'd check it out, but I'm late. Want to come along?"

"Free University? Might as well. I'm just hanging out."

We drove in Hal's Jeep to a house on Russell Boulevard and walked into a room filled with wooden chairs. Up front, a man spoke—presumably Putnam—a thin, shorthaired blond fellow with a small brush of a beard on the tip of his chin. We didn't want to interrupt, so we took seats close to the door. About ten people sat in front of us, all leaning forward, paying close attention.

"Since many of you haven't tried meditation before," Putnam said, "we will do it for only about twenty minutes tonight." He held up a long piece of paper. "I'm going to read a poem written by a master, and I want you to pick a couplet and meditate on it."

Listening carefully, I wasn't getting a vibe on anything, and then a question jumped out at me: "What is never changing in an ever-changing world?"

The soul.

Where did that come from? "Soul" wasn't a word I used. It was as though someone else had answered the question.

I pondered this a moment, and the next thing I knew, Tim Putnam spoke again. "Okay, time's up. I hope you enjoyed yourselves. We'll continue next week at the same time. Have a good weekend, everyone."

What the hell? That wasn't twenty minutes. It seemed like maybe twenty or thirty seconds at most. What was going on here? I felt weird and disoriented, but oddly quiet inside. I followed Hal to his Jeep, and we headed back to the F Street House.

"Man, that was wild!" I said.

He looked over, one eyebrow cocked in surprise. "Yeah? You liked it?"

"I don't know. I had like a timeless thing happen."

"What do you mean?"

"Well the guy said twenty minutes, right?"

"Right."

"Did it seem like twenty minutes to you?"

"Sure. Something like that I guess."

"Well, it was more like twenty seconds for me."

"No shit?"

"No shit."

Hal shook his head. "Cool."

As we climbed out of Hal's Jeep, Russ, Marybeth, and Melanie approached us. "We're heading down to Baskin's for some scoops," Marybeth said. "Wanna come?"

It was unthinkable to turn down the familiar pilgrimage to the ice cream parlor, so we reversed course and fell in with the procession.

We crossed the street, and Melanie stopped at a house a few doors down. Russ whispered, "She's got a thing for Reggie." But Reggie did the unthinkable, choosing to work on a paper over joining us pilgrims.

During the familiar four-block trek, my friends chatted as I hung back to sort out what had happened. For the first time in weeks, I didn't feel the heaviness pressing on my chest. "What is never changing in an ever-changing world?" It was like something inside me had been waiting for this question.

For some reason, I felt ripped and sharp at the same time. The elm trees looked vivid and alive, even in the dim evening light. Was this thing called soul in them too? I had to blink a few times to make sure I wasn't hallucinating.

I thought back to high school, when I went to an optometrist for the first time. Dr. Lewis had me sit in a chair beside the front window and look at the brick building across the street. It was just a brick building. So what.

Then he put a contact in each eye. I scolded myself for letting my sister talk me into this. Jabbing buttons in my eyes. What had I been thinking?

When my eyes stopped tearing, he told me to look at the building again. This time, I saw not only the building but every individual brick and even the textures and imperfections on the bricks. Wow.

That's what it felt like after "climbing the mountain"—like putting on a special pair of glasses. The quality of my sight had changed.

As the gang turned to go into Baskin-Robbins, I pointed to the pool hall across the street. "I'm going to shoot some balls." Normally, the magnetism of the ice cream parlor would have pulled me inside. But not that night.

I got a pool table and took some shots, not caring whether anything went in. I simply enjoyed the rolling and clatter of the colorful balls. It was as if I stood off to the side, watching myself play.

Then Brad came by. A robust, burly vet student, he was all muscle except for a bit of a beer belly, which he nurtured whenever possible.

"Hey, Rich. How about a game? Bet I can whoop your butt. Ha, ha, ha," he said, in his usual loud, playful voice. Brad took his responsibilities and opinions seriously, but he was also a jolly fellow, prone to contagious laughter and the use of colorful descriptions, like "It was hotter than a popcorn fart" or "It was raining harder than a cow pissing on a flat rock."

I locked my eyes on his. "We can shoot some balls together, Brad, but I don't want to play a game. I'm not in the mood for competition."

"Sure. That's okay."

He surprised me—it wasn't like Brad to agree so easily. We racked the balls and began to play. Hal, Russ, Marybeth, and Melanie showed up, all smiles, licking their cones.

As they watched, I'd take a shot and miss the hole I was aiming for. But, as if by magic, a ball or two or three would always find a pocket—and usually after multiple deflections off other balls and the table's edges. With each shot, my friends whooped and hollered. It went on like this until we had cleared the table several times.

Brad scratched his head. "Damn! Where the hell did you learn to shoot like that?"

I just smiled at him, not knowing what to make of it.

As we walked back to the house, I again floated along behind the others, craving solitude. Melanie stopped at Reggie's, and when the rest of us arrived at the F Street House, everyone else went inside while I settled on the thick concrete wall of the porch, my feet dangling over the shrubs.

I felt suspended in a warm, still, sweet soup. "Climbing the mountain" had taken me somewhere.

Not much later, Melanie glided up the front path, her movements angelic. My breath still caught at the sight of her beauty. I would have been on her like a rash if she'd made any advances, but I was happy to have her as a friend. Smiling, she sat on the wall next to me, shoulder to shoulder.

"You okay?" Her voice was like butter melting on warm toast.

"I'm good."

"That was some fancy shooting at the pool hall."

"It was unbelievable."

She touched my arm. "You sure you're all right?"

"Yeah. I went to this Free University meditation thing with Hal, and the speaker said we'd spend twenty minutes meditating. He read a lot of phrases and one stuck out. 'What is never changing in an ever-changing world?'"

As I told her the rest of the "soul" story, she watched my face, and I noticed, as always, the depth of her brown doe eyes. "So ever since then, it feels like I've been tripping."

Even the stars seemed to be twinkling more than usual that night. Melanie glowed like a goddess in the soft porch light.

"Are you stoned?" she asked.

"Totally! The weird thing is I haven't taken anything. I'm ripped, but not like on pot, which feels all warm and fuzzy and foggy. And not like acid, where the synapses go off a hundred times a second and your brain bounces around inside a hollow, echoing bell. This is tripping on clarity."

"I know. I feel it too."

"Really?"

"Yeah. Somehow I caught a contact off you. Kind of a magical feeling."

"Far out." I laughed. "That's so cool."

Her lovely eyes connected with mine. What a beautiful smile. We sat in silence for a long, long while, united in an experience of wonder and awe.

19.

I Hear That Whistle Blowin'
December 1967

I never went out with any of my female roommates, but several of them became good friends. "Big Sherri" was my favorite—and big she was. Standing at least six feet tall, with the build of a professional football player, she had a plump face, bright blue eyes above a pudgy nose, and dirty-blonde shoulder-length hair. I rarely saw her wear anything but a tie-dye T-shirt, jeans, and sandals with socks.

Her hearty laugh shook her belly—and stole people's hearts. I loved Sherri and considered her a witty, gentle giant. We'd blow a joint and spend hours rolling on the floor laughing.

We often got stoned in my room and played a game we made up called Oriental rug checkers. On my granddad's ruby-red carpet, green and golden vines crisscrossed like a chain-link fence, each intersection accented with small golden flowers. We started out with ten polished stones each, on opposite sides of the carpet. One of us threw a single die and moved, keeping on the vines and zigzagging in any direction from one bunch of flowers to the next. If you landed on flowers occupied by the other player's stone, you captured it. And, like in chess, if you reached the opposite border, you could free one of your pieces. When one player ran out of stones, the other won.

One day Sherri and I were in the middle of a game, and I lay on my side, leaning my head on my hand, waiting for her to move her piece. All of a sudden, a large Jerusalem cricket, a field-mouse–sized bug, came racing across the carpet like a buffalo in full charge, heading straight for my face. Resembling the "cootie bug" plastic toy, it has a hairless, fleshy pinkish body. Despite their mighty size and ugliness, they always seemed rather harmless to me—that is, until one took a chunk out of my friend Rod's finger.

Evidently, his story had settled into my survival neurons. Before I knew it, I had leaped on top of my steamer trunk. Sherri's mouth flew open, and she rolled on the floor, jiggling all over with enough laughter to shake the whole house. I fell off the trunk in my own fit of laughter, tears streaming down my face. Even after explaining what had happened to Rod, I knew she'd never let me live it down.

One afternoon a week or so later, Sherri handed me a joint, leading to another game of Chinese rug checkers. After she beat me, I left to meet Hal and Russ at a downtown bar. It was early evening by then and I was running late, so I took a shortcut, walking along the tracks.

Two sets of tracks came together from three different directions, forming a perfect triangle that surrounded the Davis Train Depot. The northbound tracks ran to Seattle, the westbound to San Francisco, and the eastbound to Denver. Walking from the direction of Sacramento, I had come to the point where one set of tracks angled north and the other angled west.

I glanced over my shoulder and saw a light far in the distance. A train was coming! The little boy in me jumped for joy. No way could I resist the rush of a train passing.

Looking around, I spotted something that could liven things up. If I stood just beyond where the tracks split, I wouldn't know until the last second whether the train would pass to the right or left. This sounded like a nifty idea. I found a spot far enough back so the passing train would clear me by about eight feet.

The light slowly approached. I had to wait a while, but the train was finally about thirty seconds away. This would be sooooo cool. Out-a-sight cool. God I loved trains. I planted my feet, preparing for the onslaught of metal that would soon roar by. The headlight grew larger and brighter, nearly blinding me. The tracks started to vibrate . . .

And then, without warning, a blaring air horn penetrated my brain and nearly blew me off my feet. A quick, piercing blast, followed by another one that never let up, vibrated every fiber of my body.

Jesus! The engineer thinks I'm standing on the tracks.

The horn grew louder, and the ground bounced and shook as fifty tons of iron and steel passed to my right. My heart ached in compassion for the poor guy who must have seen me as an impending bloody splash. Oh shit!

Four pairs of braking wheels screeched by, throwing off thick bands of fiery sparks. My teeth chattered and my bones shook. I froze in place, drowning in the roar and rattle and buffeting winds that pelted my face and blew my hair.

The train kept thundering past, banging, shaking, and screeching like thousands of fingernails on a chalkboard . . . for what seemed like forever. And then, after the endless strobe of cars, the caboose flashed by, and the deafening noise disappeared into an intense silence—except for a slight ringing in my ears and the residual humming in my cells and the loud stillness in my brain. My heart beat rapidly in my chest. Whew! . . . Shithouse *mouse*! How great was *that*?

My legs like Jell-O, I walked off in the direction of the bar to meet my friends. I felt a mixture of regret for scaring the engineer and total ecstasy from experiencing the power of the train. Wow—what a rush!

I kept thinking of that engineer. Soul? It's something in living things, something that connects all of us. It's so easy to affect someone's experience, even when we don't mean to. I felt sorry for the railroad man but didn't feel guilty. Like worry, guilt is always a waste of time.

Almost always, I could see the big picture, picking up on ramifications many people missed. It's something I'd done for as long as I could remember: checking to see if my or other people's actions could cause problems or hurt feelings. But that night, I had dropped the ball, failing to recognize that the engineer couldn't see the bend in the tracks until the last second.

Sometimes caring for others caused me sadness or pain. But having empathy was far better than the alternative. I'd met people who didn't give a damn if anyone suffered, and I didn't want to be like them. Once, in a monastery near Aspen, I picked up a book by Kahlil Gibran in their gift shop and opened it to a poem. I remembered a few lines that went something like this:

> *I have learned silence from the talkative,*
> *toleration from the intolerant,*
> *and kindness from the unkind.*

A passing car jerked me out of my thoughts. It was only then I realized I had stepped back into that surrealistic "climbing the mountain" space. I had resumed where I left off, working on my mystical riddle about the soul in that sweet, timeless place.

As the semester drew to a close, the heaviness in my heart continued to haunt me. Usually I didn't notice it, but once in a while, when I was alone or quiet, I felt that subtle, nagging constriction in my chest. I longed to feel carefree and content once again. And I hoped that when school ended and I could roam freely, the gloom would finally disappear.

PART 4

Big Sur

If you obey all the rules, you miss all the fun.
—Katherine Hepburn

A dog told me I was extremely wealthy
as he licked me on the cheek.
—Rich Israel, 1967

20.

Crazy Marvin

January 1968

My van was outfitted for travel. I had removed the backseat and installed a plywood bed with space underneath for a Coleman stove and lantern, clothes, blankets, towels, tools, cooking utensils, and an ice chest. A twin mattress fit perfectly on the wood frame. My roommate Tammy had sewn green corduroy curtains for all the windows and behind the front seat, creating a private bedroom in the back.

Misty and I had stayed in touch with occasional phone conversations throughout the fall while we each finished our last semester of school. When I talked to her back in November, she accepted my offer to come out and travel with me in my little home on wheels, both of us eager to leave college behind and hit the road again. Now, having graduated and turned twenty-two, I felt ready for the real world.

As for funding the trip, I had saved some money from my job at the bacteriology department and collected more from selling my motorcycle. We would travel until we ran out of cash or couldn't find odd jobs.

Misty arrived at the 3rd Street House well after eight in the evening. I made her some soup, and we talked while she ate, though she fought to keep her eyes open. The three days on the road had worn her out.

While she showered, I took off my clothes, lit a candle, and waited in bed for her to join me. I had spent time with other women since our trip to the world's fair, but I hadn't slept with anyone. My body tingled with anticipation.

Tomorrow I would show her Big Sur and Pfeiffer Beach, the first stops on our adventure. I'd dropped acid there twice with Hal and a few others, and you couldn't find a better place for tripping. Too bad I didn't have any acid for us to share. It didn't matter—Pfeiffer's beauty would still boggle her mind.

I heard her footsteps on the stairs. "How're you feeling?" I asked.

"Refreshed but tired."

"It's nice to be with you again."

"For me too."

She shed her nightgown and crawled into bed next to me. How could I have forgotten how voluptuous she was? A few gentle kisses turned into passionate lovemaking, tender and sweet. As she fell asleep in my arms, my thoughts wandered back to that French neighborhood in Montreal, and I soon drifted off as well.

Misty didn't wake up until close to noon. After a leisurely breakfast, we packed her things into the van and walked to the market for some supplies. It was the middle of the afternoon when I hugged my room-mates good-bye, and Misty and I took off. Once we passed through Bay Area traffic, I lit up a joint.

We headed south, listening to *The Magical Mystery Tour*, a new Beatles tape Misty had brought with a portable tape recorder. She and I were on our own magical mystery tour.

Several hours later, at nightfall, I pulled over to the side of a de-serted section of Highway 1 near Half Moon Bay. "The Big Sur area is far too beautiful to miss under the cover of darkness," I told Misty. "We'll spend the night here."

She took a deep breath of the salty air. "Mmmm, I love that smell."

"Just wait until tomorrow, babe. It's going to blow you away."

In the morning light, we discovered a lush artichoke field next to the van—row after row of huge thistles spread out before us, nearly reaching the ocean. As we entered the tiny town of Castroville, we passed under a large sign spanning the main drag: "The Artichoke Center of the World." Maybe "The Artichoke Heart of the World" would have been more appropriate? We stopped for breakfast at the Giant Artichoke, a local fruit stand and restaurant, and scarfed down eggs and their specialty—deep-fried baby artichokes.

Back in the van, we continued south past Monterey, where the vegetation changed. I pointed toward the ocean. "Check out those cool trees. Different, huh?"

Misty's eyes grew wide at the sight of the wind-sculptured cypresses growing out of the rocks. "It's like we stepped into a Tolkien story."

As we traveled down Highway 1, mile after mile of jagged cliffs, sparkling beaches, and huge sea boulders held us spellbound. Enormous waves exploded on the rocks, shooting clouds of white mist into the air—and gulls and pelicans flew along the coastline, accenting the marvel before us. Big Sur never ceased to take my breath away.

The narrow dirt road that led to Pfeiffer Beach wasn't marked, making it a challenge to find, but I considered that a plus—the fewer people who knew of this secret, the better. The trick was to spot a mailbox in the shape of a birdhouse slightly beyond the campground. After driving past it, I recognized my mistake, turned back, and this time found the overgrown, winding pathway, barely wide enough to accommodate one car.

When I'd gone there before, an old, bearded hippie stopped us. Looking as weathered as his rickety wooden chair, he collected a fifty-cent toll before gesturing us to pass. When Misty and I arrived at the little dirt parking area and didn't see the grizzled guy, I realized he had cleverly duped unsuspecting motorists. I had to take my hat off to his ingenuity.

We threw some food, water, and towels in a backpack and set out for the beach. The short path led us through cypress trees, and after a few dozen yards, it opened onto the mouth-dropping beauty of Pfeiffer Beach. We stood there in awe.

A stream flowed through the sand in swirling arcs, starting from the grove behind us and traveling down to the surf near a weathered, two-story boulder. Waves crashed through the jagged tunnel in the massive rock, echoing around us.

To our left, a crescent-shaped beach stretched a hundred yards, ending at towering sea cliffs. To the right, the beach went on a long distance before disappearing behind a bend in the cliffs.

Climbing on the rocks, we enjoyed the spray of the breaking waves misting our faces. We took off our shoes and strolled down the beach until we reached a second tiny stream flowing from an indentation in the cliff, another place I wanted to show Misty. But a couple had already claimed a spot at the entrance. So we settled short of our destination, high on a dune against the cliff, about fifty feet from shore.

As we sat admiring the sand and surf in the noon sun, a young guy in his twenties with bushy red hair walked along the ocean's edge, the water lapping at his bare feet. His freckled skin, presumably white earlier that morning, had turned a painful red after hours on the beach.

He wore a long bright-red woolen scarf (nearly the color of his skin), the kind you'd wear around your neck on a snowy day. But this fellow didn't have it around his neck. He had it tucked between his legs, held up with a belt, his only other piece of attire. Both ends of the scarf hung near the ground, trailing in the water, forcing him to assume a straddle-legged gait to avoid tripping on them. Except for the color, material, and length of his loincloth, he might have pulled off an Indian impersonation.

I pushed my wire-rimmed glasses up on my nose. "Am I seeing what I think I'm seeing?"

We both chuckled as he ambled away only to turn around and head straight for us, the soggy ends of his scarf now caked in sand. The mound we sat on came up to his chin.

He extended his hand up toward us. "Hi, I'm Crazy Marvin."

Crazy, all right. Stifling a laugh, I shook his hand. "I'm Rich, and this is Misty."

"Isn't this the greatest place?" he asked.

I nodded. "One of my favorites."

"You two from around here?"

"Nope," I said. "We're traveling through in my van."

"Cool. I'm a mountain man, and me and my wife live on top of a hill in Palo Colorado Canyon. That's up the coast there a ways." He nodded his head to the north. "We do all we can to live off the land. I'm the hunter and she does the squaw work. The place we're staying at is called Stony Acres."

Thrusting out his chest, he went on about his wilderness skills, and then returned to where his wife was sitting. I realized they were the couple we had seen at the mouth to the opening in the cliffs.

An hour or so later, he appeared again, this time with something in his hand. "Would you guys like to partake in some Owsley acid?"

Misty and I looked at each other and smiled.

21.

A Double-Edged Sword
January 1968

For a while, all was mellow. But soon the drug dropped me deeper and deeper into that elusive realm of acid consciousness. On our sandy mound, I sat cross-legged with my hands behind me, the liquid sand sifting rhythmically through my fingers. The warmth of the sun penetrated my bare upper torso, and a gentle sea breeze ruffled my hair.

"It's starting." My voice came from far away—a hollow sound, as if I were talking in a long, narrow tube. The rising and falling crescendo of the waves soothed me like gentle music.

Whoosh . . . Buzzzz . . . Zing . . . Whirrrr

The entire ocean turned into an immense mosaic, billions of pieces, each an iridescent mother-of pearl. My heart soared as I watched them dance and sway to a beat only I could hear. What a gift!

Toward mid-afternoon, Crazy Marvin and his wife, Nina, stopped by our dune as they were leaving. A small blonde with shoulder-length hair and a face somewhere between plain and pretty, Nina didn't say much, though Marvin didn't give her a chance with his nonstop chatter. Before they took off, they invited us to come to their place for a visit. We accepted and made plans to see them the following day.

Now that we had the place to ourselves, I showed Misty the indentation in the cliff wall where a secret grove of cypress trees silenced the pounding roar of the ocean—my favorite spot at Pfeiffer. Ten paces in revealed a different world, quiet except for the chirping of birds. The ancient trees shaded the area, letting through a few spotlights of late-day sun. A tiny stream with deep banks meandered down the right side, past wild irises and gigantic shamrock-like clover.

On the left wall, above the garden floor, shoots of oily poison oak signaled danger. Stoned on acid, I felt its menacing vibe and heard a subtle, irritating scream. Whether I was tuned into something the plant actually exuded or a protective mechanism within me had sounded an alarm, I stayed away and told Misty to do the same.

Sitting on the edge of a dune at the entrance to the cypress grove, I watched the ocean waves roll in while Misty lost herself in the flow of the stream a distance away. As I leaned back on my elbows, something caught my eye in the lower limbs of a cypress two feet above my head. I gasped.

Thousands and thousands of motionless monarch butterflies clung to the branches. I knew they migrated each year near Santa Cruz, but I didn't expect them this far south. They closed their wings vertical to their bodies, making them look like pale-orange leaves.

Moving slowly, I reached up and clasped one branch between my fingers and pulled it down a few inches. As I let go, hundreds of those beautiful creatures shook loose, expanding from a two-inch-thick mass to about eight inches, and then fluttered back to where they perched, the rustling of their tiny wings the most unusual sound I'd ever heard.

I motioned for Misty to come sit next to me, and I shook the branches again, both of us like two children watching fireworks for the first time. Her face shone with wonder and delight, no doubt mirrored in mine, and I carried a feeling of appreciation in my heart for hours.

As sunset approached, the entire ocean turned a shimmering blue-gray underneath a canvas of Van Gogh clouds. Holding hands, shoulder to shoulder, Misty and I sat quietly until the sun had disappeared into the ocean. Though now twilight, we had no trouble finding our way up the beach and back to the van.

In the glow of my headlights, the dirt road, with its ruts and pot-holes, reminded me of an abstract painting. Along with the loud noise from the tires on the road, the whirling, shushing, buzzing, ringing sounds of an acid high filled my head. When we reached the highway, I welcomed the silence of smooth pavement.

After driving south several miles, we came upon a wide, secluded vista on the side of the road overlooking the ocean far below, an excellent spot to camp for the night. Of course, sleep wouldn't happen for a while since we were both peaking on our LSD cocktail. It was dark outside, but inside we had the light of my lantern and all the amenities of my cozy mobile home.

Thinking it would be a nice time to share some tenderness, I leaned toward Misty. But she thrust her hands out in front of her and yelled, "Stay away! Stay away!"

LSD can expand whatever love and beauty you have within. If you feel love, your heart can swell to the size of a blimp. Unfortunately, it can do the same thing with your monsters and demons. It can turn a minor concern into a major panic attack.

Yeah, acid can be a double-edged sword.

Whatever Misty's mind told her she was seeing, it must have been terrifying.

"Misty, it's me, Rich. I just want to help you. This acid is strong, but it will calm down in a while." I reached out to offer support.

"No!" She crouched in a fetal position near the back of the front seat. "Stop! Stay back!"

"I won't hurt you. It's the acid. You're hallucinating. It's me, Rich, your friend."

"Don't talk! Stay back!"

"Okay, I'll stay way back here. Let me know if I can help you." I pressed myself against the opposite corner of the van, knowing all I could do was wait for the drug to subside. I sat there helpless, listening to the sounds in my head.

Whoosh . . . Buzzzz . . . Zing . . . Whirrrr

I hated that nightfall had released her demons. My friend and lover couldn't trust me in her present state of mind. I hurt inside for the pain and fear Misty was experiencing, and I ached from the helplessness of having no way to lessen her misery.

Knees to her chest, her lips quivering with fear, Misty retreated as far from me as possible in our tiny quarters. The fierce wind howled and rocked the van, muffling her whimpers. My heart felt like an animal hide stretched out to dry in the sun—rough, brittle, rock hard—far worse than the heaviness I'd been carrying around the last few months.

Dozens of vibrant, undulating colors flowed like molten lava, illuminating the walls and ceiling of the van. The hallucinations and sounds, both inside and outside my head, rose and fell for hours and eons, not settling until the early hours of the morning. Then sleep finally grabbed hold.

I woke to suffocating heat. It was near noon, and the van had become an oven. Misty was sleeping on the front seat, so I stepped outside, leaving the door wide open to give her some air. I sat on the ridge contemplating the ocean below and the night before. The calm sea breeze and the water lapping on the sand began to soften the hard lump in my chest.

What a bummer. What could have been hours of colorful, glorious love had turned into a nightmare for both of us. Our two-day magical mystery tour had derailed into a train wreck.

The heat finally forced Misty to get up. Sitting next to me, she looked wasted, her hair all tangled and her bright eyes now dark and tired. I wasn't doing much better myself.

"Are you okay?" I asked softly.

"Yeah. I just don't feel like talking right now."

I let her be, and we spent a couple of quiet hours together in the shade of a tree, watching the tide come in. After eating and letting the beauty of nature heal our withered hearts, we decided to visit Crazy Marvin and Nina.

As we drove up Palo Colorado Canyon, the twisty, single-lane paved road took us through a mossy, old redwood forest—truly the land of Tolkien. The mythical scenery eased some of the pain from the night before.

We stopped at a crude wooden gate bearing the scrawled name "Stony Acres." Passing through, we proceeded uphill, navigating more switchbacks and hairpin turns, until we reached the top of a mountain and Crazy Marvin's small trailer. Far off in the distance, we caught a glimpse of the Pacific between the hills.

A young German shepherd pup bounded over to greet us, followed by Marvin and Nina. Marvin pointed to the dog and said, "His name is Pee, because that's his thing."

They invited us to have a seat on the folding chairs outside their tiny home. Marvin turned to his wife. "Hey, Nina, why don't you cook up something for these folks." Silently, she began preparing food on a Coleman stove in the shade of a nearby tarp canopy. He never offered to help. Dressed that day in a red-checkered flannel shirt, jeans, and boots, the New York Irish bloke turned mountain man barked orders and treated her like his subservient.

"Nina, bring us a couple of beers."

"Nina, can you find my leather pouch?"

"Nina, what else we got to eat?"

Never complaining, Nina obeyed Marvin's rude requests. At first I was put off by his chauvinism, but as we spent more time with them, I saw that she had everything under control.

Wearing jeans, a brown plaid shirt, and no shoes, Nina handled Marvin the way a mother would a spoiled child. She took care of him, tolerating his eccentricities, but made sure he never crossed the line. If he pushed too hard, she gave him a hard look that stopped him cold, and he'd change the subject. A power herself, she skillfully let Marvin bask in his delusions.

"So did you see that big house on the way up?" he asked us, pointing down the hill with his thumb. "The owner lets us stay here for free, but I'm going to build a homestead deep in the forest. If I shoot a deer, I'll use everything: eat the meat, tan the hide, make tools from the bones. Live off the land the way man was meant to."

The more I got to know Marvin and Nina, the more I liked them. It became clear that this big-mouthed Irish lad was just a big teddy bear.

Misty had no hard feelings after the fateful night above the beach, but she needed some space. When we got down off the mountain, she asked me to stop at a pay phone so she could call a friend living in Haight-Ashbury. The next day we met her friend, who took her off to San Francisco.

I understood, but I felt sad to see her leave. Two people who had known each other for only a week thought they could live together in a four-by-twelve-foot box on wheels. At least we parted as friends—and I'd never forget the sweet moments we shared in Montreal.

I stayed in my van up on the hill with Marvin and Nina. I liked the area, and my new friends made me feel welcome.

Late one morning, Marvin and I sat on his lawn chairs taking in the view. He took a handful of unshelled peanuts from a paper bag and passed the bag to me.

"So where's Misty?" he asked, cracking a shell and tossing a nut in his mouth.

"She went off to stay with some friends in the Haight. That bum trip spoiled Big Sur for her. She really freaked out."

"Pretty bad, huh?"

"Yeah. To have someone look at you with such terror really hurts— a lover, no less. It was tough. At least now she's with close friends who can comfort her."

"Well, don't fret. There's plenty of fish in the sea."

"I guess . . ."

"Hey, listen. I'm gonna start making candles. I figured I can sell them to the tourist shops in Carmel. If you want to do it with me, we can make some money."

Marvin showed me his idea. Using his Coleman stove, he melted some remnants of red candles in a tin can. While the wax was heating, he tied a length of candlewick to a stick and dropped it in a glass jar, resting the stick on the rim. Next, he poured the molten wax into the jar.

He repeated the process, melting yellow and blue candles. As the last step, we placed the jar in a paper bag and gently chipped away the glass with a hammer. The result was an attractive candle layered in red, yellow, and blue.

"Hey, this is slick, Marvin. I could see someone buying one of these."

I agreed to help him with his business. As I drove north to visit my friends, I'd collect more jars, bottles, and old candles. I felt restless, so travel suited me just fine.

That afternoon, I glided along Highway 1 on the southern Big Sur coastline, taking in the scenic vistas and following close behind Marvin's rusty '53 Buick. We soon came to a turnoff that took us to an area already full of an assortment of rag-tag vehicles.

Out on the beach, at least forty Big Sur hippies scattered everywhere in their finest regalia, half of them tripping on something that made their eyes sparkle. The festivities went on for hours, highlighted by a pig roast over an open fire.

After a long day of play, I drove north toward the Bay Area, still digesting Misty's departure. Even though it may have thrown a curve in my plans, I wouldn't let it put a damper on my heart. Hell, there was simply too damn much fun to be had.

22.

Dead Bug

January 1968

I spent the night with friends in Berkeley, then took off north for a short visit with my parents. On my way back to Big Sur, I stopped to see Brad, my pool-playing buddy, at his place in Dixon, about ten miles southwest of Davis.

We sat in his dark, cluttered living room having some beers and smoking a joint. At one point, he jumped up and headed for the kitchen, calling out, "I'm so hungry I could eat the south end of a north-bound horse. Har-har. Want something to eat?"

He returned with a soiled pizza box and offered me a slice. I declined, but his black lab, Molly, jumped to her feet, eager for a bite. After wolfing down a piece of crust, she came over to me and put her head in my lap. As I pet her, Brad asked through a mouthful of pizza, "So, Rich, when are you going to get a dog?"

I had talked about getting a puppy once I was free from school and landlords. "I don't know. I haven't thought about it, but I'll keep my eyes open."

Later that afternoon, I drove to San Francisco to meet Marvin and Nina in Haight-Ashbury. After checking out the hippie scene and grabbing some fish and chips wrapped in newspaper, we headed over to the Fillmore Auditorium. Inside, the amplified sound of Traffic cranking out "Paper Sun" assaulted my ears—demanding immediate movement from every part of my body. All around me, a long-haired, tie-dyed, beaded, tripping multitude of characters glowed in an aura of love and brotherhood. A ragged lad in an American-flag shirt bumped into me, then peered back at me over his scruffy beard and held up two fingers, flashing a peace sign.

Across from me, a pretty young woman danced in a trance. Her many colorful necklaces jumped around to the music, revealing rosy nipples popping through her fishnet blouse. She sent powerful signals to both my heart and my groin, distracting me so much I stumbled over a brutish Hell's Angel biker type sitting against the wall, a huge scar carved in his forehead. I froze.

Luckily, he sat there in a daze, bobbing his head up and down as if he were watching someone dribble a basketball.

Whew! I slipped away, weaving through people, some staring off into space, some intertwined in loving embraces, some dancing to the music of the band and some to their own internal tunes.

The wonderful spectacle came to an end several hours later when Marvin found me. "Hey man, it's time to leave," he shouted.

They dropped me off at my van, tucked away on a side street, and I crawled in and fell asleep as soon as my head hit the pillow. I slept in, then headed south and turned inland to explore Carmel Valley, but it was Sunday, and the little woodland town was deserted. On a bulletin board, a simple note grabbed my attention: "Samoyed Pups—Free." Hal once had a Samoyed named Sammy I'd been fond of. I jotted down the address and asked an old man on a bicycle for directions.

When I pulled up to the house, a girl about seven was playing on the front porch.

"I hear you have Samoyed pups here."

She looked at me through stringy blonde hair. "Yep, they're in the back." She motioned for me to follow her.

A full-grown Samoyed lay in the shade, and her two pups played nearby. One had short, white hair with a big brown spot around its middle, reminding me of an English pointer. The other looked like a little panda bear—a white, long-haired fluff ball with a black mask. It touched my heart when it pranced over to me.

"Is this one a boy?" I didn't want to deal with a dog having puppies in my van.

"Yep," the young lady said.

"I'll take him."

I stopped at the market for some Puppy Chow, and we were on our way. Driving south along the curves of Highway 1, I looked down at my cute little friend. "Hi, Charlie. That name should fit you well."

He gazed up at me with what I took to be understanding eyes—and barfed in my lap.

It was dark when I arrived at Stony Acres. Marvin and Nina stayed in San Francisco and wouldn't return until the next day, so I parked above the stream at the bottom of the hill. Wherever I went, Charlie hung close to me, begging for attention. By the light of the lantern in the back of the van, I fed him and fixed a cheese sandwich for myself. Full of energy, he jumped all around, but when I crawled into bed, he snuggled next to me and fell asleep. It was nice having a pup in the family.

The next morning, I washed up in the stream and made breakfast alongside my new companion. In the sunlight, Charlie's long white hair shimmered like melted pearls. His asymmetrical mask gave him a mischievous appearance. On the right side of his face, he looked like a panda, but on the left, he looked like Batman.

I loaded him onto the front bench seat of the van, climbed in next to him, and started down the narrow dirt road toward Marvin's, looking forward to staying put for a couple of days. As I passed a wood-shed on my left and a stone cliff wall rising twenty feet above on the right, my front wheel hit the edge of a protruding boulder. Although I crawled along at only five miles an hour, the van had enough downhill momentum to direct the front right tire into a thick groove angling up the cliff face—causing the van to tip and fall gently on the driver's side.

Shit.

Wasting no time, I shoved open the side door directly above me, grabbed Charlie—now sprawled on top of me—and put him up through the opening. Then I climbed out after him, jumped down to the road, and pulled him off what had turned into the skyward side of the van.

I stared at my vehicle, my home, and basically everything I owned lying on its side up against the cliff.

"Fuuuuuuuuck!" The desperation in my voice shook my nerves.

Ignoring the empty feeling in my chest, I turned and started walking, all the way out of Stony Acres and down Palo Colorado Canyon Road.

Damn it. Life could really throw a curve, even when you were feeling good. First Misty's bad trip and now this.

I kept my eyes peeled for Marvin and Nina's old green Buick, but I had no idea when they'd return. Trying to get a grip, I kept walking, little Charlie tagging along at my heels.

How could this have happened? My car and my home eliminated in seconds. The absurdity of it all kept hitting me. It was as though someone had purposely lifted the van and put it on its side.

I needed to think about something else until I could recover from the shock. Talking with Charlie, occasionally carrying him, I focused on the trees and the view. Finally feeling calmer, I turned around, knowing that the farther I walked, the farther I'd have to walk back.

When I returned to the van, I took a fresh look at things. The only real damage was a dent high on the back corner where the van had fallen on a piece of firewood. But the tires now faced the cliff wall, at a distance of only about a foot and a half. Even if I could find enough people to push the van over, it would hit the wall first and never be upright. We would have to somehow drag the van on its side away from the wall.

Yes, except that the road was barely wide enough for the van as it was. There was no room to drag it. It seemed hopelessly caught between the woodshed and the cliff—an impossible mind-bender of humongous proportions.

I gave up taxing my brain and did something useful. Through the back hatch, I unloaded the six boxes of bottles, jars, and wax I'd collected, stacked everything in the woodshed, and set aside some essential items for camping out.

Charlie and I hung out by the creek for several hours until Marvin and Nina returned. Marvin's jaw dropped when he saw what had happened. "Are you kidding? How the hell did you manage that?"

Nina walked over to the van, shaking her head. "How is that even possible?"

The van blocked the road, so they parked, and I related my story as we all hiked up to their trailer with our arms full. Nearby, I pitched my camp in a small cluster of trees.

Over the next few days, I'd occasionally walk down the hill to fetch water from the creek or get something from my van. Whenever I crossed the bridge, I saw my great big dead bug, its headlight eyes staring off sideways into the distance. And each time I got a sick feeling in the pit of my stomach. How would I ever get that thing on its tires?

Having no solutions, Marvin and I carried the boxes of jars and bottles up the hill to his trailer and made candles of all shapes and color combinations. Most of them turned out surprisingly attractive. Our favorite was a red, white, and blue piece in the shape of a Coke bottle.

On the fifth day after my van fell over, Marvin suggested walking down the road to the home of some longhairs he knew. If we could get help, he said, we might be able to devise a way to tip the van back on its wheels. Though skeptical, I agreed to join him, unable to look at those forlorn headlamp eyes any longer.

Arriving at the house, we were greeted by the only person there: a clean-cut, shirtless, young hippie wearing a blue bandana as a head-band. I explained my predicament, and he handed me his AAA card.

I still couldn't imagine what magic could remedy my plight, but I was open to anything. When the AAA driver showed up, we hopped into his truck and returned to Stony Acres. Like us, he was in his early twenties, and I had little faith he could help.

Without a word, he studied the van for a few minutes and made two circles around it. Then he strolled back to his truck, turned it around, and backed down to a spot thirty feet from the vehicle. Whistling, he pulled his cable down to the van and hooked it onto the skyward end of the back axle, just below the wheel.

What could he possibly have in mind? On one side was a rock wall and on the other a steep drop to the creek, well beyond where his truck was parked. Did he plan to drag it all the way up the road? What would the left side of my van look like after scraping over this rough terrain?

The guy turned on his winch, and the spindle rotated with a whirring sound. The cable lost its slack, becoming rigid with a sharp "CLINK-CLANK." As it tightened on the axle, the van tipped slightly off the ground and slowly rolled back on its two left wheels, retracing its own path. It inched up the road and away from the cliff wall, and as soon as it had enough clearance from the cliff face, it fell gingerly on all four tires.

"Holy shit." This guy was either a genius vehicular engineer, a magician, or the luckiest son of a gun that ever drove a tow truck.

The van had no scratches—or any other damage besides what I'd first noticed on the upper back corner. In fact, the piece of firewood causing the dent must have kept the rest of the van a fraction of an inch off the ground.

"Unbelievable!" Marvin and I cried out in unison.

I thanked the guy repeatedly. But he just shrugged it off and unhooked his cable. After seeing I could start the van, he went on his way.

The AAA had brought my dead bug back to life. I was no longer a homeless hippie.

23.

Getting to Know Charlie

February 1968

The road now clear, Marvin and I loaded up his car with candles and took off for Carmel. We found several places willing to sell them on consignment, and a few paid us cash. This called for a celebration, so we stopped to buy some food and drinks. I wanted to get a bottle of muscatel, but Marvin talked me into cream sherry.

"Do you like avocados?" he asked as we headed to Stony Acres.

"Not really. Actually, I haven't had one since I was a kid."

"I love avocados. You have to try them the way I fix them."

"I love artichokes and asparagus, but I've never had any use for avocados."

"What's an artichoke?"

"You've never had one? They're one of the best foods on the planet. You don't know what you're missing."

Back on the mountain, we sat outside with Nina and filled her in on our success. As he talked, Marvin took out his buck knife, cut an avocado down the middle, and pitched the pit into the forest. After scooping some cottage cheese into the holes, he handed me one half with a spoon.

"Hey, this is good," I said. "Much better than I remember. I'll have to turn you on to artichokes. You'll love them."

Marvin opened the cream sherry and took a few large gulps before passing it to me. "We did pretty good with those candles. We'll have to find more bottles."

"Yeah, especially Coke bottles. They sell those only out of machines these days. Used to be you couldn't buy a Coke in anything but a glass bottle."

"Yep, the whole world's going to shit. That's why I want to live as far out in the woods as I can get. Hey, would you like to be my partner in a quartz mine?"

"Quartz mine? What are you talking about?"

He pointed his spoon down the canyon. "Al, the guy in the big house, showed me a place in Big Sur State Park where a quartz vein comes right out of the ground."

"What do you do with quartz?"

"For one thing, they grind it up fine and use it as an abrasive in Comet cleanser. And they say a quartz vein often has gold in it. But there's another angle. If you have a mining claim, you can homestead it for free. I want to build a house and live up there."

"Is that all you have to do? Stake a claim and the land is yours?"

"You have to work it periodically. But you only have to remove three cubic yards of dirt or rock a year."

"Really? That's all it takes? That doesn't seem like much."

"Yep. And I got that worked out as well. We just toss in some dynamite and blow the dirt away."

I took a swig from the bottle. "Where you gonna get the dynamite?"

"There's a hardware store in Monterey. It's no sweat. I already hauled a plunger up to the mine."

"Sounds pretty wild to me."

"Wouldn't it be cool to find a fat vein of gold? After we score the dynamite, we can hike up there and do some mining. What do you say?"

I'd never worked a mine, much less played with dynamite. "What the hell. I'm game. By the way, this cream sherry takes muscatel to another level."

We shook hands, and I became a partner in Crazy Marvin's quartz mine. We would use our candle-making profits to buy dynamite and blasting caps.

· · ·

Restless again, especially after being stranded, I headed north to see how my van would perform on a long journey. At sundown, I stopped in Los Gatos, where Hal was staying with some biker friends, and we shared a joint. The pot had an edge to it, making me jittery, so I stepped outside with Charlie for some solitude. Five minutes later, a fellow named Tim joined me.

He looked peculiar—tall and thin with a long face and piercing eyes. His narrow nose supported owl-like glasses, and a bush of black curly hair sprouted from his head in all directions, reminding me of one of the Fabulous Furry Freak Brothers in Zap Comix.

He crouched down to pet Charlie. "Nice dog. What's its name?" His voice squeaked like a rusty hinge.

Tim's feral appearance made me more tense. "That's Charlie," I said, aware of my sharp tone.

"What kind of dog is he?"

"Part Samoyed and part drifter." I took a deep breath to calm down.

Tim looked up, his wild eyes boring into mine. "How come you hate me so?"

His question shot straight to my heart. "Gee, it's not you, man. I'm off—something's going on in my head."

"Relax. It'll pass. Things are cool."

Most of my nervousness dissipated with this welcome confrontation. As freaky as he was, I was grateful for Tim's blatant honesty.

Charlie rolled over on his back, begging for a tummy rub. "Ain't that true, Charlie? Things are cool." Tim tilted his head toward me. "Hey, you do know this dog is a girl, right?"

"Huh? You're kidding. I never bothered to look."

"Yep. No balls, man. This is definitely a chick dog."

I stepped closer. "Shit. I'll be damned. That's the last time I'll ever trust a seven-year-old." I shook my head, feeling foolish. "Oh well, you're still my Charlie."

I traveled all the way to Reno, and my van didn't seem to have any problems, despite its run-in with the cliff. On my return trip to Big Sur,

I stopped in Davis to see tiny, giggling Gina, a lighthearted redhead with a contagious enthusiasm for life. I'd had a crush on her since we met the previous fall in the entomology department, where she worked part time for one of my professors.

On this visit, we drove to the shores of Putah Creek and made out on the bed in my van for a long time. After taking her home, I headed over to the F Street House and parked next to their unfenced yard for the night. When I climbed in back, I discovered that Charlie had peed on my bed, the first time that had happened. She must have been jealous of Gina.

I held her nose in the pee spot and told her in a strong voice, "No! No!" Avoiding her big, sad eyes, I put her outside the van and scolded her some more. "You don't get to be in the van if you're going to act like that. You'll have to sleep outside tonight."

At a nearby faucet, I washed the urine off the soiled blankets. Luckily, her puppy bladder was small, and the damage was minimal. I left the two blankets to dry overnight on the clothesline in the F Street House backyard.

When morning came, I opened the side doors of my van. There was Charlie sitting in the apex of the "V" shape of two stretched-out blankets. She had dragged each one from the clothesline right up to the van—her peace offering.

I picked her up and hugged her, told her I loved her, and explained again why I had to be strict. It was the last time she ever messed up in the van, or, for that matter, in any indoor area.

Like kids, dogs are only as dumb or smart as we teach them to be. If parents constantly tell children they're stupid, in most cases they will believe it and grow into clueless, incompetent adults. The same holds true for dogs. If we talk frequently and intelligently to them, they will more likely understand the meaning of many words. If they can learn "sit" or "stay," why can't they learn hundreds of words?

Uninterested in having a circus dog, I treated Charlie like an intelligent being from the start. I didn't need to teach her useless tricks. It was more important for her to learn how to stay safe and respect others.

To teach her about the danger of moving vehicles, I would conjure up fear in my body when one approached. When it passed, I would release the fear. If she could pick up on the feeling, she would stay away from cars and trucks.

To be welcome in my friends' homes, Charlie had to have good social skills. She needed to know how to lie down, stay, not jump up on people, and keep out of garbage cans. With these basic skills, she could travel with me nearly everywhere.

As we grew closer, I wanted Charlie with me all the time. She learned fast, and before long, she had gained many human friends.

24.

The Art of Choking
March 1968

Charlie and I developed a vagabond routine. We'd spend about ten days at a time in Big Sur with Marvin and Nina, and then we'd travel a week or two, sometimes wandering as far as Reno, before returning to Stony Acres.

Marvin tagged along on one of our trips. As we passed through Castroville, I decided it was time to turn him on to artichokes. We stopped at the Giant Artichoke, and I bought a dozen decent-sized thistles.

"When we get to Berkeley, we'll have a feast," I told Marvin. He looked at the bulging plastic bag and gave an unconvincing nod.

We arrived around dinnertime, and when Sam opened the door, I saw a bunch of people behind him.

"Richard, what the hell are you doing here? I thought you'd have choked on a Pacific oyster, by now."

I knew Sam through his girlfriend, Lil, a matter-of-fact, fun-loving woman with a deep, gravelly voice. I'd met her the year before in Davis, and after going out a few times, we decided we made better friends than lovers (not that we'd ever slept together). Sam, thin with short dark hair and ears nearly perpendicular to his head, looked the studious type in his black horn-rimmed glasses, but he was far from serious. He and his riotous buddies loved to spar with verbal cuts and jabs, and in their presence, I became another bantering fool.

"The only chokes I've got are in this bag, Sam. This is Crazy Marvin. I've been staying with him down in Big Sur."

He shook Marvin's hand. "Well, you *must* be crazy to hang out with Richard. Lucky for you, we take pity on the deranged. Come on in."

We stepped inside and Marvin's face lit up. "Hey, looks like a party." He wandered across the spacious room to where a few folks were passing around a pipe of weed.

Sam and I headed down the hallway to the kitchen. "Now that you're a Berkeley student," I said, "I thought you'd be studying or protesting or doing something meaningful."

"Do I look like a dummy? You do that stuff only when you absolutely have to."

"We brought plenty of artichokes. There's enough for everyone."

"I love thistles. Let's get them started."

In the kitchen, Sam and I put on the chokes and a big pot of rice and then joined the rest of the group. In one corner of the living room, Marvin was talking with a couple of fellows and seemed to blend in just fine. Sam and I sat with Lil and Doug at the other end of the large room, and Doug offered me a pipe full of pot. He told me he had already met Marvin and gotten him ripped.

It was always good to see Doug, a longtime friend of Lil's. Sporting a well-trimmed full brown beard, he had sparkling blue eyes, a stocky build, and a warm, jovial disposition. We hit it off from the beginning— one of those cases when you feel you've always known the person.

"Hey Rich," he said, taking the pipe from me. "I've gotten some good use out of that minister's license." Inspired by my experience, he, too, had sought out Reverend Kirby Hensley, but he didn't have to fork over ten bucks. When he asked Kirby to be a minister, the reverend said he'd fill out the paperwork if Doug helped him fix his water pump. Kirby's wife had even given him lunch.

Blowing out a stream of smoke, Doug said, "A buddy of mine was arrested for going AWOL, and they threw him in the brig down at Camp Pendleton. He listed me as his minister, so I showed up wearing a collar, and they let this scruffy twenty-year-old past the guards and guns. Talk about a trip!"

After more puffs on Doug's pipe, we gabbed and jabbed plenty. During a rare lull, Lil turned to Sam and said, "Shall we tell them?"

"Sure, why not. They already know we're crazy."

Lil snickered. "Believe it or not, guys, we're going to get hitched." A faint southern inflection appeared in her voice, as it always did when she was stoned.

"You guys really are nut cakes," I said. "When are you going to do it?"

"March first, up at Tilden Park. But you haven't heard the best part."

"What's that? You're pregnant with twins?"

"No way. I'm crazy, not stupid." Lil paused, looking back and forth between Doug and me. "You two are going to perform the ceremony. You're both Universal Life ministers so we want you guys to do it, and, of course, you don't have any option of saying no." She clapped her hands and gave a defiant, hearty laugh.

"You're kidding," I said.

"Way cool," Doug said. "Now I'm really glad I got that license."

I didn't share his enthusiasm. "You want us to put a ceremony together?"

"No, don't worry," Sam said. "We'll have some things for you guys to read. We wouldn't want to strain the few brain cells you have left."

"Hey, if you want to compare brain cells, look who's getting married," I threw back.

I glanced at my watch, and Sam and I went in to check on the food. When it was ready, he called everyone into the kitchen. I filled my plate and returned to my seat in the living room, continuing my conversation with Sam, Lil, and Doug as we ate.

When I took my empty plate to the kitchen, I ran into Marvin. I had forgotten all about him. "Hey, how did you like your artichoke?"

He grimaced. "I really didn't like it very much. Mine was really chewy. I only ate half of it."

He pointed to a plate on the sink nearby. There sat a choke with half the leaves left and not a single discarded leaf. I realized that nobody thought to tell him how to eat it, and Marvin was way too proud to ask.

"Oh, no. You're not supposed to eat the whole leaf, just the tips. I can't believe you ate all those leaves." I almost gagged at the thought.

"Let me show you how to do it. They're really good if you eat them the right way."

But the damage had been done. No way would Marvin try more. What a horrible experience. I should have taken the time to instruct him, but I'd been caught up in the smoke and conversation. I couldn't imagine eating one full outer leaf, let alone the thirty he must have "choked" down.

Talk about getting your roughage. Shit!

25.

The Quartz Mine
February 1968

Marvin's olive-green backpack bounced along up ahead of me, framed by his flaming-red hair and bright-red plaid flannel shirt. Twelve sticks of dynamite joggled inside, and over his left shoulder, the barrel of his deer rifle stuck out at an angle.

How had I let him convince me to carry the more volatile blasting caps? "If I see a deer, I can't shoot with blasting caps on my back," had been his argument. Still, after drinking a few beers, we'd made it in one piece all the way down curvy Highway 1 from Monterey in a car packed with explosives, so we could probably make it up this trail to the mine.

Following Marvin's instructions, we kept a twenty-foot gap between us. In case one of us got blown to smithereens, the other would be safe. I envisioned the survivor covered with the entrails of his friend. Not much of a consolation prize.

Early that morning, we had driven to the end of Palo Colorado Canyon and hiked uphill from there, and three hours later, we were still hiking. Marvin said it was four and a half miles to the mine, and my legs could attest to it. It felt strange not having Charlie at my side, but because of the explosives, we decided to leave the dogs with Nina.

The beautiful forest reminded me of the raw Kentucky wilderness you might see in a Daniel Boone movie. Marvin pointed out animal signs and other backwoods details with certainty, playing up his mountain-man persona the entire time. Along with deer droppings, we saw evidence of wild boar rooting around in the forest leaves, and Marvin even speculated about a mountain lion, but the "footprint" he found—some indentations in the dirt—didn't convince me we had to worry. The only wildlife we'd actually seen were birds, chipmunks, lizards, and insects.

I had to admit that his ability to follow this obscure trail was beginning to convince me that a little mountain man did exist in the guy after all. But I didn't take his deer-hunting talk too seriously—I'd grown accustomed to his boasts and tales.

At one area where the terrain leveled off, Marvin came to an abrupt halt, and I stopped just as fast. He aimed his rifle to the left, and a loud blast echoed through the forest. Looking in the direction of the muzzle, I saw a large form stumble through the trees. Marvin took off running and I followed.

We came upon a young buck on the ground struggling to get up. An excited Marvin shot again at close range, but he missed the head, blowing off the tip of one antler. Then he steadied himself from a few feet away and put a bullet though the unfortunate deer's skull. It jerked hard once and lay still.

Adrenaline and despair collided within me. When I was young, I hunted birds with my dad and concluded I didn't like to see wildlife die. I'd never seen a large animal gunned down, and it shook me to the core.

As Marvin stared down at the creature, the glee on his face disappeared, replaced by a somber expression that made me think he had some reservations about it as well. It was probably his first deer, but true to his style, he didn't discuss his feelings. I held my tongue.

Taking out his buck knife, Marvin set about butchering the animal. He removed about ten pounds of what he said was the best cut of meat from the rear flank, wrapped it in plastic, and tucked it away in his pack. The rest, he said, he'd leave for a mountain lion, but I suspected that only beetles and flies would benefit from his brutal act.

I watched him in silence. What a waste.

We trudged on, neither of us saying much, and soon Marvin angled off the trail into the woods. At last we came to a small clearing, where a large, milky-white boulder stuck out of the ground, glistening in the early afternoon sun. The rock came up to our belts, its circumference the size of a kitchen table. A few narrow black lines streaked through it, and about a third of the way from one side, a wide crack ran down almost to the ground.

The deer incident behind him, Marvin stretched out his arms and beamed. "This is it—our quartz mine."

Removing my hat, I wiped a river of sweat off my brow with my sleeve and sat on the pale boulder. This wasn't at all what I expected. I'd had visions of an opening in the face of a mountain, an actual tunnel—like the old mine shafts I'd seen in TV westerns.

It turned out I was part owner of a lousy rock.

Marvin walked off to the bushes nearby and reached underneath, returning with a brown wooden plunger box for igniting our explosives. For the best protection from flying debris, we placed the plunger twenty feet from the "mine," behind a three-foot outcropping of rocks.

After we ran the wires from the plunger to the boulder, Marvin placed a stick of dynamite deep in the crack and packed it down tight with newspapers, making sure the fuse stuck out the side. "The man at the hardware store said the newspaper will help direct the blast downward," he said.

When he reached for the blasting cap, I said, "Careful, man! I've heard blasting caps can be temperamental."

Slowing down, he hooked up a cap and connected it to the wires from the plunger. We checked everything one more time before taking cover behind the stone outcropping.

Marvin turned to me. "Ready?"

I nodded, and he pushed down hard on the plunger.

A loud boom echoed around us, followed by some small pebbles and dust flying over our heads. We scrambled to the quartz vein and looked in disappointment at the crack. The gap had widened only slightly, going from maybe one inch to two. That was it.

So we placed two sticks of dynamite in the groove, packed it with more newspaper, rewired another blasting cap, and again took our position behind the outcropping.

It was my turn to push the Wile E. Coyote plunger, and the explosion sent a bigger swarm of rocks over our heads. Again, we scrambled to see what damage we'd done. A large white rock, about the size of a flat watermelon, had been dislodged and now leaned against the mother stone, which had a slightly wider crack. Other than that, we hadn't made much progress.

"We have to remove three cubic yards?" I asked with a touch of sarcasm.

He shrugged. "Looks like we'll have to try four this time."

I nodded.

After stuffing, packing, and wiring four sticks of dynamite, we started walking toward the plunger.

"Wait a minute," Marvin said. He turned back and placed the watermelon-sized rock directly on top. "That should push the blast downward."

Once again we crouched behind our shelter and Marvin pushed the plunger. The deafening blast reverberated against the surrounding hills. Our watermelon rock shot at least a hundred feet into the air and flew completely out of sight, landing somewhere on the next mountain. When the dust settled, we stood up from our fortress.

It looked like it had snowed. Our milky white boulder had vanished—the dynamite had reduced it to ground level.

I scratched my head. "Damn. You think maybe we should have gone with three sticks?"

Sh-i-i-i-t-t-t!" Marvin shouted, his eyes as wide as his smile.

Surveying the situation, we agreed we'd had enough mining for one day. It was a long walk back, and we needed to leave soon to make it before nightfall. After wrapping the plunger and remaining explosives in plastic and stashing everything, we started our long trek down the mountain.

We rested several times on the way down. At one shady spot, we sat on a ledge overlooking a view that went on for miles.

Marvin stared at the ground, kicking at some dirt. "You know, that was the first deer I ever killed."

I could sense he wanted to say more, but I didn't press him.

"Rich, you can't tell anybody what I'm about to say, okay?"

"No problem."

"When I lived back East, I used to drive an ambulance."

"Really? Were you a paramedic?"

"Not officially. I had some training, but not the best. People died in that ambulance, and when I found out they hadn't trained me right, I didn't know if I could have done more to save them. It really haunted me, so I quit and moved out here with Nina."

Sometimes, when you see what people are dealing with, you understand why they act the way they do.

"Well, Marvin, if they didn't teach you properly, you can't take responsibility for their mistake. At this point, there's nothing else you can do but move on."

A bulky blue-belly lizard scooted across in front of us. It stopped to check us out, tipping his head, then disappeared into a pile of rocks.

Wiping the back of his neck with his kerchief, Marvin said softly, "I know, but it still haunts me. Killing that buck today brought it all back. I didn't think I would really hit him. I wish I could change that too. It would be different if we were closer to home. I could have used all the meat—and the hide too."

"At least you learned from it. You can't ask for more than that."

As we walked on, I felt flattered he had shared such a private matter with me, and I found I had more compassion for his brash, insecure behavior. And now I understood why Nina was always so patient with him.

The next day I sat in the woods on the side of a hill, alone except for Charlie, who lay in the shade under a nearby manzanita bush. It was a warm afternoon, the Big Sur forest as beautiful as always. I soaked in the panorama of green hills stretching to the small blue wedge of the Pacific, shimmering like an aquamarine gemstone—the perfect place for some mellow music. I pulled out my Blues Harp and played a serene tribute to the mountains, ocean, and sky.

As my mind wandered, it happened again. For the fourth time, I found myself in that mysterious place, right where I'd left off on my "climbing the mountain," soul-searching journey—in that timeless, parallel reality that took me into a deeper comprehension of life. My thoughts flowed like a lazy river toward a sea of understanding. Sweet. It came to me that only one real emotion exists: love. All other emotions—jealousy, hate, fear, anger—are simply bent forms of that primary emotion, a distortion of our true nature. It was like white light passing through a prism and separating into different colors. Love runs through everything, and in its purest, unspoiled state, it is simply magnificent. *Maybe this is what they call soul?*

After I returned to earth, the feeling and understanding stayed with me for the rest of the day, along with an undeniable sense of completion. I had reached the top of the mountain. I would probably have more mountains to climb, but this particular journey had come to an end, leaving me in a tranquil state of calm and comfort.

26.

Canyon Lands
March 1968

I rambled down the narrow, winding road leaving Pfeiffer Beach, my van stuffed with an assortment of friends from Davis: Todd, the tall, lanky, red-bearded biologist who lived with Hal and Russ; Ann, the pretty, petite blonde from the F Street House; and my good friends and former housemates Rod and Big Sherri. Counting Rod's dog, Tessie, and Charlie, we were a merry band of seven.

We were heading to the Grand Canyon. It all began with a conversation I had with Sherri about this amazing place, and she decided she needed to see it for herself. Our plans and group had grown from there.

People can tell you how big and beautiful the canyon is, but you can't grasp the magnitude of that ditch until you stand at its edge and gaze down into it. I'd never forget that moment. Since I loved to turn people on to great experiences as well as blow their minds, I wanted my friends to feel the same rush. And no trip south through California could be complete without a visit to the Giant Artichoke and Pfeiffer Beach.

Not on our itinerary, the next stop was in Bakersfield, where my van blew a gasket. After spending four boring days behind a Fireball gas station, we arrived at the Grand Canyon in time to catch a jaw-dropping orange and purple sunset over the canyon rim. Everyone agreed it was a hell of a hole. We camped and started early in the morning so we could hike the Bright Angel Trail to the bottom.

Close to the trailhead stood a big sign that read "MULE TRAIL—

NO DOGS ALLOWED." But Charlie and Tessie wouldn't cause any trouble, so I pointed at the canyon and said, "Rod, check out that view." He spotted the sign anyway, but we continued past it, pretending not to see it.

On our walk down, the temperature and stunning vistas changed dramatically, going from partial snow cover to hot desert a mile below. At the lower elevation, the ground leveled off, and we walked by a ranger's cabin, a few trees, and some picnic tables. About a quarter mile ahead, we stopped at a scenic overlook, where the canyon dropped 1,300 feet straight down to the river. A refreshing breeze cooled us, and Sherri passed a joint as we gazed at the breathtaking scene.

Soon, Rod's eyes widened, and a familiar mischievous expression spread across his face. He climbed up and sat on the metal railing facing me, hooked his feet under the second rail, and said, "Hey, Rich, come over and hold my feet."

I did as he'd instructed, making sure I had a secure grip on both ankles. He took a deep breath, and bent backward over that 1,300-foot chasm, hanging from his knees. When he came back up, his eyes had grown to the size of dinner plates. "I saw Buddha!"

Well, naturally, I had to try it too. With my feet tucked under the lower bar and my ankles and life in Rod's hands (and my heart in my throat), I leaned backward over the edge. I hung there for a bit, my arms dangling in the breeze, looking at that muddy ribbon of the Colorado River far below. Even though I didn't see any significant Eastern holy men, I had to admit it was the most righteous rush I'd ever experienced.

Rod and Ann wanted to walk all the way down to the bottom of the canyon and took off with Tessie on the river trail. After a while, Sherri and Todd said they were ready to head back. I was comfortable where I was, so Charlie and I stayed put for another hour, soaking in the sites.

As we began the trek back to the top, two hikers came toward me.

"Hey, man, you better watch out. The ranger is waiting to bust you for having your dog down here."

"Thanks for the warning." I wasn't concerned. The pot combined with the serene environment had mellowed me to mush.

Close to the ranger's station, I climbed a mound of huge boulders to get the lay of the land. Feeling like I was Clint Eastwood in *Fistful of Dollars*, I took out my Bull Durham tobacco and rolled a cigarette. I had a perfect view. The trail weaved through the middle of the station, two picnic tables on the left and the ranger's house and a small shed on the right, everything located in a narrow passageway with no easy escape.

I had only one option: bend low and hug the right side, slide past the back of the ranger's building, and then sneak out on the other side of the clearing. I discussed it with Charlie, finished my cigarette, and savored the rugged, untamed country.

I climbed down to the trail, but when I was about to walk into the ranger's lair, I realized how much energy my plan would require. Too tired from climbing the mountain of rocks, I abandoned the whole thing and simply followed the trail with Charlie by my side.

To the left, two young hikers sat at one of the picnic tables. Far to the right, the ranger stepped out of his house.

Shit.

A gruff voice came blaring across the clearing. "HEY YOU!"

I pretended not to hear, looking straight ahead at the trail as I continued walking.

"HEY YOU!" came the aggressive, man-in-power voice.

I pointed to my chest. "Who, me?"

"Don't you know you can't have dogs on the trail? Didn't you see the sign?"

"Jeez, I guess I missed it." I spoke as humbly as possible.

The red-faced ranger scolded me for a time, but after he'd unloaded his rage with little response from me, his tone changed and he began to soften. I didn't pose much of a threat with my half-grown, furry pup.

"I don't make the rules. They're waiting for you at the top of the canyon. You need to at least have that dog on a leash. Do you have something to tie him up with?"

I fumbled with the strap on my canteen, the only thing that resembled a leash, but it was sewed to its case. I shrugged. "Dang, I guess this won't work."

"Let me see if I have something in the shed. Maybe I have a rope you can use. Come with me." He turned and walked toward the shed, and I followed with Charlie at my heels. The two hikers at the table looked stoned, and their long faces at my predicament made me feel sorry for them. "Don't worry. It's cool," I said in an assuring voice.

Well, that touched off the ranger once more, and he regressed to his original tough-man stance. "Don't you understand how serious this is? They're going to throw the book at you when you get to the rim of the canyon. They're waiting for you up there. We don't have rules for nothing!" He continued ranting, and I watched all that pent-up aggression in respectful amusement.

But I kept my mouth shut and a concerned expression on my face. When he calmed down, he went to the shed and came back with four feet of clothesline rope. I tied it around Charlie's collar as she sat on the ground. Then I tugged on it gently, watching just her head move sideways with each tug. It was obvious she had no idea what a leash was for.

"I'll let her get used to it for a while. Thanks for your help," I said in a polite tone. I picked up Charlie, turned, and followed the trail out of the clearing. Once we were around the bend and out of sight, I put her down and took off the rope.

The trek back was a never-ending vertical ascent, and I needed to stop from time to time to gather my strength. At one point near the end, I lay down in a snowbank to catch my breath. I wasn't sure how long I was out, but I woke to Charlie licking me on the cheek. Dusk was descending, and the temperature had dropped. "Good going, Charlie. You might have saved my life, girl."

We pressed on, keeping a steady pace to beat the darkness. Not far from the top, we came to a sign that read "MULE CORRAL" and another trail branching off. Charlie and I took that path, which led me over and her under fences in and out of the corral. Approaching the parking lot from that direction helped us avoid any rangers waiting for us—and the mules didn't pay us any attention. Back at the van, I found Sherri and Todd cooking dinner on my Coleman stove.

Rod showed up a few hours later, well after dark. "Ann has bad blisters. I left her with Tessie in that hut about halfway down the upper trail."

"What're you going to do?" I asked.

"Hike back down with food, water, and sleeping bags. We'll stay in the hut and hike out in the morning."

"You can take my flashlight and some Band-Aids."

After he left, we were ready for sleep. Somehow Todd managed to fold himself into the front seat of my van, while Sherri, Charlie, and I squeezed in the back, all of us tired enough not to let the tight quarters interfere with our sleep. I couldn't imagine how exhausted Rod must have been.

Around noon the next day, Rod, Ann, and Tessie arrived at the van. We drove along the canyon rim, enjoying the vistas, and later got stoned with a Hopi Indian boy named Frank we'd met along the way. He invited us to spend the night with his family. We lined our sleeping bags on the floor of their living room, already packed with several of his siblings.

Back on the road in the morning, we drove a day and a night straight through to Davis. I dropped off my friends and settled at last outside the F Street House, restoring the calm of just Charlie and me. With my magical mystery tours behind me, my van felt like home again, quiet and cozy.

PART 5

A Pipe Dream

Once you make a decision,
the universe conspires to make it happen.
—Ralph Waldo Emerson

Only dead fish go with the flow.
—Anonymous

27.

Too Many Chickens
March 1968–January 1969

Back in Davis, I needed to find a job. My generous parents had allowed me to use their credit card to cover repairs on my van. For years I had carried that emergency card and never needed it, but it sure came in handy in Bakersfield. Grateful for their help, I wanted to make things square.

Gina told me her boss in the entomology department was looking for another lab assistant. I met with him the next day and began work the following week. It was an outdoor job—ideal for me—involving the study of insect pests on vegetable crops in the greenhouse and in the field. The required overtime earned me frequent three-day weekends, giving me the freedom to take short trips.

Rod had been renting a room in Brad's place out in Dixon, and when he moved out, I moved in. I liked living in the country, and so did Charlie. Soon after, Albert, the mechanical genius, moved into a weathered, twenty-foot trailer parked in Brad's side yard.

In early July, I had the day off and the place to myself. It was quiet except for an occasional vehicle racing by on the county highway or a train rumbling on the tracks out back. Albert had given me a hit of mescaline, the hallucinogen found in peyote, and this was the perfect day to give it a try. It turned out to be more relaxing than LSD—no internal noises or wild visions exploded in my mind. In fact, at times, I would even forget I was stoned.

Behind the house, Brad kept a dozen chickens in a fenced-in pen.

That afternoon, I found myself lying in the shade of grapevines along one side. A thick carpet of fresh straw covered the ground, making the area soft and clean. We didn't let Charlie in there, so she curled up in the shade of a nearby bush.

At first the chickens stayed on the other side of the pen. The head rooster eyed me with suspicion, then ruffled his iridescent brown and green feathers and gave out a hearty crow. I crowed back with a lousy imitation. He crowed again, and I answered once more. I must have said something right this time because the rooster and all the chickens relaxed and went about searching for seeds. But they still kept their distance, never venturing closer than about five feet.

I watched how they scratched away at the straw, and when they uncovered a seed or something resembling one, they pecked at it. Spreading two fingers wide, I scratched at the straw too and exposed small particles that had sifted below to the ground. As if on cue, the entire troupe of chickens lifted their heads in my direction and then returned to their own search.

Livening things up, I scratched a little and took an excited deep breath, staring with wide eyes at the spot under my fingers as if I'd found a great treasure of seeds. To my delight, several of the chickens scampered toward my hand. But they immediately realized they didn't want to be that close to the new guy in the pen and retreated back to safety. Again and again, they would sense my excitement and forget the danger until they got close, then scatter away.

Their funny antics entertained me for close to an hour—of course, it didn't take much in my stoned state.

One day, a coworker told me about a nearby poultry barn that was giving away chickens. I dropped by on my way home and found six wire cages, each containing twenty half-grown white chickens. The man in charge encouraged me to take the whole lot and even loaned me his truck to haul them away. I zipped home, released them in the chicken yard, and returned the cages and truck in no time. I could hardly wait to surprise Brad.

When he got home, it was nearly 8 p.m. Strutting with pride, I led him out back with a powerful flashlight. "I want to show you something" was my only response to his inquiries. By now, all the chickens had found refuge for the night in the makeshift henhouse.

To call it a henhouse was a stretch. In reality, it consisted of five hay bales, set end to end to form a crude pentagon. Brad had created a five-inch opening between two of the bales, just large enough for a chicken to squeeze through. A four-by-eight plywood sheet placed over the top served as the roof.

As we approached the low-standing henhouse, I handed the flashlight to Brad and motioned for him to look inside. Getting down on his hands and knees, he shined the light through the opening.

Excited, I stood there waiting for his shouts of joy and gratitude when he feasted his eyes on all those free chickens. I imagined him saying something like, "Wow, Rich. What a score! Makes me happy as a junkyard dog with a grisly bone." Or, "Shucks, man. There're enough drumsticks in there to make Gene Krupa smile like a fool."

But instead of showering me with praise, Brad yelled, "HOLEEE SHIT!" and jumped up and stamped around like a wild horse, his eyes as wide as silver dollars.

"Fuck man! What the hell have you done? That is way too many fucking chickens. Oh shit! What the hell are we going to do now? What were you thinking? Oh shit! Damn!"

He started pacing like an angry mountain lion. My mouth dropped. Hey, not even a thank-you? I took the flashlight out of Brad's flailing hand and knelt down to have a look. When I peered through the tiny doorway, it took everything I had not to roll on the ground with laughter. Before me, like Popsicle sticks, 132 white necks poked out of a white-feathered cloud stuffed into a space the size of a bathtub, and 264 piercing red eyes stared directly at my light.

My buddy's irrational behavior, along with my self-preservation, forced me to keep a straight face, but I really had to work hard at it. I finally managed to calm the "Oh shits!" out of him by suggesting we give away the extra chickens to some of the neighboring farms.

I'd often thought that they should make "blowing minds" an Olympic event. If so, I probably would have medaled with my poultry prank—though even I had to admit that 132 pairs of little red eyes staring into your soul was a bit freaky.

The next morning we stopped by the farm up the road, where a Mexican family was more than happy to take any extra poultry off our hands. Our flock now reduced to thirty, including Brad's original twelve, we "feathered" the storm admirably.

It was around then that Marvin made a poor decision and helped himself to two loaves of bread from the Boy Scout camp down in Palo Colorado Canyon. "They had forty loaves there. I didn't think they'd miss a couple."

While he was the county's guest for thirty days, Nina came to stay with Albert. Even though she kept Marvin supplied with pot brownies the whole month, by the time he was released, his admiration for Big Sur had diminished. He also had no place to live since the manager of the Boy Scout camp owned Stony Acres.

So Marvin stayed with Nina in Albert's trailer—until his dog, Pee, led Charlie astray, and they killed some of Brad's chickens. Then Marvin and Nina rented a farmhouse about twenty minutes away, and mild-mannered Nina took a job at a local gentlemen's bar as a topless waitress. We'd drop by with Marvin to keep her company. You could see how proud he was of his lady and her cute little bobbling breasts.

I continued seeing my favorite redhead, Gina. I loved being with her, but we weren't really a couple, even though we had dated off and on for the past year. One warm summer evening, after hanging out with my F Street House friends, I took a walk with Charlie and noticed Marna sitting on the front porch of her little house next door. We'd met before but talked only briefly.

Her long, flowing dark hair and sultry brown eyes bewitched me, not to mention her lovely body. When she laughed, it came from deep inside, and I knew right off that she loved having a good time. Somewhere during our long conversation, I took a chance and kissed her. As our passion ignited, she suggested we go inside to her bed.

After that, we spent a lot of time together, and one weekend, she invited me to her family's beachside house on the Marin coast. When her parents and sisters fell asleep, she sneaked outside to my van—the wind wasn't the only thing rocking my vehicle that night!

Marna often called Charlie "Chuck," making me laugh. She told me she thought Charlie was jealous of her, but I think it was the other way around. Charlie represented constant love and loyalty, and I reciprocated with the same vigor. For anyone who knew me, there was no question that Charlie came first.

Even so, I had a major dilemma: I had fallen hopelessly in love. The problem wasn't love itself but that I had fallen in love with Gina *and* Marna! Just my luck: I met someone special I grooved with, and she showed up in stereo. After pondering my situation, I did the only honorable thing a man could do. I confessed to the two women that I loved them both.

Whoa! I guess I was too honest or maybe too naïve. I couldn't lie to the women I loved, though, could I? It simply wasn't in my nature. The result was tragic—I lost them both. They each respected my honesty and remained good friends, but romantically I was doomed in duplicate. It was just another case of too many chickens!

28.

What a Riot
February 1969

I met Mitch in an entomology class, and our mutual involvement in draft resistance cemented our friendship. Tall and slender, he was down to earth and intelligent, the kind of guy you could always count on. When he spoke, I was confident he knew what he was talking about. He also loved nature as much as I did.

One early evening, Mitch and I rambled southwest along Highway 505 toward Vacaville in his Ford station wagon. The sun was setting behind the low hills, and some of the oncoming cars already had their lights on. Over the past few days, we had heard about the riots at the Cal campus in Berkeley and wanted to see what was going on. Curiosity motivated us, not any interest in participating. We firmly believed that peaceful change was more constructive, and I hoped the homicidal lord of curiosity didn't have an appetite for us cats.

As we approached the Vacaville area, I asked Mitch if he'd like to meet a few friends of mine. Sure, he said. We turned off on Midway Road and came to a humble little farmhouse with a barren front yard, where a few weeds kept company with Crazy Marvin's '53 green Buick.

It was late February, and there was a chill in the air. We gathered on the carpet, close to the roaring fire in the hearth. In the light of the dancing flames, Nina filled a pipe, lit it up, and passed it around.

The bud was pretty hot, and we partook with much coughing and snorting. I passed the pipe back to Nina. "We're heading down to Berkeley to see what the commotion is all about."

Marvin poked at the fire. "I heard about that shit. They trashed the windows of the Bank of America building. Sounds crazy, like Telegraph Avenue is a real combat zone. Are you guys ready to fight?"

"No way," Mitch said, shaking his head. "Violence isn't our bag. We're only going down to observe, to see what's really happening. And it's not only Berkeley. Stuff like this is going on in Chicago, Madison, and other places. People are fed up with the war. I heard *Esquire* magazine even has an article about the protests."

Marvin cocked an eyebrow. "Really? I can just imagine their slant on it. Damn. Watch your butt, guys. Those cops can be vicious."

We spoke more about the protests and riots, the government, and the war. Then Marvin said, "The back acreage is fenced in, so I want to get a couple of horses."

"That would be cool," I said.

Marvin took another hit. "Man, I wish I lived a hundred years ago. Wouldn't it be great if you could jump on a horse and ride to Wyoming like they used to?"

When Mitch and I got back on the road, I kept thinking about what Marvin had said. "Ya know, it would be far out to do a cross-country horse trip."

"I could groove on that."

"Except it would be kind of a drag to ride a horse through miles of Nevada and Utah desert. The heat and the boredom would do us in. It's hellish just hitchhiking through that no-man's-land."

"You have a point there." Mitch thought a moment and then said, "How about a ride from Colorado to Wyoming?"

"Wow! I could get behind that. Why don't we do it?"

He turned to me. "You really think so?"

"Why not? We could buy horses in Colorado and sell them in Wyoming. It would be a blast. What's stopping us?"

"We could do it this summer."

"Bitching!"

I told him I'd been on the back of a horse no more than ten or twelve hours in my entire life. "And a good part of that time I was just sitting on an old chestnut mare I discovered in a small corral near the Davis campus," I said.

Literally out to pasture and practically abandoned, "Horse" and I forged a great bond the minute I found her. I had plenty of friends, but Horse was my confidant. All through college, when I needed someone to talk to, I would drive out to see my equine buddy, sit on her back, and spill my heart and guts to her.

Mitch made a sweeping curve onto I-80. "Well, you have me beat. I've ridden only a couple of hours, tops. But hell, we can't let the little crap stop us, right?" He laughed.

I rubbed my hands together. "Totally. A horse trip from Colorado to Wyoming is way too cool to pass up."

We agreed to meet in Aspen in late June, after Mitch returned from an insect-collecting expedition in Mexico. Each of us would buy a saddle beforehand, and together we'd look for horses.

As we drove on, I thought about Horse. She was the only one who knew I'd always wanted to be a cowboy—ever since I was a kid walking with friends to the western movie at the Tower Theater Saturday matinee. We'd dodge from bush to bush, shooting imaginary guns at each other, dying, only to rise again.

It could be a pipe dream, but cowboy life was in my blood.

Mitch and I crashed that night with my Berkeley friends and the next morning walked up Telegraph Avenue to Sproul Plaza on campus. What a scene! Around and through the main part of the plaza, several thousand people moved three- or four-wide in a counterclockwise direction. The line undulated like an enormous python, creating a block-long, lopsided star. On each of the building's massive staircases, enthusiastic cheerleaders with bullhorns whipped up the crowd while the human snake chanted back slogans.

We ambled around the periphery, feeling the hyped-up energy. Once we made our way to the north end of the huge plaza, we stood off to the side, observing the spectacle. Not long after, someone shouted through a bullhorn, "I hear that Governor Reagan is meeting with the regents across campus. Why don't we go over and pay him a visit?"

The giant line broke apart, and everyone surged toward the gates next to us. Mitch and I squeezed through with them and veered off to the right up a grassy mound fifteen feet above a wide concrete path that wandered through campus.

The angry mob, now five or six abreast, their fists pummeling the air, marched down the walkway. The power of that focused energy reminded me of a strong undertow in the ocean. I had to consciously plant my heels in the grass to keep from being dragged along by their wave of unified determination.

Once we had our footing, we followed alongside, but apart from the fury of the crowd. A line of cops charged, hammering at the protestors with long wooden clubs. Time to split! We found an escape route and ran to a safe distance.

"Could you believe the pull of that mob?" I asked, still catching my breath.

"That was scary. There's a war going on down here."

"I hope they don't hurt too many people. Marvin was right—those cops looked brutal."

"Unbelievable! Shit, that was unreal."

It took a while to shake off the adrenaline. I saw how easy it was to be swept away by violence and mob mentality—and I never wanted to witness anything like that again.

29.

The Collar
March 1969

Three weeks before Lil and Sam's wedding, I visited Berkeley and hung out with my friends in their gigantic living room. At one point, Lil sat next to me on the couch and nudged me with her elbow. "I need to talk to you," she whispered. I followed her into the kitchen, intrigued by her mysterious behavior.

When we were alone, she blurted out, "Richard, would you sleep with me?"

I jerked back. "Huh? What do you mean? You're getting married next month."

"That's the point. I don't want to get married without ever knowing what it's like to be with another man. I've already discussed it with Sam, and he's okay with it. We both decided you would be the best candidate to have sex with me."

"Hmm. I don't know. Let me think . . ." I pretended to give it serious thought.

Lil put her hands on her hips and got in my face. "Hey!"

I burst out laughing. "Sure! Of course. Tough job, but somebody's got to do it, right?"

She sighed with relief and smiled. "Cool. The guys said they'd go out for drinks this evening so we can have the place to ourselves."

After everyone left, we undressed and slipped into Lil and Sam's bed and started touching and kissing. It all felt nice, but I couldn't get into it—sex without romantic love wasn't much of a turn-on for me.

We sat up and smoked a cigarette. I told her, "My friend Jeanette used to say, 'A good friend is better than a good fuck.'" After some discussion, Lil came to the conclusion that her love life with Sam was enough. We laughed about it, chalked it up to experience, and agreed to tell him when he returned.

Lil laughed. "Well I guess I shouldn't complain, Richard. I have a good friend in you and a great lover in Sam. Of course that doesn't mean you aren't both a bit strange."

"And what does that say about your taste, girl?"

When Sam returned, he eyed us with a crooked smile. "So what have you fuckers been up to?"

Lil gave him a hug. "Less than you think, sweetie."

"I couldn't do it, Sam," I said. "Too much like sleeping with my sister. I return her to you unspoiled."

"Oh shit. I was hoping she might learn some new tricks."

Lil socked him a good one in the bicep.

On a chilly, overcast March morning, about twenty of us joined Sam and Lil in Berkeley's Tilden Park. I wore my usual jeans and boots but replaced my blue work shirt with a black turtleneck and a white minister's collar I'd bought at a Bible supply store. A large metal peace symbol and some beads hung down my chest.

Standing behind a small, antique podium Sam and Lil had brought along, I read a chapter on marriage from Kahlil Gibran's *The Prophet.* Then Doug, dressed in similar attire, read something Lil had put together, and we both pronounced them man and wife, or woman and husband, depending on the preacher you listened to.

Lil asked me to pick up some paper cups and ice from a liquor store on the way back to the house. When the guy behind the counter eyed my collar, he got jumpy, diverting his eyes while going out of his way to help me. Calling me Reverend, he wouldn't even let me pay for the bag of ice.

At the reception, I sat on the couch with an elderly gentleman. If I had been wearing my typical work shirt, this man would have probably looked me in the eye, told me a great story from the past, and offered some fatherly advice. But because of the white ring around my neck, he seemed nervous, paralyzed, like a deer caught in headlights. I hated it. The collar created a wall and made him act artificial, reinforcing my disgust for guilt-tripping religions.

It was a good thing most of us at the reception weren't crippled by negative beliefs. We had a blast, fueled by exquisite marijuana brownies.

Not long after the wedding, I spent one of my three-day weekends in Reno with Greg and Jeanette. Greg now had a job as a bingo caller at Harrah's Club.

"Rich, you have to come in for the 2 a.m. game. If you win, you get to play bingo for seven days."

"Why would I want to do that?"

"If you play that much, you're bound to win some of the time. You could make a lot of money. It's worth a try."

I shrugged. "Okay, I'll be there."

"When you come in, ask for nine cards. It'll give you the best chance of winning."

Greg went to work, and Jeanette and I toked up and visited for a while. Then I managed to sleep for an hour before heading to Harrah's. Jeanette thought it would be a hoot for me to surprise Greg by wearing my minister's collar.

At five minutes to two, I arrived at the bingo parlor and spotted Greg on the opposite side of the room, sitting on a stand next to a metal basket full of numbered balls. When he noticed me and the collar, he turned away, fighting to stifle a laugh. I paid for my nine cards and took a seat at a long counter that circled the room, having no idea what to expect.

Each card contained three individual games, so I was actually playing twenty-seven cards at once. Given that I'd just woken up and had zero experience with Bingo, I was out of my league.

"B10" came over the microphone.

I looked down the left side of one card after another and had almost gotten to the end when I heard "N19."

Grabbing more markers with my other hand, I tried to finish the B10s while starting on the N19s. About halfway through came "O57." Holy shit! I tried to pick up speed but fell further behind.

I had looked at only half my cards before the next number was called. And as more numbers came rushing at me, I knew there was no way I could possibly keep up.

Call it the power of the cloth or whatever you like, but the woman playing on the left of me started covering some of my numbers, and the man on my right did the same. To top it off, the casino worker wandering through the room to keep an eye on the game pointed over my shoulder at some spots I'd missed. With all this assistance, you'd think I would have won, but some heathen shouted "Bingo!" before my righteous team could come up with a winning card.

Without doubt, no one would have helped me if I hadn't been wearing that white collar. It had been worth getting out of bed in the middle of the night to witness this chain of events, but I couldn't wait to take the damn thing off. People behaved too strangely when I had it on. It made folks *collar-blind*.

30.

Road 97-D
March 1969

The end of March brought two unexpected developments. Brad's girlfriend decided three was a crowd, forcing me to seek refuge elsewhere. Just west of Davis, my buddies Hal and Russ rented a farmhouse on Road 97-D, and they offered to let me park my van in their yard and use their kitchen and bathroom. Russ had a black, long-haired cocker mix named Arlo, who was Charlie's age and one of her longtime gentleman friends. They played together while I was at work.

Then I discovered Charlie was pregnant. I had tried diligently to keep her away from males while she was in heat, but she managed to get laid anyway. I suspected a persistent black lab of the felony. He had slept under the van and chased us halfway across town.

So we had to deal with imminent motherhood. The farm had an old water tower, a three-story wood structure with twelve-foot sides. The upper area held an out-of-use storage tank, while the lower portion formed a tall room with a concrete floor. The warped door was stuck half-open. Not the Ritz, but it would make an excellent puppy nursery.

I filled a large cardboard box with old blankets and nailed a small board across the door frame to contain the pups but still give Charlie easy passage outside. When the birth was near, she settled into her nursery, rearranging her blankets at least a dozen times. I parked my van with the side door open beside the tower so she wouldn't feel abandoned. It wasn't long before she gave birth to four tiny black-and-white creatures.

Charlie did well in her new role until the pups got larger and more demanding, stressing her out. Fortunately, finding homes for the pups took no time at all. And I promised Charlie she'd be spayed before the next heat. "No more puppy stress, girl."

I had my own way of dealing with stress. The students at the next farm allowed us to use the rope swing in their old barn whenever it struck our fancy. Hanging from the middle of the ceiling, the thirty-foot rope was as thick as the grip on a baseball bat. The end of the rope, about three feet above the ground, had a softball-sized knot.

Holding the knot in one hand, I would climb a ladder and then jump onto a wide beam that ran horizontally across the back wall, twelve feet above the ground, working my way to the center. Before me was the barn door, a large opening forty feet away.

The next step was a big one—literally. I had to muster my courage and grab the rope with both hands while jumping and clamping both feet on the knot. This propelled me at high speed all the way through the barn and out the front door, bending the rope against the top of the opening just a few feet above my hands. The momentum took me back into the barn, almost to where I had taken the original leap.

Now I could push off the back wall and swing until the pendulum motion slowed and finally stopped in the middle of the barn. Here it was safe to jump off.

I felt a major adrenaline rush every time, helping me escape the doldrums. If I woke up a little foggy, a little down, a little stressed, or a little bored, I'd hike up the road and take a morning swing. When I jumped off that beam, any preoccupation with my problems disappeared. Facing ultimate danger, we focus, and focus leads to clarity.

After a swing, I'd always walk back whistling, exhilarated, with a brand-new outlook on life.

Several times that spring, Hal, Russ, and I passed out leaflets at the Oakland induction center, where young draftees went for their physicals. We'd get up at 3:30 a.m., cook a hearty breakfast (usually one of Hal's tasty omelets), and head for the Bay Area. Keeping a low profile, the three of us would walk into the center and mingle, informing the nervous teenagers that when it came to the military, they had a choice. Some were sympathetic to our message, and a few took our leaflets, but we never persuaded anyone to walk out.

At Travis Air Force Base, a military man had petitioned for a conscientious objector status, and when he was denied, they ordered him straight to Vietnam. Considering this a kidnapping, thirty of us stormed the area with protest leaflets. We were rounded up and held for most of the night.

By now, I detested the establishment. So much in the past year had steeled my resolve to fight back: the Tet Offensive, the assassinations of Martin Luther King and Robert Kennedy, the police brutality against peaceful protesters in Chicago, and LBJ's and then Nixon's refusal to end the bloodshed. All the antiwar protests and campus takeovers, including the destruction of draft records by Catholic priests, convinced me I belonged to a growing number who despised the war and the military mentality.

Couldn't our political leaders see that hate, intolerance, and killing led to more of the same? How could people be so narrow-minded? The military trained kids—indoctrinated them—to hate and kill, stripping them of any compassion. It was all so senseless.

At some point, though, it didn't feel right. I was involved with politics because I believed that peace was more meaningful than war, that love was a better choice than hate, that killing was wrong. But now I abhorred those who were ignorant of my principles, making me feel conflicted and hypocritical. I couldn't stand up for love with hate in my heart. I had to step back if I wanted to feel nonjudgmental and compassionate again.

To be true to myself, I couldn't let the thoughts and actions of others sweep me away, the Berkeley mob and its scary pull still vivid in my mind. It's important to dig your heels in and hold on to your integrity, no matter how noble the cause. To keep in balance, I wanted to respect the people I disagreed with, even if I thought their beliefs were wrong.

31.
House Raising
March 1969

Arms crossed, I stood with Russ looking at the faded-green '55 Chevy three-quarter-ton pickup.

"It runs great," the farmer said. "We have to leave by Monday, so we've got to sell it. You can have it for a hundred bucks."

That's all he wanted for a three-quarter-ton truck?

After taking a test drive, I knew I couldn't pass up such a deal. The farmer said, "I need to use it tomorrow, but you can buy it Saturday." He also offered us a free roll of hog fence and some wood fence posts, which we loaded into Russ's yellow '53 Studebaker truck.

On our way back, Russ agreed that I scored big. I pulled out my harmonica and composed a piece of music to mark the occasion. After playing several stanzas, I broke in with a low, gravelly voice, singing "hog fence," then played a few more bars and another "hog fence," a little higher this time. Toward the end of the tune, I added "chicken wire" to the lyrics.

Somehow the simple song caught on, and whenever Rod, Russ, Albert, Crazy Marvin, and I (or any combination of the afore-mentioned loonies) would get together to play our blues harps, we'd always include "Hog Fence" in our repertoire. It became our anthem.

A week later, I sat out in the yard with Russ and Hal drinking a few beers. "You know," Hal said, pointing to my recent purchase, "you oughta build a camper on that truck. A three-quarter ton could haul a good-sized house."

Russ nodded. "Yeah, it could look really cool."

At the time, both of them worked as carpenters, and they volunteered to build me a camper as long as I paid for materials—another deal I couldn't pass up.

The open shed behind the house became their workshop. Hal backed the truck into it so a spring shower wouldn't dampen their creation. They stretched an extension cord from the house and sawed and banged out there most evenings. And they made the shed off-limits to surprise me with the finished product.

When it came time to shop for a window, we scoured a Woodland wrecking yard and found a hinged side window from a VW van. As we walked by a broken-down school bus, Hal's eyes filled with glee. "Oh, man, wouldn't it be great to have running lights?" We removed them from the bus, paid the grungy yardman, and left with our treasures.

After three weeks of construction, Russ called me out to the shed. They had pulled the truck outside, and on its back was a complete miniature house. The left and right walls of the camper extended a foot out from the pickup bed, and the front extended halfway over the cab. They had painted the camper a deep chocolate brown and attached the red running lights to the top corners, each set in a yellow frame. The slightly peaked roof looked like one on a real house.

I walked around the back and found a tan-and-green two-part Dutch door, the top part open. To the right, a matching checkered flower box hung below a small black mailbox.

Russ opened the bottom section of the door and motioned for me to go inside. A bed frame stood on the right side. Hal said, "We measured your van's mattress, so it's a perfect fit." He pointed to a Plexiglas skylight above that was almost as large as the bed. "You can sleep under the stars regardless of the weather."

"How very, very cool!" I couldn't believe what they had done.

"And check this out." Russ showed me several partitioned storage slots over the truck cab, a three-tiered bookcase, and a mirrored medicine cabinet. Then he demonstrated how the window worked.

"This opens just enough to provide air," he said, "but not enough for someone to reach in and snatch anything."

The right side of the little cabin was an engineering masterpiece. The bed folded up and hooked to the right wall, the hinged bottom leg folding flat against the bottom of the bed. A hinged table folded down and hung on two small chains from the bottom of the bed. They hadn't overlooked a single detail.

"I'm blown away—you guys thought of everything!" I said, in awe of their gift.

The following week I decorated and added some amenities. A green corduroy curtain over the window offered privacy and a cozy touch. I placed my ice chest on the roof of the truck, securing it with baling wire. Then I moved my things in, including my mattress and Charlie. Gazing affectionately at the green Chevy with my new home on the back, I gave her a name: Evergreen.

My VW van hadn't run the same since tipping over in Big Sur. Though it had served me well, I'd lost confidence in it. I put out the word that it was for sale, and David, a fellow Hal knew, dropped by to check it out. Having received his conscientious objector status, he needed to be in Denver in six days for alternative service and didn't want to ride his motorcycle all that way. I told him about the problems I'd been having with the van, but he wasn't concerned. We worked out a deal for two hundred bucks and two ounces of weed.

Several weeks later, Hal told me, "You won't believe what happened to David. He took off for Denver with his bike aboard. The van broke down somewhere in the middle of Nevada, so he hopped on his bike because he needed to report for alternative service on Monday morning. Somewhere in Utah, the bike broke down too. Then he put out his thumb and arrived in Denver Sunday evening. When he walked in the next morning, he was told that they didn't expect him until two weeks later."

I felt for the guy. "What a royal bummer. If I ever feel like I'm having a shitty day, I'll think of David, and things won't seem so bad."

32.

Tequila Trickery

April 1969

One day, Albert, Crazy Marvin, and I were driving through Sacramento when Marvin pointed to a woman standing on a street corner. "Wow. Look at that hot chick in the mini skirt. She sure didn't waste any money on material."

Albert glanced over. "She's a hooker. You usually see one or two on this corner."

Marvin sat up straight, craning his neck. "Really?"

We found out that big-talking Crazy Marvin had never been with a prostitute. In fact, that afternoon was the first time he'd ever seen one. We agreed that this bordered on deprivation and set our minds to remedy the situation. Albert offered to drive his truck to Mexico that weekend. Russ said to count him in.

Our new buddy, Ralph the Triple-A man, also decided to join us. A month before, when Brad's van had gotten stuck in the mud "tighter than a lid on a honey jar," he called AAA, and lanky, baby-faced Ralph showed up with a tow truck. Brad got him stoned, and from then on, he was a member of our gang.

Early Saturday morning, the five of us loaded into Albert's truck and left for Mazatlán via the border town of Nogales, the perfect place to correct Marvin's deficiency. I took over driving shortly after midnight, somewhere in the middle of the Arizona desert. Ralph the Triple-A man sat next to me in the cab, and Crazy Marvin rode shotgun while Albert and Russ grabbed some shut-eye in the back of the pickup.

I missed Charlie. It was the first time I'd left her behind for more than a few hours. At least she was with Arlo, Russ's dog. I thought about Nina allowing Marvin to leave so he could experience a whorehouse. What a unique woman.

As we cruised along Highway 93, the cool night air blowing through the open windows, I couldn't help but think about my first trip to Nogales three years before.

It was spring break, and I was a junior at Davis. My friend Al and I drove down to Tucson to visit my pal Gary. I hadn't seen him for close to a dozen years, but we had stayed in touch.

I'd never traveled out of state on my own before. My folks had loaned me their '62 Nash Rambler station wagon for the trip. Every couple of hours, Roger Miller's "King of the Road" came on the radio, and we belted out the lyrics. It became our theme song on that maiden journey—we couldn't get enough of it.

Arriving in Tucson, we discovered that everything was done in cars. We spent most of our waking hours in Gary's emerald green '65 GTO. When we weren't cruising the main boulevard, we were drinking beer with his buddies in the back room of a Phillips 66 gas station.

It was during that stay that Gary introduced us to Nogales. We reached the border late one afternoon and left the GTO on the American side. After walking through the border crossing, the three of us stopped at a nearby bar for a few too many beers, each one followed with a shot of tequila.

Shortly after dusk, we caught a cab to the red-light district, the infamous Canal Street. Gary led us to his favorite whorehouse, where scantily clad girls surrounded us. Fifty percent of their English vocabulary consisted of the words "fucky" and "sucky." We had more beers with tequila chasers while enjoying the off-key music of a mariachi band.

One by one, each of us chose a girl and began to bargain for their services. I liked Lupe for her friendly smile and soft voice. She wanted ten dollars, and we went back and forth a few times before settling on eight. My friends had disappeared by the time we completed our transaction.

Lupe gave the money to the bartender, who slipped her a key. Pretty bombed at that point, I staggered along behind her through the back door out into the evening air, the stars sparkling overhead. We walked through a small plaza of crude stone and tile, dimly lit by makeshift streetlights, a dry, dusty fountain in the center. Half a dozen pastel-colored cabins surrounded us amid a scattering of tropical trees.

At a faded-yellow cabin, Lupe unlocked the padlock and opened the door, leaving the padlock hanging on the latch. She gestured for me to step into a small room with a wood floor and pale-yellow walls. A velvet painting of a man in a sombrero hung at a slant on the wall. Next to the bed were a chair and a small table that held a cheap, low-wattage lamp with a flowered shade. The soiled lace curtain at the single window offered little privacy, but I was too out of it to care.

Lupe undressed and I did the same, tossing my clothes on the chair.

We crawled into bed and kissed. I was nervous, never having been with a prostitute before—and my head was spinning circles from the alcohol. She crawled on top of me. A few minutes later, she paused and said something I didn't understand.

"Peederslipi."

"*No comprende*," I said.

"Peederslipi."

"*No comprende*." What was she saying?

She slowed her speech, taking greater care. "Pee . . . der . . . sli . . . pi," she repeated.

I thought for a moment. "Oh, now I get it. Peter sleepy."

She nodded.

The booze had reduced my manhood to the consistency of a limp noodle. I was faced with a pickled penis—too plowed to poke, too bombed to ball, too sauced to screw, too trashed for a trick. Man, I was altogether too fucked up to fornicate.

Disappointed but too inebriated to be embarrassed, I shrugged, got up, and put on my clothes. Giving her a quick wave, I stepped outside. Still in an alcoholic haze, I closed the door and secured the metal hasp of the padlock. It all happened in an instant—one innocent, continuous motion. The second that padlock clicked into the locked position, the realization of what I had done came crashing down on me.

I stumbled back into the bar, trying to figure out what to do next. I wasn't just drunk—I was drunk in a rough part of town in a foreign country, with a severe language barrier. The imminent danger associated with my actions sobered me right up. There's nothing like personal survival to clear your head.

Al was drinking a beer at the bar next to Gary and his lady. I sat in the seat on the other side of Gary and whispered in his ear, "We have to leave. I locked her in her room."

"What?" he shouted.

The blaring music and bar noise forced me to raise my voice. I couldn't allow either the bartender or Gary's lady friend to hear, but I had to relay this vital bit of information ASAP.

I shouted as softly as I could, cupping my hands to his ear, "I LOCKED HER IN HER ROOM."

Gary's eyes widened, and he calmly got up and went over to Al. He said firmly, "Let's get out of here."

We walked out the door and hailed a cab, which appeared as if on cue from out of the night. The dilapidated '51 Chevy had only one headlight, and it didn't work. The space left by the missing headlight gaped black and eerie like an empty eye socket. Even in the faint light seeping from the cantina, we could see the dents, dust, and rust covering every inch of the chassis—but our consumption of alcohol and the danger back at the cantina left us no time to sweat the small stuff.

"To the border!" Gary yelled as we piled into the vehicle and raced off. I was glad to put some distance between Canal Street and our vulnerable necks. How our driver stayed on that dark, bumpy dirt road was a mystery.

After five hours of driving south through Arizona, Ralph by my side, I started feeling the weight of fatigue. Close to the border, I turned to my Triple-A buddy, his ever-present company shirt and cap visible in the orange glow of dawn. "Hold the wheel for a minute."

"Huh?" He took the wheel with his left hand as we rolled along the razor-straight highway. I opened my door and climbed out onto the running board. The wind whistled through my hair as I held on to the frame of the truck.

Slamming the door behind me, I worked my way over Albert's and Russ's bodies, both buried in their sleeping bags in the bed of the pickup. Once on the other running board, I opened the passenger door and climbed in as Marvin slid to the center.

"Your turn, Ralph," I said.

I settled into the seat and marveled at the spectacular sunrise as pastel colors rained over the desert. *Mexico, here we come.*

33.

Viva Carmen
April 1969

We arrived in Nogales late in the afternoon and found a motel room on the American side. I headed straight for the shower to wash off the road grime, my four companions too busy joking around to notice. While they primped and preened in front of the mirror, preparing to rock the world, I sat propped against a pillow on one of the beds, consumed by thoughts about the evening ahead.

As I had discovered with Lil, sex without romance and affection didn't do much for me, so I wasn't too keen on paying for it—particularly when it wasn't that hard to get a good lay for free.

I considered the unfortunate girls in the Canal Street brothels. What if I offered some genuine love? Yes, that's what I'd do! I would muster all the love I could and give my heart to a lady of the night. Maybe for a short time, I could brighten her dreary existence, adding something special to a life of empty, mechanical sex.

It was already dark when the five of us walked across the border. We stood under a dim streetlight on a dingy street corner. Two weathered, middle-aged Mexicans sat in a nearby pickup truck.

I walked up to the driver. "*¿Dónde está Canal Street?*"

He said something to his friend I couldn't understand. They both laughed, and with a big smile, he motioned for us to climb in the back of his pickup. We piled in and bounced out of town on a rutty dirt road, a trail of dust and exhaust billowing behind us. Soon we came to a long block of buildings with four or five cantinas on either side, just as I remembered it from three years before. Our driver pulled over, and we gave him a few bucks and more than one *"muchas gracias."*

After taking in the scene, we stepped into the closest cantina and gathered around one of several large, round wooden tables. Three men with sombreros played mariachi music far back in the room. A long bar with stools ran along most of one wall, and ten girls in skimpy dresses lined up at the end near us.

When a waiter came over, Russ pointed around to all of us. *"Cerveza, por favor."*

"Tequila, también," I added, holding up my hand to indicate five.

When the waiter brought our beers and shots of tequila, he placed a bowl of limes and a saltshaker on the table. I showed everyone how to apply juice from the lime to the web of your thumb, and then shake salt on it. It was a ritual I had learned the last time I was in these parts. The others grabbed a slice of lime and did the same.

I raised the shot of tequila and held it to my nose. It smelled like a mixture of kerosene and burned leather. Still, I lifted my glass high in the air and poured it down, my eyes watering as the tequila scorched my throat. Then I licked the salty citrus off my hand, shook my head with a wince, and picked up my beer to put out the fire.

Everyone nodded approval, lifted their glasses, and repeated the process. As we drank, some girls came to the table and tried to woo us. One lady sat in Marvin's lap and said "Fucky" as she rubbed the inside of his thigh. He smiled, enjoying the attention, even though his ears turned as red as his hair.

"Hey, I got an idea," Albert said. "Let's check out all the places, one at a time. And once we all know who we want to be with, we'll split up and then meet when we're done with our fun."

Good plan. I surveyed the assortment of girls—tall and short, skinny and plump, natural and painted, pretty and downright raunchy. Only one caught my eye: a petite woman with a beautiful, kind face and shiny black hair reaching her shoulders. Her pink mini-dress had blue embroidered flowers and delicate buttons down the front. Standing poised and confident, she seemed to have more class than the other women. *I could love this one.*

After downing our drinks, we left the club and began our tour. At the neighboring building, we stood evaluating the girls, not much different from those at the previous place, and then moved on to the next.

At the last cantina, following another round of drinks and our umpteenth mariachi serenade, we agreed to meet back there when we finished our business. Before we split up, Albert gestured for us to lean in toward him. "Remember, guys, this is Mexico," he said, lowering his voice. "Bargaining is what they do. Everything is negotiable, and they're always going to ask for more than they're willing to take."

Armed with his advice, we rose and stepped outside.

I returned to the first place since no one else could compete with that pretty little lady in the pink dress. When I walked through the door and scanned the room, I saw her sitting near the back of the bar beside a tall woman wearing way too much makeup. Behind the bar was a heavy lady whose use of cosmetics made the tall one seem conservative.

I walked over to the lady of my affections. "*¿Cómo se llama?*"

"Carmen." She looked at me with alluring, doe-like dark eyes.

I pointed to my chest. "Ricardo. *¿Quantos?*"

"*Quince dólares.*"

Fifteen dollars. Higher than I thought. "*Diez dólares.*"

"*Quince dólares.*"

"*Doce.*" I flashed my best smile.

"*Quince dólares.*"

So much for Albert's negotiating tips. I hesitated a moment, then gave in. We both knew she was well worth every *centavo*.

After paying her, Carmen took my hand and led me through the back door. "Come theese way, señor."

So she spoke English. Her hand was warm and silky in mine. She led me down a corridor to a small, well-lit courtyard surrounded by rooms. Carmen stopped at a door and opened it without a key.

The simple room had a bed with just a bottom sheet, a chair, and a mirror on the wall. The only light came from the patio through thin white curtains carelessly hung at the tiny window. My mission was still clear: to give this lady all my love for the short time we were together.

The beautiful Carmen made this an easy task.

She stood before me and began to unbutton her dress. I held up my hand to stop her and stepped forward. Gazing deep into the rich brown pools of her eyes, I coaxed the love from my heart and directed it into her chest. Smiling, I slowly unbuttoned her dress, working my way down until I could slip it off her shoulders. It fell to the wood floor with a sound like a gentle breeze.

The soft light cast a golden hue on her smooth skin. I cupped her cheeks in my hands and brought her lips to mine, directing love from my heart up through my mouth.

Her dark nipples reminded me of fine buttercream chocolates. I bent down to give each one a long, tender kiss, eliciting a sigh of pleasure. She unbuttoned my shirt and let it drop behind me as I unhooked my belt, the buckle clanging as my pants hit the floor. Both of us discarded our underwear in a swift, effortless motion. Her eyes on mine, she lay back on the bed, extending her hand for me to join her.

Unlike my last trip to Canal Street, I had no problem beckoning my manhood. Without hesitation, I was on top of her, thrust deep inside. That was when Carmen showed me her hidden talent. With the ease of a contortionist, she somehow pulled her toes into position and commenced to play a piano concerto on the top of my testicles. *Ohhh myyy God!* Any effort to prolong this ecstasy was fruitless. My inner juices soon exploded, and our divine rendezvous came to a short but ever so sweet end. I lay there in her heavenly arms for a few minutes, cherishing the moment.

As I dressed, I looked over at her. "That was wonderful, Carmen."

She stood and gave me one more extended, tender kiss. "You are a good lover, señor." I said good-bye and let her clean herself in private. As I walked across the street to meet my friends, Jerry Lee Lewis's song "Great Balls of Fire" played in my head. My feet barely touched the ground. I had experienced something special while giving a little sincere love to a fine woman.

It hit me how strange it was that a random roll of the dice could define people's entire lives. This woman had the elegance to be anything she wanted—but fate had led her to Canal Street. Regardless, there was no doubt that Carmen was a lady, and one I wouldn't forget.

My thoughts drifted away as I entered the saloon to meet my friends. I joined Albert, Ralph, and Russ at a table and signaled the waiter for another beer. "Is everybody happy?" I asked. Smiles all around—until Crazy Marvin sat down looking grim.

"How'd it go?" Russ asked.

"Everything was going great. She was a pretty lady, and we had fun in bed. As I was leaving, I decided to ask for her name. And do you know what she told me?" His voice rose an octave. "Daphne! I can't believe it. Daphne. Not Carlotta or Maria or Josefina. No. I get a Daphne. I finally score at a Mexican whorehouse, and it's with a Daphne. Shit! What kind of luck is that?"

Of course none of us gave him any sympathy, just lots of laughs. When we had our fill of drinks and jabs, we took a taxi back to the border, again jerking and jostling our way along the rough road. Carmen still on my mind, I decided my old green truck would no longer be called "Evergreen." She'd now be known affectionately as "Evergreen Carmen"—a tribute to that lovely lady.

The following morning, we struggled to get going but managed to leave before the sun hit high noon. We drove seven hundred miles south to Mazatlán, stopping only for tacos, tamales, or beer. Occasionally, someone would try to grab some shut-eye in the back of the truck—a challenge considering the bathtub-sized potholes littering the roads.

It was dusk when we finally arrived in Mazatlán and found a place to camp on the beach. Russ pointed out some strange, wide tire tracks in the sand. Even Albert couldn't figure out what kind of vehicle they came from. Exhausted, we collapsed in our sleeping bags.

I awoke in a sweat and crawled out of my bedroll, the Mexican sun beating down on me. Crazy Marvin waded in the surf, and Russ sat nearby, rubbing his eyes and scratching his beard. I scanned the beautiful beach and noticed that the strange tire tracks had increased during the night. They crisscrossed one another all around our makeshift camp, producing a well-defined circle that came within a few feet of our sleeping bodies.

"Those aren't tire tracks," I said. "They belong to creatures of some kind—and they were observing us while we slept. That's pretty damn creepy."

My friends gathered around, but we still couldn't figure out what made the tracks. Later, when we took a walk, Russ pointed off in the distance and shouted, "Check it out!" On the rocky cliffs, a family of giant iguanas basked in the sun, some stretching five feet in length. Mystery solved. Content to hang out on the beach for a few days, we went to town and stocked up on food and beer.

On the third day, Russ and I both woke up feeling the wrath of Montezuma's revenge, and Albert, Ralph, and Marvin went to town to fetch us some nausea medicine. As the sun rose in the sky, it got hotter and hotter, and we felt sicker and sicker. A few hundred yards down the beach, we could see a cabana covered with palm fronds—the only protection from the sun—but we felt too weak to get more than a few steps before collapsing.

By noon we were delirious from the pounding heat. What had happened to our friends? Lying in the water with the waves washing over us, we took turns reassuring each other with the little bit of strength we had left. "They'll be back soon." "They must have gotten lost." I imagined my bones lying in the wet sand.

Somehow Russ managed to prop up a suitcase and a gas can and drape a blanket over them. He signaled to me, and we both crawled under the low sun-break and passed out.

I woke up needing to relieve myself. By now the sun was starting to approach the sea. While taking a pee, I watched the hills in the distance zoom into view and realized I'd had blurry vision all day. A high fever must have broken. Russ was also feeling a little better. Finally, we heard the sound of Albert's truck approaching.

"Hey, where the hell have you guys been?" Russ asked.

Crazy Marvin strutted toward us. "We got drunk and ended up in a whorehouse. You wouldn't believe it. A pig ran right through this place while we were drinking. I couldn't leave Mexico after only sleeping with a Daphne. This chiquita was a fat one, but at least her name was Juanita!"

34.

Home on the Go
May 1969

I loved working in the entomology department. In fact, I loved my job so much that I saw a distinct danger of becoming complacent and getting stuck. So I did what I had to do—I gave notice.

Ready once again for the open road, I talked with Mitch about our cowboy adventure, and we agreed to meet in Aspen around June 20, saddles in hand. In the meantime, I had more than a month to kill, plenty of time to test out my new home on wheels. After saying my good-byes, Charlie and I climbed into Evergreen Carmen and headed east to visit my friends in Kansas City.

En route, I stopped for a short visit in Reno, then picked up two hitchhikers near Winnemucca, who helped with the driving as far as Denver. Continuing on alone through the monotonous eastern plains of Colorado and endless wheat fields of Kansas, I entertained myself with the AM radio blaring country tunes. I wasn't raised on that music, but something about it massaged my heart: simple stories about people and their feelings. Unfortunately, the sad songs fueled my longings for Gina and Marna.

Marna was incredible, but the sultry brunette was with someone else now. Though Gina was also in a relationship, I clung to the hope that someday we might rekindle the spark we once shared. Memories of her infectious laughter consumed me as I drove, and I promised myself to be patient.

Charlie, in her usual state of travel recline, stretched out on the seat, her head cradled on my thigh, its weight and warmth comforting. I stroked her soft fur and told her of my heartache, and then read to her a string of red-and-white Burma-Shave signs stretched along the highway.

Well past midnight, I caught a couple hours of sleep at a rural truck stop and took a shower before getting back on the road. Close to noon, I arrived in Kansas City and worked my way to Bill's house, a modest light-green, two-story Victorian that had been converted into several apartments. Up a narrow staircase, I had no trouble finding his place—tacked on his door was a poster of Mr. Natural from Zap Comix in a trucking stance: "Don't gag on it. Goof on it!" All Right! I knocked, feeling at home.

Bill appeared, his curly hair in disarray, and smiled at me, then down at Charlie. Calling out over his shoulder, he said, "Hey, Tote, come see what the dog dragged in. Hi, dog, where the hell did you find this guy?"

Tote, the Mia Farrow look-alike who used to be Andy's girlfriend, was now Bill's squeeze. As soon as she saw Charlie, she fell in love with her and told her so in that refreshing country-girl drawl.

Shortly after I arrived, the door opened, and an attractive young woman with long reddish-blonde hair strolled into the apartment. Susanna lived in the unit above Bill and Tote. Shaking her hand, I was captivated by her soft chestnut eyes, sweet smile, and the light freckles dancing high on her cheekbones. Her smoky voice tugged at me like a siren's call.

In an instant, she wiped out all thoughts of Gina.

The four of us, five with Charlie, set out on foot for Volker Park. Susanna, a psychology student, needed to stop off at the university, and I accompanied her. Along the way, she shared two things with me: one, she had taken acid that morning and was beginning to soar; and two, she wasn't interested in getting into a relationship. Okay, I respected her wishes—being in her presence was a prize in itself.

When we caught up with our friends at the park, Bill pulled out a joint, and I put on a nice buzz. We spent the afternoon playing Frisbee and exploring the park, and that evening, following dinner at a nearby diner, I fell in step with Susanna on the way back.

After only a few hours' sleep in three days, I felt dizzy with fatigue. I walked her to her door, Charlie at my side, and Susanna turned to say good night—or at least that's what I thought she was about to do. "Would you like to stay with me tonight?" she asked in a dreamy voice, her warm eyes devouring me.

"Uh, sure." I grinned, my weary body coming to life.

I tagged along behind her up a narrow stairway, watching the roundness of her butt and the sway of her hips under her thin dress. When we entered her small, untidy apartment, she said, "Get naked, then come outside." She giggled as her dress slipped to the floor.

I shed my clothes and followed her well-proportioned body through a small window, Charlie jumping out after us. Out on a level extension of the roof was a mattress with sheets, skirted by the leaves of an ancient oak. We sank upon the smooth sheets under a blanket of stars and moonlight, our naked bodies caressed by the warm night air. We played around for a while, but my exhaustion left me with little to give. I fell asleep feeling as if I were floating on a cloud.

The next evening, Susanna stopped by Bill's place. "I'm going to this talk at the university. Rolling Thunder is speaking. Have you heard of him? He's a Shoshone medicine man and prophet. Wanna join me?"

Before we left, a nervous fellow named Don dropped by. I talked with him for a while, or actually, I listened—he seemed to enjoy the sound of his own voice too much to give anyone else a turn. At first he offered his intellectual take on higher mathematics and quantum physics, but he lost me when he attributed spiritual ramifications to these bland academic subjects. Then the conversation digressed.

"I bought a bunch of Benzedrex inhalers the other day. When you break them open, you'll find a piece of cotton inside drenched with Benzedrine. I soak them in water, then shoot up the solution. Man, what a bitchin' high."

"Doesn't sound like something I'd do. I hate needles." I didn't mention I had no interest in speed either. His nervous energy made me uncomfortable. The more he talked, the less I found to admire. At one point, he pulled up the front of his shirt revealing the butt of a handgun.

"What the hell?" Bill asked. "Are you insane, man? What are you going to do with that?"

"I gotta protect myself." Don pulled out the squared-off automatic weapon and showed it off. "There are a lot of crazy motherfuckers out there who'll shoot you in the blink of an eye. You can't be too careful."

"Put that thing away. Don't you know you're asking for trouble carrying heat? What the fuck's the matter with you?" Bill shook his head. "You're probably going to shoot your dick off, fool."

It was a waste of time—you can't reason with a paranoid speed freak racing towards disaster.

At the university, we filed into the small classroom and chose seats in the middle of the second row. I sat between Susanna and Don. What a contrast! After the room filled with two dozen spectators, an Indian gentleman, decorated in fringe and feathers, walked into the room. The creases and wrinkles in his face revealed a mixture of age, wisdom, serenity, and power. I felt relaxed in his presence.

Rolling Thunder began to speak of the ancient ways and tales of the Indians. "The prophets foretold that the great native tribes would be nearly wiped out, but they would return again before a great turmoil."

While he talked, I observed how he studied one person after another in the audience, slowly working his way down one row after another, making eye contact for several seconds with each person in the room. That is, except for Don. As I watched him work his way up our row, he barely stopped when he came to Don. Nothing there of interest? No depth? When he came to me, he looked deep into my being, and we shared a moment of recognition that made me feel reunited with an old friend. He also took his time connecting with Susanna.

When he was done familiarizing himself with everyone in the room, he said, "I see many Indians here today. Not all Natives have red skin."

Rolling Thunder went on to describe prophecies of the last days, when the skies would turn red and the earth would shake. But he concluded his talk with an unexpected exception: "Remember, all prophecy is subject to change!"

Incredible! Who ever heard of a prophet making such a statement? My admiration for this enlightened, humble being had just grown logarithmically.

I whistled for Charlie, and she came bounding after us as Susanna and I strolled back to the house behind Don, Bill, and Tote. "That was amazing," I said in a low voice. "Thanks for letting me know about it."

She reached over and squeezed my hand. "I loved his face. What a remarkable man."

When we arrived at her door, the glint in her eye made me wonder if I might get lucky again tonight. Respecting her wish to avoid a relationship, I left her to call the shots—and sadly, the shot she called left me sleeping alone in my truck with Charlie.

Dang.

35.

Field of White Daisies

June 1969

I left early the next morning, heading east to visit a friend in Ann Arbor. The rolling, wooded expanse of Missouri always made me come alive. It seemed so familiar—had I lived there in another lifetime?

IF DAISIES

ARE YOUR

FAVORITE FLOWER

KEEP PUSHIN' UP THOSE

MILES PER HOUR

Burma-Shave

Arriving in St. Louis late that afternoon, I parked in a secluded place facing the Mississippi River. As I sat in my truck with Charlie and stared at the water, I thought about how I'd always preferred the West.

When I was twelve, my family spent a month circling the country in our '56 fire-engine-red Packard Clipper. My dad helped plan the Interstate Highway System (championed by President Eisenhower), and he wanted to check it out. I remembered not being impressed with the eastern states. Most of the people I'd met seemed uptight and narrow-minded—no doubt from a lack of open space.

After much contemplation, I decided not to go east—the other direction had more to offer—namely, Susanna. I couldn't deny the mysterious, irresistible pull to spend time with her. Where Gina once reigned, Susanna now dominated my thoughts. My groin stirred in anticipation.

So as the hot sun melted into the horizon, I started up Evergreen Carmen, turned around, and headed back toward Kansas City.

Susanna occupied my mind. Hours later, although terribly tired, I kept driving, eager to see her. It was well past three, the road dark and empty and Charlie fast asleep curled up next to me.

Out of nowhere, a man appeared a few feet in front of me on the highway. Oh shit. As I went to slam on my breaks, his image zoomed off into the distance, turning into a speed-limit sign a hundred feet down the road. My heart thumped in my chest. Jesus fuck!

I had heard about this guy who shows up for weary drivers. The truckers talk about "the little man who isn't there"—some ghost who has taken on the mission of warning tired drivers off the road. Maybe someone who left this world driving while under extreme fatigue? I found a wide shoulder on the interstate and parked. We crawled into my camper, and I sank into the depths of unconsciousness.

I woke from a vivid dream. Susanna and I were sitting across from each other in an immense, rolling field of tall white daisies, both of us naked. Under the warm sun, the daisies formed a nest around us, enveloping us in love and joy. Nearby, a large rattlesnake worked its way toward us, but we understood there was nothing to fear. It crawled slowly into my lap, and I welcomed the serpent as my friend.

A brilliant image of white flowers and green leaves stayed with me long after I awoke. Feeling refreshed, I climbed behind the wheel and continued to Kansas City, the sun already high in a cloudless sky.

When Bill opened the door, he did a double-take so fast he looked like a cartoon character. "Wait a minute—weren't you just here?"

"There's nothing east of the Mississippi for me," I said, laughing. "Besides, I missed you guys." *Not to mention Susanna.*

"Come on in. Tote and I were talking about some beautiful camping places in the Ozarks."

"If you want to take a trip down there, my truck's warmed up and ready to roll."

So we decided to embark on a weekend trip. Because I needed to have Charlie spayed before she went into heat again, I made the tough decision to leave her with a veterinarian while we ventured south into Arkansas. I assured her I loved her and would return soon. Except for my time in Mexico, we hadn't spent a single night apart. Though racked with guilt, I knew we needed to put this procedure behind us.

We left early Saturday morning. Built-like-a-box Ruth joined Susanna in the front seat, and Bill and Tote rode in the camper. That afternoon, we stood outside Fayetteville, Arkansas, at a turnoff to a little-used dirt road near the Kings River, wondering whether to follow it.

"I think it would be posted if it was private property," Bill said.

"Have you been here before?" I asked.

"It's been a long time, but we should be able to find a place to camp."

"Should we ask at one of the farms around here?" I looked at a run-down, unpainted house and barn set far back from the road.

"They're afraid of strangers down here. Sometimes these people won't even come to the door if you knock. Or they'll come out with a cocked shotgun. Lots of people in the Ozarks live in an isolated reality."

As if on cue, a '57 Chevy convertible, the top down, raced around a turn. Three teenage boys with Elvis haircuts stared at us as they drove by, their radio blasting old time rock and roll. We all watched, speechless, until Bill broke the silence: "I think we just stepped into a time warp."

"I bet we look strange to them too," I said.

In the end, we took the dirt road and, to our delight, came to a lush meadow bordering a small river. Susanna passed out some acid as we went to work setting up two tents: one for Bill and Tote and the other for Ruth. Susanna could stay with me in the camper.

The river beckoned. We stripped down and waded in, the water deep enough in the middle for us to sit up to our shoulders.

Whoosh . . . Buzzzz . . . Zing . . . Whirrrr

People's voices seemed distant. I got lost in the water's glare as my heart grew in my chest. I missed Charlie, but I knew I had made the right decision. Then I went through a guilt-laden, moral debate about calling a female dog "Charlie," a mental discussion I'd had before.

Bill got out of the water on the opposite shore and motioned for us to come. "Hey, guys, you gotta check this out."

All around him, we found dozens of small stones embedded with fossilized leaves and shells. As we searched for more up the shore, the rocks hurt my feet, so I went back to fetch my boots. In my pile of clothes, I spotted my hunting knife on my belt—*hmm, that might come in handy.* I removed the belt from my jeans and wrapped it around my waist, then grabbed my hat.

As I approached my friends, Bill pointed at me, his eyes wide. "What does this mean? What does this mean?" He burst out laughing.

"Huh?" I pondered my appearance: my Redwing cowboy boots, my black cowboy hat, a belt with a hunting knife hanging off my hip—and that's all. Buck-naked except for accessories.

We hiked a short distance up the river, where a steep bank rose to the left. Bill, Tote, and Ruth continued on ahead while Susanna climbed up the incline, disappearing over the top. I hung back, tripping on some shiny rocks at the water's edge.

Hearing my name, I looked up to see Susanna's smiling face peering over a boulder high above me. "We've been good children," she called, beckoning me with her index finger.

When I scaled the bank and pulled myself over the top, I entered an enormous, rolling meadow with tall white daisies as far as I could see. We were like comic-book children, small and tender against an ocean of flowers. Susanna's lovely breasts seemed out of place on her childlike body.

It took a moment to register, but then the defiant déjà-vu finally pierced my swirling brain. The dream. Next to the interstate. It was that field of daisies! Here we were naked as jaybirds just like in the dream.

Shocked and excited, I grabbed her arms. "Susanna, you won't believe me, but I dreamed this exact scene the other night. It was the two of us, alone, naked among a million daisies, and a rattlesnake came to visit us. We let it crawl in our laps without fear. This is not just a field of daisies but the field from my dream!"

"For real?"

"I swear it's true. This is blowing my mind." The cosmic acid sounds hummed as I tried to make sense of it.

Whoosh . . . Buzzzz . . . Zing . . . Whirrrr

Warmed by the sun, we reveled in the glittering flowers and the gift of the moment. Then we heard something rattle. I was too stoned to tell what it was. I only knew that mixed in with the acid symphony of buzzing and whizzing in my head was a rattling sound. Was it a cicada, a grasshopper . . . a rattlesnake? The prospect of meeting a poisonous, fanged reptile in our condition, regardless of my dream, freaked us both out. We scurried down the bank and joined the others, who were swimming back near camp.

As evening descended, we ate trail mix, fruit, and celery. Celery had become my favorite food when tripping. Full of water, it satisfied my constant thirst, and the sound and texture of eating celery was also cool, like biting into tree trunks. The downside was that it's impossible to hear anything over all the snapping and crunching.

When the sun went down, I saw a tiny flash of light in the distance. "I must be really stoned. I thought I saw a light over in that field."

Bill looked where I was pointing. After a few minutes, it appeared again. "Oh, that's a lightning bug," he said.

"Way cool. They don't have them out west." I had considerable knowledge about fireflies, but I'd never seen one in nature before.

Before I knew it, more and more of the little creatures danced around me in the dim light. I sat there a long time, marveling at their luminescent displays. I thought about Susanna and how wonderful it would be to have her in my bed that night. Imagining her skin against mine evoked a deep longing. Golly, I was hornier than a billy goat.

When one firefly glowed so close I could see his entire body illuminated, I was satisfied with my bug watching. I returned to the others sitting around a small fire. Bill and Tote said good night and retired to their tent. Soon after, Ruth disappeared into hers.

Opening the door to my camper, I saw Susanna heading toward me, and I broke out in a huge grin.

She touched my arm. "Rich, I'm going to sleep with Ruth tonight."

What? No! She might as well have cut out my heart and fed it to the fish.

As my chest fell into my boots, I put on my best poker face to hide my disappointment. "Whatever's best for you."

I watched her walk away, loneliness crushing my rib cage.

Inside my camper, I got into bed and looked at the sea of stars sparkling through the skylight. I had forgotten about this group of girls being bisexual. But dumped for Ruth? Ruth, the one with table-like legs and ho-hum looks? Damn. The rest of the night passed in pain and frustration. I missed Charlie too.

My drug-tired brain made it impossible to process the shock. I played it over and over in my head, trying to ignore my hunger for Susanna. Such rotten luck. A single firefly streaked by just outside the skylight. I finally drifted off to sleep, my heart a bruised plum.

Waking late the next morning in a sweat, I walked out naked and jumped into the river. My heart was still numb, but I had moved past the strange events of the evening before, ready to get on with my life. When some menacing clouds appeared midway through the afternoon, we broke camp and loaded everything into the camper. Bill and Tote rode up front with me.

As we drove north, the rain began, and by the time we crossed into Missouri, it was coming down in torrents, accompanied by sheet lighting. The dark clouds blocked out the sun, and the pounding rain reduced the visibility to almost zero. I couldn't see more than one or two segments of the dashed white line on the narrow highway.

Every now and then a barrage of sheet lightning would flicker for up to five seconds at a time, lighting up the view as far as the eye could see, and then darkness would return. Buckets of water washed across the windshield, and the wipers struggled to keep up.

For more than an hour, we crept along like this, almost every dark minute interrupted by bursts of light. Strangely, the intense weather excited me. I loved seeing the power of nature and actually felt relaxed and alert. When we approached the suburbs of Kansas City, the savage storm finally broke, and the rain tapered off.

Damn, I missed Charlie—I treasured her loyalty now more than ever. She wouldn't have ditched me for Ruth, that's for sure.

The following morning, I busted Charlie out of the Kansas City Pet Prison. Boy was she pissed. She scolded me for three or four minutes, zigzagging back and forth at my feet, yelping and whining all the while. When she calmed down, we climbed into the truck, and she nestled against my leg. "I missed you too, girl. And if it's any consolation, I didn't get treated exactly the way I wanted to this weekend either . . . At least you'll never have to worry about puppies again. I'm glad to have you back."

I stroked her for a long time. My love for Charlie filled me with a warm, weightless feeling. She was definitely my best friend.

Back at Bill's house, I asked him where I could buy a saddle. He laughed, and it took several minutes to convince him I was serious. He described a place north of town and agreed to guide me there. A half hour later, we pulled into a western shop with monstrous cow horns over the front door. They had a dozen saddles on display, and I examined each one.

I told the clerk about my planned journey, and he pointed to a well-crafted model with intricate ornamentation all over the rust-colored leather. The seat was pale yellow and well padded. "This here's a Vetch saddle," he said in a drawn-out Missouri drawl. "They have a reputation for sturdy saddles. You can't get one much better than this. It's in great condition. I'd be surprised if you or your horse ever got a saddle sore from this baby."

Even I could see it was a fine piece of workmanship. "How much is it?"

"One hundred and forty dollars."

"Is that your best price?"

The clerk rubbed his chin. "For this saddle, I couldn't go any lower. I won't have any trouble selling it for that."

Before making a decision, I walked around and glanced again at the other saddles. With my back to the man, I turned over the seam of my jeans. From a tiny slit visible only to Bill, I removed a roll of hundred-dollar bills. Bill's mouth dropped, and his eyes nearly bulged out of his head. I took out two bills and replaced the rest.

"I'll take it," I said to the clerk.

As I loaded the fine leather saddle into my camper, Bill stood there shaking his head. "You're too much."

Now all I needed was a horse.

36.

The Men on the Flying Trapeze

June 1969

The golden wheat fields stretched from here to tomorrow as I followed the ruler-straight interstate west, the warm Kansas air rushing through the open windows. Country music and Charlie's head on my thigh massaged my heart.

DIM YOUR LIGHTS

BEHIND A CAR

LET FOLKS SEE

HOW BRIGHT

YOU ARE

Burma-Shave

As the driving part of my brain took over the operation of Evergreen Carmen, I tried to make sense of the charming and mysterious Susanna, now elevated in my mind's eye. She had poisoned me with her scent. What a woman. Images of our night on the roof quickened my pulse, and I wondered if I'd ever feel her warmth again. "What is it about the ones who get away, Charlie?"

I took a deep breath and concentrated on the road. By the time I hit the Rockies, I was beat, and I'd run out of things to discuss with Charlie. I found a roadside rest stop where we ate and slept.

In the morning, on our spectacular ride down Glenwood Canyon, outcroppings of gray and blue rock rose from river to sky like ancient Gothic spires. Varied shades of green vegetation clung beyond reason to rocky niches. Evergreen Carmen lumbered along the narrow, curvy two-lane that followed the Colorado River, straining above fifty-five. Out of respect for her and because I was in no hurry, I kept my speed down and had to pull over occasionally to let strings of cars pass.

The last stretch towards Aspen got me excited. In just a couple of weeks, Mitch and I would be embarking on the adventure of a lifetime.

Who else lives as pure a life as a cowboy, a man at one with nature and his horse? Who cares less than a cowboy about what the world thinks? True to his lifestyle and his actions, he represented free spirit. Hot damn.

After stopping in Aspen for supplies, I drove to Difficult Campground, located on the banks of the Roaring Fork River, where I found an empty campsite. Our national parks are amazing gifts, the one thing the government does well.

Charlie and I walked around the area meeting folks along the way, a good number of them longhairs. Posted in several places was a crude flyer announcing a love-in at the end of July, featuring almost every notable band and legend: the Beatles, Rolling Stones, Grateful Dead, Country Joe and the Fish, Jefferson Airplane, Janis Joplin, Joan Baez, Bob Dylan, Jimi Hendrix, and Santana, to name a few. The love-in of all love-ins.

I spent an afternoon writing postcards to my friends in Davis, Berkeley, and Kansas City, inviting them to meet me at the event. At the top of each card, I inserted a line borrowed from Hal: "Scenery is here, wish you were beautiful."

At the campground, I met Ira, a tall string bean of a man with a small bush of curly black hair. He wore bell-bottom jeans and a gaudy, multicolored shirt, louder than a hawk's screech. Ira's claim to fame was the Free Speech Movement at Berkeley, when he stood with Mario Savio shouting "Fuck!" and "Shit!" through a bullhorn from the

steps of Sproul Hall. A fun, good-natured fellow, he wanted to see
Taos and Santa Fe, and since I had some time to kill, I offered to drive
him down to New Mexico.

Outside Taos, we stayed for a couple of days at the New Buffalo
Commune with a gracious group of laid-back, clothing-optional people.
We helped with the goats and chickens and did some garden work,
then drove south to Santa Fe, where we stopped at the Hog Farm
Commune, made up of remnants of Ken Kesey's Merry Pranksters.
This infamous group of crazies organized "acid test" LSD parties and
traveled the country in a psychedelic painted bus, blowing minds any
way they could.

Three scruffy fellows sat around an old stump, sniffing the vapors
from a gigantic tin of glue. They invited us to participate, but judging
from the daft look on their faces, we declined. You could almost hear
their brain cells frying. Good thing I had some discrimination when
choosing my drugs.

The following afternoon, we arrived in Durango, Colorado, and
learned from a storekeeper that the Shrine Circus was hiring. Ira and
I looked at each other and grinned. We took off for the high school
football field where they were setting things up—after all, it's every
kid's dream to work for the circus, right?

A beefy man named Jack, whose large red nose could have quali-
fied him as a clown, hired us on the spot. "Come back at 6:30. You
can watch our final show, and then I'll pay you $4.50 an hour to help
us pack up." When we returned that evening, he told us to sit on one
of several painted wooden crates.

Keeping with tradition, the circus had three rings. The one on the
left, enclosed by a large cage, held lions and other big cats, and the
one on the right was surrounded by large balls, platforms, and other
props stacked in piles.

The center ring, featuring the aerial acts, was supported by tall aluminum posts piercing the air. From different positions on the posts,
wire cables connected to trapezes, strings of multicolored lights, a
tightrope, and a sweeping woven net that dropped to a point six feet

above the ground. We sat at the base of one of those posts, the best seats in the house, eagerly awaiting the show.

Soon the bleachers filled with townsfolk, and the ringmaster began, introducing the first act. A gaggle of clowns rushed out and entertained the crowd with their hysterical antics, followed by a troupe of acrobats defying gravity with their tumbling and balancing. Next came the jugglers, tightrope walkers, and lion tamers.

As the grand finale, two men in flamboyant red-and-gold leotards performed several maneuvers to a cheering audience. Then one did a double flip from one trapeze into the arms of the other man, who hung from his knees on the adjacent trapeze—at least that's how it was supposed to go.

Actually, he missed and fell deep into the net, bouncing several times in slow motion before scrambling to his feet. The man above looked down and said with disgust, "Whiskey heads better stay off the damn bottle." The man below raced up the pole and managed to complete the trick, all to a standing ovation, no one privy to what we had overheard.

After the performers took their final bows, a flurry of activity let loose on the field. Everyone associated with the show pushed or pulled or moved or carried or hoisted a cart, vehicle, cable, or prop. All the equipment attached to the posts slowly descended to the ground.

Jack barked orders in all directions. He told us to open the colored crates, and as a string of lights came down, we were to disconnect the bulbs, separate them by color, and place them in their corresponding trunk. All the trunks had layered holes to protect the bulbs and a place for wires.

When we finished packing the lights, we helped move the big cats, each in its own cage on wheels. "Don't put your fingers too close to the wire mesh," Jack told Ira as we pushed the spotted leopard cage. "You might lose one." In just two hours, the circus was loaded up and several of the trucks had departed. Jack paid us only a few bucks, but we came away a lot richer in experience.

Ira and I camped outside of town and at daybreak headed north.

After smoking a reefer, we started on Route 550, what they call the Million Dollar Highway. All along the two-lane road, we saw beautiful, towering rock formations. Reds, grays, browns, and blues shone in metallic pastel hues. We must have uttered a hundred jaw-dropping "wows" during the three-hour ride.

In Glenwood Springs, Ira bailed, eager to hitchhike west to California. I shook his hand and wished him luck. "Don't take a ride that strands you in the middle of the desert."

Then I turned south, back to Difficult Campground, taking in more gorgeous scenery. "Charlie," I said, "we're a couple of lucky dogs."

37.

Horse Traders
June 1969

Free national park and forest campgrounds provided convenient stopping points for long-hair migrants to Haight-Asbury and elsewhere. I spent the rest of the week with a constantly changing band of colorful hippie folk, generous in sharing adventures, laughter, insight, food, drink, and weed. One pixie-like wood nymph, whose first words to everyone were "What's your sign?," gave me a hit of acid along with some advice: "You need to read John Steinbeck's book *Travels with Charley*."

A couple of days later, I picked up a copy of Steinbeck's memoir at a used bookstore in Aspen. Sitting on a log in the morning sunlight, I started reading about his journey across America with his French poodle. But it struck me as a boring version of my life, and I quit after three chapters, leaving it on an empty picnic table for someone else.

On the afternoon of June 20, as I sat on my tailgate in the shade, sharpening my hunting knife on a wet stone, Mitch drove up. Shawn, Mitch's silver-black Samoyed-husky, jumped out to reacquaint himself with Charlie.

Grinning, Mitch offered a warm embrace. "It was easier finding you than I thought. Your home is hard to miss." He sported a new straw cowboy hat and some fancy shitkickers.

"Looks like you're ready to play cowboy." I laughed. "Did you get the hat and boots in Mexico?"

"Yep, and come see the incredible saddle I found."

Sitting in the back of his green '59 Chevy station wagon was a crazy kind of saddle. It didn't look finished—the rawhide stretched tightly over a wooden frame, but some of the wood still showed. The seat sat taller than an ordinary saddle, and it didn't appear to have much padding.

He beamed. "Cost only forty US dollars."

"Is it comfortable?"

"Yep, seems to be. I've sat on it—but not on a horse. They all use them in Mexico where I was. I got a saddle blanket as well."

I nodded in the direction of my truck. "Come see what I picked up in Missouri."

When I showed him my Vetch saddle, he whistled. "Wow, that's a beauty. Check out that leather work."

"Yeah, I lucked out. The guy assured me it'd be comfortable for both me and the horse. Speaking of which, I found out horses are really cheap in New Mexico. Maybe we should ride from Taos to Aspen. There's going to be a monster love-in here at the end of July. It would be bitchin' to ride back in time for that."

Mitch didn't need much convincing, and we scrapped our original plan to ride to Wyoming. That settled, we drove to the US Forest Service Headquarters in town and picked up four national forest maps covering the area from Taos to Aspen. Over a tomato beer at Woody's, we plotted our course, occasionally interrupted by Mitch's stories about his new flame, Jasmine.

"Man, it was tough leaving her," he said, a tortured look in his eyes. "I've never met anyone like her."

"You sound smitten, my friend."

"You don't know the half of it. If I wasn't dead set on this horse trip, you might not be sitting across from me right now. She said she'd send me letters, so I need to give her our route."

The next morning, I left my truck in a gravel parking area near Maroon Bells. We drove south all day making plans and lists of things to carry with us—and Mitch carried on about Jasmine. We arrived in Taos at dusk, and after eating at a diner, we camped north of town, near the Rio Grande Gorge.

I woke at dawn to the sound of hundreds of sheep moving past our sleeping bags. We watched the unexpected parade in the crisp morning air while pulling our clothes on over our long johns.

As soon as it opened, we went inside the Taos County Tack and Saddle Shop, the rich smell of leather filling my nostrils. Behind the counter stood a bearded, middle-aged gentleman sucking on a toothpick. Under the brim of his cowboy hat, his clear-blue eyes observed us in a lazy fashion as we checked out the bridles and halters.

I called over to him, "We're going on a ride to Aspen. Do you have any idea where we can buy a couple of horses?"

The man didn't respond. Stroking his beard, he studied me for a moment and then shifted to Mitch. We must have passed some kind of test because he strolled over to us. "Are you experienced horsemen?"

I laughed and shook my head. "Hardly. I've been in the saddle about twelve hours, and my friend here has about two hours on his résumé. By the way, my name is Rich." I extended my hand, and he took it in his strong grip.

"Thomas," he said.

Mitch introduced himself and shook his hand.

Thomas went back to stroking his beard as he looked back and forth at us. What was going on behind those blue eyes? "So why do you two want to ride all the way to Aspen?"

"Well, we were talking about how incredible it must have been in the old days to ride across unspoiled country. We decided we wanted to do it."

He paused again. "You need to know what you're doing when you buy horses. Horse traders can be a crafty bunch. You might get an old horse that wouldn't make the trip or one that's too spooky for trail riding. And you need to know how to care for your horses and equipment."

This didn't sound as easy as I thought. Still, I knew we weren't going to turn back. "Yeah, I'm sure we have a lot to learn. What do you suggest?"

To our great fortune and relief, Thomas took pity on us naive hippie boys. He helped us shop for the rest of our horse gear and showed us how to care for it. As we washed and oiled our gear with saddle soap and neatsfoot oil out in front of the shop, he made some calls.

When we completed our saddle-care assignment, Thomas came out to inspect our work. "You fellows can camp behind the store by the corral if you want. Get up early. We've got some horses to look at."

"Cool. We'll be ready," Mitch said.

Soon after daybreak the next morning, we were sitting on the shop steps when Thomas pulled up in his sparkling red Dodge pickup. He told us to put the dogs in the back. "I want to see how the horses react to having dogs around."

Our first stop was less than a mile from his shop. In a meadow, along with two other horses, stood a three-year-old gelding—a castrated male, we discovered.

"This horse is 'green-broke.' That means he hasn't been cut long, but he's been broken to the saddle. He hasn't been ridden much either, and because he's not far from a stallion, he still has a lot of youthful spunk."

A "buckskin roan," the gelding had a golden-tan coat and a thin black line running down the middle of his back. His jet-black mane had been trimmed to about two inches, making it stand up on his neck like a Mohawk haircut. He also had a strangely rounded Roman nose, not what you'd associate with a "handsome steed."

Smaller and shorter than the other horses, he stood only about as high as my shoulder. But Thomas told us he was still strong enough to carry a man and his gear. Actually he looked more like an Indian pony, and I could envision a painted warrior riding low on his back.

Working his way up to the young horse, Thomas pulled some oats out of his jacket pocket and held out his hand. The gelding hesitated but soon took some of the grain. While he ate, Thomas stood to the side and smoothly slipped a lead rope out of his back pocket and around the horse's neck, snapping it into a loop with its clasp. With his eyes and hands, he examined the animal's body and legs, and then led him around the pasture to see how he moved.

After stopping the horse, Thomas pulled back his lips to check his teeth, peered into his eyes, and lifted each foot to inspect his hooves. He also waved his hand gently around the horse's head to find out how he'd react, but he didn't do much more than make slight, jerky movements with his head. Finally, without a word, Thomas unhooked the gelding, patted him on the backside, and headed back to his truck. Mitch and I followed, and we were soon rolling down the highway.

This time, we headed north toward the town of Questa. Thomas told us how some horse traders were downright crooks. "That's where the term 'getting taken for a ride' came from," he said, waving his index finger in warning. "Sometimes, though it happened more in the old days, a horse trader will put a fishhook under the hide of an old horse to make him seem more spirited. And that's where the term 'getting hooked' came from. That's why it's important to know how to read a horse's teeth—so you can determine the accurate age."

"Man, we use a lot of expressions related to horses," Mitch said. "Here's another one: 'don't look a gift horse in the mouth.'"

Thomas nodded. "Yep. Horsing around, kicking up your heels." He paused. "A long trail ride like you fellows are going on requires able horses—or you'll never make it to Aspen."

I felt a surge of gratitude. What would have happened to us had Thomas not taken us under his knowing wing?

Near Questa, we took some side roads to a funky little ranch, where we saw a weathered barn and a small, poorly painted house. A homemade horse trailer, large enough to transport a small herd, sat next to the barn. There were eight or nine horses in various corrals and almost as many kids of all sizes and shapes hanging around the porch. "Tiny Sanders lives here," Thomas said. "From what he told me, he has a horse worth looking at."

A short, thin fellow in his thirties, his clothes covered in dust, Tiny had dirty-blond hair and ears so huge they could have carried him away in a strong wind. He sent a boy to fetch a horse from a small corral next to the barn. Meanwhile, Thomas grabbed a couple of cinderblocks, a wooden fence post, a rake, and a bucket and lined them up on the ground.

The kid came through the gate leading a haltered brown "paint" with white splotches on his chest and rump. Three of the young Sanders boys jumped up on top of the corral fence to watch. As he had with the buckskin, Thomas inspected the horse's teeth, eyes, and hooves and then led him around, studying his eyes and feet. He brought him through the obstacle course he had laid out, observing how the horse dealt with objects in his path. After a few more passes, he talked price with Tiny and said he'd be in touch.

On our way back to Taos, Thomas told us we had two more horses to check out: one that evening and another the next day. At six o'clock we met up with Thomas again and drove thirty miles to Eagle Nest.

On the way, he pointed toward the turnoff to Angel Fire. "I live up this side of town with my lovely wife, Maria."

Along with his admiration, I sensed a sadness I couldn't place.

Riding shotgun, Mitch leaned around me and asked, "How long you been married?"

"A couple of years. I love her to pieces, but my in-laws are tough. They don't like me much."

"How come?" I asked. What was there not to like about this guy?

"She's Spanish, and her people don't like outsiders. I hope they'll get used to me after a while. Other than that, we're mighty happy together."

We arrived at a ranch that boarded horses. A couple was waiting for us with a saddled, large chestnut mare named Doña. Thomas had told us, "They bought Doña for their young daughter, but they were concerned because the horse bucked a few times."

He performed his usual inspection on the ground and then mounted the jittery mare. Once he got her to settle down, he took her through some maneuvers, turning in different directions and walking her around and over obstacles.

We drove back, and Thomas dropped us off at his shop. "I'll see you boys in the morning. We still have one more horse to see. Then we'll have to make a decision."

After a long day, Mitch and I stood quietly, watching the taillights of his truck disappear down the road.

38.

Rodeo Time
June 1969

Late the next morning, we again headed for Questa, driving through barren countryside until we reached a good-sized ranch. Thomas hopped out and went over to two men standing outside one of the buildings. After a brief discussion, the men got into a white truck and Thomas returned to us, saying we would follow them. We bounced and rattled down a little-used dirt road onto a wide open prairie.

Thomas pointed to the herd of horses grazing in the distance. "We're going to look at a mare in that herd," he shouted over the noise of the truck.

Ahead of us, the two men made a wide arc to the left of the horses, and when slightly past the herd, they turned and headed straight toward them. As their truck angled to the left rear flank of the herd, Thomas angled his truck to the right. The horses stopped grazing and eyed us with suspicion.

When both drivers started honking their horns, a tall chestnut took off in front, and soon all the horses were galloping together. A magnificent sight. More than two dozen chestnuts, paints, palominos, whites, blacks, and browns all racing at full speed twenty yards in front of us—tails high, manes waving, hoofs kicking up dust and clods. Talk about the Wild West. This was, hands down, one of the coolest moments of my life.

We bounced along, bones rattling, for a half mile or so, the dirt from the horses' hooves glancing off the windshield. The two trucks herded the horses into a corner where two fences met, then slowed and stopped. Jumping from their pickup, the two men stretched out their arms and waved their cowboy hats, coaxing the horses into a small corral, closing the gate behind them.

We parked and walked over to the other men, who introduced themselves: Hank, the ranch owner, and Willie, his hired hand. Grabbing a rope from the back of the pickup, Willie stepped into the corral and gently waved his hat to separate the nervous horses. When he had isolated a brown mare, he threw the rope over her neck in one smooth movement.

She pulled back, shaking her head, as Willie led her to our side of the corral and tied her to the fence. Hank brought over a saddle and halter from the truck, and while Willie saddled her, Thomas conducted his exam. When he finished, Willie led the mare a few feet from the fence and motioned for me to mount up.

Already pumped with adrenaline, I hopped on without a thought and grabbed the reins. But the mare had other ideas. As soon as Willie stepped away, she arched her back and kicked out her hind legs. *Jesus! Whoa!* I held on with both hands while she bucked, weaved, twisted, and heaved. Somehow I managed to keep my butt in the saddle and my composure, cussing silently the whole time. *Fuck! Sonofabitch! Damn!* No way in hell would I act like a tinhorn in front of those hardened cowpokes.

Finally, the wild horse tired of her orneriness and settled down. I slid out of the saddle and hit the ground running, stooping on the way to retrieve my hat.

"I don't know," I said, reaching the others. "She seems a little spooky."

"Green broke," Willie said.

"Mighty green," Thomas added.

As he talked to the rancher, Mitch and I climbed out of the corral. "That was quite a ride," he said. "I'm surprised you hung in there."

"No shit. That was nuts." But I was actually proud of myself. I had been initiated in the cowboy way, maybe even earning a bit of respect from Thomas, Hank, and Willie.

On the ride back to Taos, Thomas turned to me in the cab. "So you don't want that one, huh?"

I laughed. "Not a chance. I need a horse with a better disposition."

"Just kidding. Already made up my mind. Rich, you'll take the buckskin roan up the road behind the shop. And Mitch, the chestnut mare up in Eagle Nest should be reliable. I'll make the calls, and we'll pick them up in the morning."

So that was it. In one day we would have our horses and be on our way.

The next day, Mitch went with Thomas to fetch his chestnut in a horse trailer, bringing along $150 for his purchase. The night before, Thomas had taken my $125 to the owner of my horse, and I took off on foot that morning to get him. Armed with a short rope and halter, I had to catch the gelding and lead him back to the corral behind Taos County Tack and Saddle. Easy enough.

After walking with Charlie for about a mile, I spotted the gelding with the other two horses on the opposite side of the pasture. I approached with a generous bouquet of fresh green grass in my hand, my rope and halter hidden inside my shirt. It took patience and a steady soft voice before he finally accepted my offering.

I left to get more grass. When I approached him the second time, he was still cautious but came to me faster. I was able to pat him on the chest and soon worked myself close to his shoulder. Then I slid the rope out of my shirt and up and around his neck.

Once he was on a rope, putting the nylon halter over his head was a breeze. I removed the lead rope from his neck, clipped it onto the halter and led him to the gate. As we began the walk down the road, I observed my new friend. His coat was a beautiful golden brown, and he did resemble an Indian pony. "I'm going to call you Geronimo, my friend, after the Apache warrior. We are about to have the ride of our lives together. And I promise to treat you well."

We were almost out of sight of the other two horses when Geronimo whinnied to his friends, who answered in kind. Then he bolted and pulled back and spun and twisted and complained. His wide eyes bounced around, wild and nervous. I held tight and talked softly, trying to calm him. After a few minutes, he settled down—but missing his stable mates, he soon went at it again.

What the hell had I gotten myself into with this guy?

This time he rose up on his hind legs, his front feet rotating high in the air above my head. My lead rope was short so it was tricky holding on while keeping clear of his spinning front hooves. When he'd finally come down, we would walk a short distance before he'd erupt again, pawing at the air. "Hey, buddy, cool it. Man, I should have called you Crazy Horse."

It was one of the longest and most action-packed miles I'd ever traveled. At last we made it to the corral, and I released him. He continued to stomp around and carry on, missing his friends. But I figured when he saw the lush meadows of Colorado, he would forget what he'd left behind. When Thomas and Mitch pulled up and unloaded the mare, Geronimo calmed down.

Now that we had our horses, Thomas wasted no time. He taught us how to care for them, brush and curry and clean their feet, feed and water them—and we learned when it was appropriate for them to drink.

Next, he showed us how to saddle them properly and hold the reins so we had control but didn't hurt their mouths. He even taught us a trick to make sure our saddles were secure. "Cinch up the saddle like this, and then leave to do some other things. You see, the horse is smart, and while you're cinching, he'll take a big breath and puff himself up so the saddle won't be tight. So futz around for a few minutes and wander back and pull the cinch another notch before he suspects. Then you tie it up like this."

It was a crash course in horsemanship, and after two days, we were ready to hit the trail. Our great adventure, once a mere pipe dream, was about to begin.

PART 6

Horsing Around

*There's something about the outside of a horse
that's good for the inside of a man.*
—Winston Churchill

*A horse fart can blow your hat off and
drain away your will to live for the rest of the day.*
—Gerry Souter, *American Shooter*

39.

Hang On Tight

June 1969

It took us all morning to pack our supplies and gear and saddle up the horses. Geronimo and Doña stood patiently while we reviewed the list we had made and amended over the past week:

General: harmonicas, pocket knives, hunting knife, hatchet, canteens, small shovel, coffeepot, cooking pot, mess kits, collapsible cups, fishing lines, hooks and weights, salmon eggs, flashlights, batteries, binoculars, maps (4), wood matches, sewing kit, grill, towels, toilet paper, toilet kits (toothbrushes and paste, soap and soap dishes, razors), dog food, dog dishes (gold pans), first aid and snake bite kits, insect repellent, tomato sauce (for skunk scent removal), bedrolls, plastic tarps, leather gloves, clothesline rope, compass, pliers, edible plants book, extra pairs of socks and underwear, denim shirt, long johns, extra jeans, neckerchiefs, jacket/poncho

Horse gear: two 50-ft ropes, hobble, saddles, blankets, bridles, halters, 6-ft lead ropes, saddlebags, hoof picks, curry comb, comb, brush, feedbag, saddle soap, neatsfoot oil, oats (10-day supply)

Food: Bisquick, oatmeal, rice, raisins, sugar, cinnamon, coffee, trail mix, Crisco, egg mix, milk powder, packaged soup, canned beans, salt, pepper, dried fruit, Campfire marshmallows, candy bars, beef jerky, dry milk, apples, cheese, potatoes, onions, hot dogs

As we packed our duffel and saddlebags, we tossed in a couple of books: for me, *Journey to the East* by Hermann Hesse, and for Mitch, *Siddhartha* by Hesse and *Stranger in a Strange Land* by Robert Heinlein.

Using clothesline rope, we secured our bedrolls in a tarp and attached them to the leather straps on the back of our saddles. Our saddlebags fit nicely between the bedrolls and the back of our saddles, and we draped our duffel bags in front of the saddle, looping their handles over the saddle horns. We kept any items we might need during the day in our pockets or saddlebags.

For a belt, I used a horse hobble—a thick leather strap with two silver-dollar-sized iron rings. If I needed to secure Geronimo, I could weave the belt in and out through the rings and around his ankles—and hope that my pants didn't fall down.

I threw on my lightweight rawhide jacket over my bare chest and did a final run-through of our list. Up to this point, we had focused on planning and preparation. It suddenly hit me that we were actually going to do this.

By the time we were ready to leave, it was almost noon, the sun high in the deep-blue New Mexico sky. We led the horses around the front of the saddle shop, and I called through the open door, "Hey, Thomas, we're about to take off."

He stepped outside, tilting his hat back with his thumb. "You fellows are mighty lucky, you know that? I always wanted to do a long ride north into the Colorado high country. Sure wish I was going with you." He reached over and rubbed Doña's neck.

"We'll be forever grateful, Thomas," Mitch said. "Couldn't have done it without you."

Geronimo bent around to nibble on the fringe of my jacket. "We learned so much from you," I said. "Thanks for helping us find our horses."

"You boys take good care of those fine animals now."

Our cowboy hats firmly in place, we mounted up and headed north, single file, along the gravel shoulder of the highway. Mitch took the lead, his green-and-white neckerchief flopping up and down as he bounced in the saddle. I glanced back to check on the dogs. Both of them followed behind at a safe distance, knowing to stay clear of the motorway and the horses' hooves.

Ten minutes later, I pointed ahead to a break in the fence. "Good. There's the trail." Already roasting, I took off my jacket and laid it across the front of my saddle.

Happy to leave the busy highway behind, we turned our horses through the entryway and found ourselves on a narrow, dusty dirt road overgrown with weeds. After riding alone for nearly an hour, we spotted a figure on horseback on the horizon. As he approached, we could see a giant of an Indian sitting atop a tall, beautiful Palomino stallion.

Everything about him sparkled in the sun: his bright turquoise-and-gold western shirt, white wide-brimmed cowboy hat, silver spurs, and the silver medallions on his saddle. Behind him, a long black braid swung left and right with the stride of his massive horse. He held his reins high in the air with one hand while his other cradled a whiskey bottle, already three-quarters drained.

Oh boy. Careful. This guy's been hitting the firewater.

Stopping alongside us, he reached out with his bottle and slurred, "Have a drink with me?"

Mitch and I both took a sip, not wanting to offend the fellow, and complemented him on his magnificent horse. After inquiring if we were headed in the right direction, we thanked him and continued on.

A ways down the road, Mitch let out a long breath. "Oh, man. That could have been ugly."

"No shit."

We rode the next couple of hours saying little. The simmering New Mexico sun made talking only worsen the dryness in my mouth. Sweat poured down my face, and my inner thighs ached something fierce. "It sure would pay to be bowlegged."

"Roger that," Mitch said, swatting a fly with his hat.

"It's apparent we weren't born in the saddle, partner." I laughed. "I need to walk for a while."

I dismounted and stretched to loosen my strained muscles—a welcome relief. Mitch did the same. We both staggered a bit until the kinks worked themselves out, and before long, we felt comfortable enough to mount up again. After several more hours of riding and walking and riding and walking, most times single file, we came to the edge of a cliff.

Below, a few farmhouses dotted the narrow, green valley, the inviting lushness in sharp contrast to the surrounding desert hues and dusty brush we'd been riding through all day.

My stomach growled. "I'm starving. Maybe we can camp down there."

"Yeah, let's look for a place," Mitch said, glancing up at the sky. "Only a couple of hours left until dusk."

Following the dirt road down the cliff, we descended a hundred feet at a gentle angle, heading toward the east end of the valley floor. Before us, to the north, a wooden bridge crossed a creek, and the road turned west again, passing farmhouses and well-tended, fenced green fields.

By now, the sun had disappeared behind the canyon wall. Just this side of the bridge, along the stream bank, a small meadow beckoned—a perfect spot for the night. There was plenty of tall grass and water for the horses, and the grass would provide a soft mattress for our bedrolls.

We unsaddled Doña and Geronimo, tied each to a fifty-foot rope, and fed them first, giving them their ration of oats. The dogs came next, and then we gathered firewood for our dinner. While the fire gained strength, we cleaned the horses' hooves and used the brush and curry comb on their coats, as Thomas had taught us. We also worked the burrs out of their tails—a time-consuming chore.

Famished, Mitch and I feasted on hot dogs, packaged soup, and toasted marshmallows, simple yet satisfying.

"Well, that was a hot, dry, and painful ride today." I laughed, rubbing my aching thighs.

"No lie." Mitch smoothed his short black beard with his fingers. "I bet I'll sleep like a baby in this tall grass."

Once we finished eating, we brushed our teeth over the creek and donned our long johns. Physically tired, but feeling a sense of accomplishment, I slipped into my bedroll and drifted off, the smell of grass in my nostrils and a lullaby of crickets and the bubbling stream in my ears.

. . .

Day two of our journey began with the first hint of dawn. I threw twigs on the smoldering coals from the past evening's fire, and soon the smell of coffee filled the air. We ate oatmeal with raisins, sipped our coffee, packed up, and saddled the horses.

The trail led west, up the valley, for a quarter mile before turning north into dry, dusty terrain. According to our map, the small town of San Cristobal lay seven miles ahead.

We rode through a sparse forest of small thirsty oaks, past a number of arroyos, or gullies. Centuries of erosion had carved these channels—hard to imagine in an area so parched.

Over the course of the day, the dirt road diminished into a jeep trail, then a single-lane walking path, and finally a faint deer trail. As the shadows lengthened in the late afternoon, the trail disappeared altogether. We circled around and around, crisscrossing for an hour with no sign of a trail.

A tired, thirsty, and hungry Doña had had enough. She arched her back and kicked her hind legs high in the air, swaying back and forth. Geronimo danced nervously, and the dogs scattered for cover while Mitch held on. After a half-minute rodeo, he convinced Doña to calm down. When the dust settled, I rode over to him.

He took off his hat and mopped his brow. "Sh-i-i-i-it! I wasn't expecting that."

"That was some bronco ride," I said, laughing. "You did better than the eight seconds the pros hang on for."

Sitting next to each other, surrounded by scrub oak, we admitted we were lost. What the hell were we going to do?

I thought about how eager the horses had been to get back to the barn—it's a horse thing. For the past two days, whenever we hesitated on the trail, the two of them would spin around, facing south. My arms ached from the constant struggle to maintain our direction.

"Let's give the horses free rein," I said. "They'll lead us out of here."

"Are you sure? It's getting dark. There's a lot we can get tripped up on."

"I don't think we have a choice—though I have a hunch that if we let them have their way, they'll take us right back to Taos."

He shrugged his shoulders. "It's worth a try."

"Hang on tight and protect your face."

So we loosened the reins. Within minutes, Geronimo and Doña were galloping side by side through the forest. I gripped the reins and saddle horn with one hand and kept my hat on my head with the other, tipped down to block out any surprises. Dry branches snapped at the onslaught of my speeding body.

We plunged downward into a deep arroyo, heading up the other side. The terrain would open up, then, with little warning, I'd be slapped by small branches. One dry limb crashed into my right shoulder. Another scratched my left arm, while a larger one whipped my left thigh. Sounds of breaking limbs and thundering hoovesF bombarded us.

My pulse surged as we tore through the fading light. Dogs have excellent night vision, but I didn't know about horses.

Mitch saw it first. I heard an "OH SH-I-I-I-I-T!"

Three yards ahead was a gully, four feet across and three feet deep. In a split second, we reached the edge of it. Holding on with white knuckles, I gritted my teeth as we took flight.

"FUUUUCK!"

A strange silence filled the air as the horses' hooves no longer clattered against the earth. I felt suspended for at least a minute. With a great crash, we hit the other side, thundering through the trees again.

I was confident Charlie and Shawn were close behind, but I couldn't look back to make sure. Once again, Geronimo lunged down an incline, only to bound upward seconds later. The terrain zoomed by, its speed mirrored by the flow of adrenaline through my body.

After what must have been a quarter hour, I could make out a wide pathway in the faint moonlight. It was the dirt road! We reined in our horses and caught our breath. Turning, I saw Charlie and Shawn running up from behind with their tongues hanging out.

"Far out! We made it. Are you okay?" Mitch asked.

"Just a few scratches. I'm cool. Man, that was a rush."

We got down and stroked and patted our horses, trying to calm them, and then gave some attention to the dogs, offering them water from our canteens. Leading Geronimo and Doña, we walked until we came to a creek. Here we made our camp.

Though this patch of arid land offered little, it had water, some patches of grass and shrubs for the horses, and enough wood for a fire—the three essentials we needed before we could call it a day. We looked over the horses and dogs carefully with a flashlight and found no injuries, a miracle really. When the horses cooled down, we led them to the creek to drink.

Our only loss was my string of lucky Navajo ghost beads. The aged woman who had sold them to me said they had "good energy" and would "protect from bad spirits." Who's to say they hadn't? I imagined them hanging on some distant branch, a testament to our ordeal.

Now we had a place to fill our hungry stomachs and rest our weary bodies. Hell of a day!

40.

Half-Baked

June 1969

First light showed up around 5 a.m. Eager for another day, I built a fire and started coffee. Since grass was scarce, I undid the horses' ropes for wider grazing. I assumed that while dragging and snagging fifty feet of rope, they wouldn't notice their lines weren't anchored.

Big mistake.

As I rolled up my bedroll, I noticed the horses moseying side by side down the dirt road. Geronimo's head faced straight ahead, but his large right eye stared back at me with a sheepish look. I casually walked toward the sliding ropes.

When Geronimo saw I was on to him, both horses took off running. I made a flying dive, just missing the ends of their tethers, and then jumped to my feet, yelling, "The horses!"

I took off in full pursuit while Mitch cut across the meadow, leaping a stand of sagebrush. The dogs raced merrily at our heels.

For more than three miles we ran, slowing at times to catch our breath. When we came to the lush canyon we had camped in two nights before, I yelled, "I'll go across the fields to cut them off. You stick to the road." I slipped through a barbed-wire fence and plunged into the hay field with Charlie alongside. Mitch followed the road to the left and waved to show he understood.

About 150 yards ahead, I could see the cliff face with the road cut diagonally into it, where we had descended into the valley. I headed for the midpoint of road elevation, eighty to a hundred feet above the valley floor, running with strength I didn't know I had. If I didn't get to that road before the horses, we would be chasing them all the way to Taos.

As I crossed through two barbed-wire fences in the center of the hay fields, I took care to leave clothing and flesh intact. Up ahead, a farmhouse came into view. Trespassing was a worry, and I had better things to do than pick buckshot out of my butt. But I had a mission.

Another field passed behind me. Slipping through a fourth fence, I reached the cliff wall—it was steeper than I'd remembered. I scaled it on all fours, mustering what little energy I had left. My heart pounded fiercely. *Move! Move! Gotta get there!* Charlie led the way, her tail arched as she scurried upward.

At last, more than exhausted, I pulled myself onto the road. I caught a glimpse of the horses spinning around and disappearing down the trail toward Mitch. All right! Drained but relieved, I walked on shaky legs down the road. At the bottom, I rounded the bend in sight of the bridge, and there were Mitch, Shawn, and both horses in the grassy meadow, our home from a few nights before.

"They stopped as soon as they saw the tall grass," Mitch said.

I pointed at the cliff. "I saw them turn around when I got to the road up there."

"No way. They've been here the whole time."

"I swear I saw them up there." Had I imagined it? Had I been so worn out and determined to beat the horses to the road that my mind played a trick on me? What the hell? But it didn't matter. The horses were back.

While we rested in the shade, the horses expressed no complaints, gorging themselves on the fresh green grass. The dogs lay in the shallow, cool water. Removing our boots, we soaked our feet and watched the sun rise over a ridge. The cool water and the sound of the tumbling stream calmed my nerves.

After a while I turned to Mitch. "Well, I guess we need to get back on the trail. Maybe we can figure out where we went wrong yesterday."

He nodded and started putting on his boots. "Someone in the valley might know the way to San Cristobal. Maybe there's someone in that house." He pointed to a rustic, wood-framed building just across the bridge.

"It won't hurt to ask. Your Spanish is better than mine."

I held the horses while Mitch went over and knocked on the door. An older Hispanic woman peeked out. She told him to stay to the left at a subtle fork in the road.

We walked back to our campsite, gathered our gear, and saddled the horses. As we headed up the trail, sitting in a saddle felt like a luxury. When we came upon the fork in the road, Mitch groaned. "How the hell did we miss this yesterday?"

After several dry, hot hours, we rode into the tiny town of San Cristobal. No booming metropolis, it had only a dozen buildings, including a church and a small market. We stopped in a shady spot to enjoy a cold soft drink and some chips. Refreshed, we mounted up and rode off again.

The scorching heat of the New Mexico sun showed us little mercy. When we passed a faded-blue trailer, Shawn went over to lie down in the shade, as if saying, "You guys go on. I've had enough of this." After we gave both dogs more water from our canteens, Mitch scooted Shawn along, and we continued down the trail.

Late in the afternoon, we intersected Highway 522, now within a few miles of Questa. The sun continued to pound on us. Man, it was hot. Parched, I drank from my canteen and felt my tongue expand like a thirsty sponge. "It's really boiling."

Mitch wiped his forehead with his neckerchief. "It's gotta be close to a hundred."

We walked the horses along the highway shoulder. It had taken us three days to get this far—only a twenty-minute ride in a car—and we had so much farther to go. The sun reflecting off the asphalt made it even hotter. I took off my hat and wiped the sweat from my brow with my sleeve. Sheesh.

Another hour passed. I glanced over my shoulder to check on the dogs and saw Charlie lying down twenty-five yards behind. Handing the reins to Mitch, I hurried down the road. "How are you, girl?" When I lifted her to her feet, she slumped back to the ground. I offered her water, but she stared at it with glazed eyes.

"The heat's gotten to her." I pointed to a lake and large tree off to the right. "I need to get her to that shade—over there."

I boosted Charlie up onto Geronimo's saddle, but she started to slide off. I called to Mitch, "She can't even hold on to the saddle." He led both horses as I walked alongside Geronimo, balancing Charlie on the saddle, shading her with my hat.

The lake and tree were farther away than they appeared, but eventually we made it. I placed Charlie in the shade and stripped down. Greedy for moisture, Shawn was already drinking from the lake. Naked, I cradled Charlie in my arms and waded out into the water. When it was deep enough, I sat down, holding her so only her head was above the surface. With my free hand, I stroked water over her head.

"I'm sorry, girl. You'll feel better soon." My heart ached to see her so despondent.

As the lake cooled her, I touched her mouth with my wet hands, and she managed to lick the moisture from my fingers. When her eyes started showing some life, I waded to shore and laid her in the shade. Mitch unpacked a gold pan, dipped it in the lake, and set it in front of her. Sitting on a rock close to her, I let the warm air dry my body.

It was a nice spot to camp. There was water and enough grass for the horses. Once Doña and Geronimo had cooled down, Mitch led them over to the lake for a drink. Good thing he had the presence of mind to remember what Thomas had taught us: "An overheated horse can kill itself drinking."

Shawn preferred lying in the water, so Mitch stripped and joined him. A welcome breeze came along, making us all more comfortable.

"How's Charlie doing?" he asked.

"She's coming back." I gently stroked her wet fur. "Dang, she gave me a real scare."

Mitch stepped out of the water. "I'll gather some wood and get a fire started."

"I'll brush and feed the horses." I got up and pulled on my pants.

As we set up camp and tended to chores, I kept a watchful eye on my canine companion, grateful beyond measure she had survived.

The next morning, Charlie looked better and had more energy, but she still wasn't back to her bouncy self. She'd probably need another day before she could travel.

"It's too damn hot here for the dogs," Mitch said, the temperature already unbearable. "And there's hardly enough feed for the horses. Hell, this state isn't all that kind to humans either."

"You know, we're not too far from Tiny Sanders's ranch," I said. "He has that big homemade horse trailer. Maybe we can pay him to take us to a higher elevation in southern Colorado."

"That's a good idea. The horses would have better grazing."

"What do you think it would cost?"

"Not a clue. But it doesn't cost anything to ask."

"If he doesn't want to do it, he might know someone who will."

"Tell you what," Mitch said. "I'll grab something to eat, then hitch up to his place and ask him. You stay with the animals. I remember how to get there."

While he was gone, I waded in the lake from time to time to keep cool and sprinkled water on Charlie. Shawn kept his eyes on the road waiting for his master, while the horses foraged as best they could on the meager dry grass and weeds.

A couple of hours later, Mitch returned with news that Tiny would take us to Colorado the next morning—for only forty bucks. We would have paid much more to rescue our animals from this unforgiving, arid land.

By morning, Charlie had fully improved. As Mitch cooked breakfast in the crisp air, a lone hawk made a lazy circle in the soft-blue, cloudless sky. After eating, we packed up, snuffed out the fire, and spread around the fire pit rocks, leaving no trace of our camp.

When Tiny showed up, it was hard to tell the difference between the rust and the faded red paint on his old Ford pickup. Hitched to the bumper, his sturdy white horse trailer, built with wide-set welded pipes, looked like a topless circus cage.

We loaded the horses, enticing them with chunks of alfalfa, and placed the dogs, saddles, and gear in the pickup bed. Up front with Tiny, we listened to his fun stories about horses and other exploits—though some of his tales challenged the imagination.

"I once had a saddle slip on a running horse." He scratched the back of his head, making his cowboy hat bounce up and down. "I couldn't jump free because of all the cactus, so I hung on upside down until the dang mare stopped. Lucky I didn't get my head kicked in."

"You were upside down under her belly?" Mitch asked.

"Almost. I was tilted off to the side a bit. Must have been a sight."

The truck was cruising at about fifty on the lightly traveled highway when we heard a loud bang from behind. I turned my head just in time to see Shawn take flight, leaping from the pickup. Charlie was ready to follow but quickly came to her senses. Fortunately, Shawn jumped clear of the trailer, but my heart sank as he bounced high in the air like a limp rag doll and tumbled at high speed, over and over and over again.

Alerted by our shouts, Tiny feathered the brakes and pulled over. We flew out of the truck. What a relief to see Shawn jump up and come running to Mitch. By some miracle, he escaped with only a nasty cut on the forehead. Peering over the side of the truck, we discovered that the summer heat and a possible defect had caused the spare tire to burst.

Shaken but undeterred, we piled back into the truck, keeping the dogs with us in the cab. A few miles down the road, we stopped in Alamosa for supplies, and then Tiny drove us to a trailhead north of Del Norte. Though it was early afternoon, the temperature was closer to what it had been the last few mornings in New Mexico.

Here, the sun was a friend, not a cruel master.

We welcomed the bountiful green meadows, teeming streams, and wild flowers—you could even smell moisture in the air. After unloading the horses, we readied them for travel and thanked Tiny for delivering us into this woodland paradise.

Once we had mounted up, we began moving through the trees. Cool and relaxed, I couldn't help but think about our journey so far. In the last four and a half days, we had gotten lost, galloped through the forest in the dark, chased horses for miles at daybreak—and both dogs had nearly died. Man. Besides the distance we had ridden with Tiny, we had covered only ten miles as the crow flies. And Aspen was still a couple of hundred miles away.

Despite it all, I wasn't discouraged. Quite the contrary—I couldn't wait to experience whatever lay ahead. That's what adventure was all about, right?

41.

Green Pastures
July 1969

We followed a trail through pine, fir, and an occasional aspen grove, the sweet scent of the trees intoxicating after the harshness of the previous two days. The verdant flora contrasted beautifully with the iron-rich red in the rocks, capped off with a robin's-egg-blue sky and a spattering of fluffy white clouds. No wonder they nicknamed the state "Colorful Colorado."

As had become our habit, we alternated walking and riding, covering about seven miles before settling by a brook for the night. The area was loaded with tender, juicy miner's lettuce and young, sharp-flavored dandelions, making for a tasty dinner salad to round out our meal of brown rice with raisins and onions, hot dogs, and toasted marshmallows. While we ate, Charlie and Shawn chased each other in and out of the trees.

I took a long sip from my tin coffee cup. "The dogs sure have more spunk here in Colorado, which is surprising given what they've been through. I tell you, man, I keep seeing that awful image of Shawn's body flopping along the highway. I thought he was a goner."

Shaking his head, Mitch poked at the fire with a stick. "I never want to see anything like that again. Poor guy. He's been a little off since it happened, not listening to me the way he did. Makes me think he left a few of his marbles on that stretch of New Mexico asphalt, along with some of his fur."

Both exhausted, we turned in soon after eating. Lying in my sleeping bag, I breathed in the clean smell of the pine branches I had cut for my mattress before falling asleep, grateful for the gifts of the forest.

On the sixth day, we broke camp just as the sun peered over the horizon, following a hearty breakfast of oatmeal (with *more* raisins), coffee, and stick bread, a delicacy Mitch had turned me on to. The recipe was amazingly simple. We made dough out of Bisquick, milk powder, and water and rolled it into two strands, about two feet long and an inch in diameter. Then we wound each strand around the end of a long stick, pressed raisins (of course) into the dough, sprinkled the coil with cinnamon, and cooked the pair over the fire. Before long, the mouth-watering aroma of baked pastry permeated the air. The stick bread filled our stomachs and stayed with us for hours.

Most dinners consisted of potatoes or brown rice with chopped onions and raisins, supplemented with packaged soup and coffee. When fresh greens were available, we included a salad of miner's lettuce, dandelion, lamb's quarters, or red-stemmed purslane. By far, miner's lettuce was our favorite—lucky for us, it grew everywhere. We bought a package of hot dogs in Alamosa, but we had to finish them by breakfast. At night, we chilled them in the creek.

While we traveled, Mitch and I fell into an easygoing silence, not talking much except to point out a wonder of nature or a breathless panorama. The dogs stayed close, occasionally chasing a chipmunk or an enticing scent.

By now we had learned that it takes incredible strength and persistence to keep a horse moving straight ahead. Our steeds wanted to nibble at every stand of luscious foliage, and Colorado offered lots of temptations. Eating is at the top of the list of equine desires—after all, a half-ton horse requires a great number of bites to survive.

When I led Geronimo on the ground, he'd often stop me in my tracks or jerk me backward as he grabbed a bite of greenery, nearly yanking my shoulder out of joint.

"C'mon, pal. You're killing me."

When the horses weren't putting on the brakes or pulling us to the side for some delectable shrub, they were spinning us around to face their former stomping grounds. Though Taos had grown distant, Geronimo and Doña still hadn't lost their eagerness to go home.

Though we considered ourselves gentle-natured men, we had to constantly dominate the relationship to make any forward progress. As soon as I relaxed the reins even slightly, Geronimo would take over. In short order, he and Doña had taught us they needed an alert, confident leader to direct them, or they'd pursue their own agenda.

We followed our Rio Grande National Forest map up various trails, and if they disappeared, we followed streams or mountain landmarks, estimating our location on the map. Now deep into the wilderness, we wouldn't see signs of civilization for at least another week. Gunnison was only seventy miles as the crow flies, but those big black birds have the advantage—we'd travel two or three times that distance. Seldom straight, the trails, streams, and other passable routes wandered back and forth, at times taking us south before turning back in our desired northwesterly direction.

The map spoke of "English Valley" or "Canadian Hondo," and a history long forgotten. Had these places been named after the miners and ranchers who settled there, or after folks just passing through? What had it been like to leave their homeland so far behind? What had become of them?

After twelve hours of riding and walking, we made camp on La Garita Creek and set about our routine of unsaddling, brushing, combing, currying, and cleaning hooves. As Mitch grabbed one of Doña's back feet, she kicked at him, but he grabbed it again, pulling it out to the side and hooking it against his knee as Thomas had taught us.

Surveying our gear, I came up with a brilliant idea to give the horses a greater range to forage for food. I knotted the two ropes together to make a hundred-foot rope for Doña, then took off the hobble I used for a belt and secured Geronimo's front ankles, restricting him to small steps so he wouldn't wander too far.

An ideal arrangement—at least it seemed so at the time.

As dinner was cooking, Mitch crouched near the fire stirring the rice. "This trip is so cool and all, but I can't stop thinking about Jasmine. I sure miss her. A lot of my heart is still in California."

"Got it bad, huh? I know how it feels. I've thought a lot about that lady I met in Kansas City—Susanna. If she's in Aspen when we get there, I have this fantasy of sweeping her up onto Geronimo and riding off into the woods."

"I'm not going to tell you my fantasy." He gave me a sheepish look. "I hope there's a letter waiting for me in Gunnison. I sent Jasmine one with our route, and she promised to write."

"She has some time to get it there—we're still a week away."

"And, Rich, she has a totally bitchin' sister. She's cool and super pretty with long blonde hair. Rosehips told me she'd like to meet you."

"I'm good with that, man. After this ride, I'll be more than ready, especially if that Kansas City girl doesn't show up in Aspen."

After we ate, I played my harmonica by the warm glow of the fire. We washed the dishes using sand from the stream as a scouring pad and headed to bed.

It never took long to fall asleep after a day on the trail. We had walked and ridden about thirty miles so far, and the next day would be more of the same. As the day's scenery passed through my head, I reached out to Charlie leaning up against my hip. My body tired and sore, I drifted into dreamland, lulled by the rustling of the horses and an owl's song.

The next day we followed the La Garita and Geban creeks until they narrowed into a mere trickle. Mitch showed me on the map that a few miles northwest, we'd run into the headwaters of Bear Creek, which would lead us toward Gunnison. His eyebrows knitted in concentration, he went back and forth between his compass and the map, taking his role as navigator seriously—and he was good at it. After carefully refolding the map, he shoved it back into his saddlebag, "I hope we can find a primo place to camp for a few days."

"I'm with you on that." I took a large gulp from my canteen. "We could use a break from riding. And if we find good pasture, the horses won't complain."

When we moved west deeper into the forest, we collided with a thick wall of young aspens and brush that a human couldn't penetrate, much less a horse. It took several attempts and a half-mile detour to find a passageway we could squeeze through.

Leading our horses, we angled down a steep slope and came to an open area covered with iridescent shale, reflecting metallic gray and blue hues in the sunlight. A striking sight, but on an incline, the flat chips of shale can slide over one another, making it as slippery as ice. We inched our way forward.

At one spot, I slid and fell hard to the ground, jerking on Geronimo's reins. He stepped forward onto one of my calves, then the other.

My howls of pain ricocheted off the rocks, followed by a storm of cuss words.

Geronimo jerked his head up, the whites of his eyes showing in panic. Squirming in agony, I held fast to the reins.

By some miracle, he had missed both knees. I could stand and walk, though my legs throbbed, and I couldn't help wincing when I reached over to rub Geronimo's neck to calm him. "It's okay, boy. No real damage done."

Soon we dropped down into thick but passable old forest. A fire must have swept through the area decades before because fallen trees littered the ground. Here, the angle of decline steepened ever more and became less maneuverable, so we mounted our horses and let them take us down the mountain. Some debris rose as high as their bellies, yet they stepped around or over the large obstacles with the grace and precision of ballet dancers, never missing a step.

Finally, after descending more than four hundred feet, we burst through the trees and entered a huge valley. The pristine splendor sent chills down my spine.

Several small tributaries of Bear Creek began their flow through a two-hundred-foot-wide meadow surrounded on three sides by steep, densely wooded slopes. The valley continued north before bending out of sight, leaving a bowl about twice the size of a football stadium. A small herd of elk grazed in the distance, and gnawed tree trunks indicated the presence of beaver, but the water where we stood flowed clear and clean.

Mitch whistled. "Wow!"

"Double wow!" It was right out of a Hamm's beer commercial: "From the land of sky blue waters . . ." Their silly jingle with the tom-tom drumbeat started playing in my head. "Let's settle here for a while."

"Agreed." He smiled. "Hey, the day after tomorrow is the Fourth. We'll celebrate."

"This is the perfect place to trip on acid. Wouldn't want to be unpatriotic."

He pointed to some dark clouds off to the west. "Looks like a weather front moving in. It may not get to us for a while, but we'll need shelter tonight."

After lapping water from the stream, Charlie rubbed up against me. "What do you think, girl? Is this nice or what?"

Near the meadow where our horses grazed, we built a lean-to out of the plentiful supply of branches, logs, and sticks. By now, gigantic thunderheads were pushing and shoving one another in the sky, and the air was heavy with moisture. We secured one tarp over the lean-to and the other over a mattress of pine boughs.

The back of the shelter cleared the foot of our bedrolls by less than two feet, while the front was nearly five feet high and faced an open area where we constructed a good-sized fire pit. The tall, dense trees would offer some protection from the rain as well.

As we sat to eat, the first drops fell. All our gear was stashed deep in our lean-to, safe from the elements. Our saddles, placed for pillows at the head of our bedrolls, reflected in the firelight. And our ponchos and wide-brimmed cowboy hats kept us dry.

Ravenous, we dove into our delicious meal of brown rice and soup, accented with miner's lettuce, plentiful in that area. I leaned over, rain dripping off my hat brim, to protect my tobacco as I rolled a handsome cigarette. Offering the makings to Mitch, I settled back and watched the wispy blue swirls mix with the gray smoke from our campfire.

Lying next to me, Charlie stood and stretched, then slipped into our lean-to and plopped down at the foot of my bedroll. Soon after, I finished my cigarette, said good night to Mitch, and joined her, my hunger satisfied but my legs still sore as hell.

42.

Independence Day
July 1969

It drizzled throughout the night, and we woke to a cloudy dawn that promised more rain. After breakfast, we gathered a huge pile of firewood so we didn't have to worry about fuel. As the rain came and went, we cleaned and oiled our saddles and in the afternoon sat on our bedrolls playing five-card draw, using sticks and pebbles as poker chips.

So far, I was ahead.

Humming to himself, Mitch drew three cards. "You know, I bet there are lots of trout in that stream. It would be great to have a fish dinner tomorrow."

I took one card for myself. "We could go out early and see if we can catch anything. Then come back to camp and drop acid."

"That'll work. Let's say we meet up around ten. Man, I would love some fresh trout."

"No shit." I looked out toward the meadow. "Rain or shine, this place is totally bitchin'."

"Love it." Mitch laid down two pairs.

I showed him a king-high flush—and a shit-eating grin.

By the next morning, the rain had let up, but the sky was still dense with clouds—ideal weather for trout fishing. We found sticks to serve as fishing poles and attached lines, then turned over rocks until we found enough grubs for bait.

I would go downstream, while Mitch stayed close to camp. Before leaving, I grabbed a handful of nuts to ward off hunger. "We'll meet back here in about two hours."

Busy baiting his hook, he didn't look up. "Sounds perfect. Good luck."

Though fishing had never been my strong suit, I was determined to catch something. Fresh trout cooked over the fire would add some variety to our repetitive meals. Fifteen minutes downstream, I found a deep, slow-moving fishing hole with plenty of shade from overhanging branches for trout to hide in, but after almost an hour without a bite, I walked farther downstream and tried a second spot, and a third. Even tried a salmon egg. No success. And now it was time to head back.

Damn. Fishless. I was doomed to failure. Maybe Mitch had had better luck. Walking toward camp, I noticed a large trout in a small, slow-moving pool. All right! I dropped a baited line into the water, several feet in front of the fish, and stood watching, but it didn't budge.

I moved the bait forward until it was less than half a foot in front of its nose. *Come on, baby. Come to Daddy.* Still nothing. I waited and waited, and just as I was ready to give up, in one quick movement, the trout moved forward, grabbed my bait, and spit it out again. Damn.

What do I do now? I waited a little longer. At last, the fish put his mouth around my bait, and this time I didn't hesitate. I jerked the pole upward, and the fish flew right over my head. A ten-inch trout danced on the end of my line, the hook set deep in its mouth. I hit its head on a rock so it wouldn't suffer, and with great pride, I headed back to camp with the fish still on my hook.

The enticing smell of coffee reached me before I arrived. Mitch hadn't caught anything, so his face lit up when he saw my trophy. I cleaned the fish and set it on a string in the water to keep it chilled until dinnertime.

After breakfast, Mitch took out his wallet and unfolded a tattered three-inch-square piece of paper. "There are twenty hits of blotter acid on this sheet," he said. Tiny stains of LSD dotted the paper in neat rows. "Easier to conceal and carry than sugar cubes." He tore off a little piece for himself.

I did the same and said, "Bottoms up." We swallowed our hits and washed them down with coffee.

It began to drizzle again. We sat by the fire, the dogs content to curl up in the lean-to, and soon the acid kicked in. The smell of moist earth filled my nostrils, and sparks from the fire danced in the air like hundreds of tiny fairies. Everything took on a soft, magical quality. Mitch whittled on a piece of wood while I drifted off into my own thoughts.

Whoosh . . . Buzzzz . . . Zing . . . Whirrrr

My brain raced. Every sound in the forest, including the falling rain, blended into an unending chorus. As the storm turned violent, we threw great mounds of wood on the fire. BOOM! BABOOM! Powerful thunderclaps bounced off the surrounding peaks and shook the canyon. I shouted to Mitch across the fire, "How's this for Fourth of July fireworks?"

"Super-cool pyrotechnics, man," he shouted back. "But we better check on the horses. I bet they're freaked out."

"Oh shit. You're right. It's like cannons going off out there."

We hurried to the meadow but found the horses unfazed by the crashing storm, even after a dozen lightning explosions shook the valley. As the water poured off the brims of our hats, we relaxed and watched the light show before retreating to our fire. One angry cloudburst after another rolled in until the rain finally let up and the sun broke through the clouds.

Everything sparkled from the moisture. And the colors! The greens and mineral hues from rocks blasted my senses. My heart opened like a spring flower.

As we approached the horses, Geronimo stood a few steps ahead of Doña, his moist coat shining like gold in the sun. His black mane, ending in a tiny, tapered black line at the top of his rump, glistened like chipped obsidian.

Nearing him, I said, "Hey, Geronimo. How're you doing?"

When he lifted his head from grazing, my mood took a hairpin turn. All the life had drained from his eyes, all the glimmer, replaced by a vacant stare. I could feel his sad heart, and it weighed him down like a heavy stone. He stood in his hobble like a criminal waiting for the gallows. I felt his pain.

What I thought would give him more freedom was instead a manacle crushing his spirit. "I'm sorry, Geronimo." I squatted down next to him and reached for the buckle on the hobble.

Mitch asked, "Hey, man, what's up?"

"It hurts to see him so down. If he runs all the way back to Taos, so be it. He needs to regain his spirit." I removed the hobble from his front legs. "I can't stand to see you like this, boy."

What I saw in his eyes I'll never forget—a mixture of surprise and gratitude and joy. He took a step and another, and galloped off. At full speed, he made a wide arc that followed the perimeter of the valley, his black tail high in the air like a flag. When he came to where he could have disappeared down the valley, he continued his arc until he was heading straight for us again.

When he reached Doña, he pulled up behind her and attempted to mount her. But intimacy wasn't on her mind, and her wicked back hooves kicked high and hard, catching him a good one in the chest. *Shit. That had to hurt.* Men and dogs scattered in a hurry. This was as rough as horseplay gets.

Geronimo got the message and returned to grazing, content to be close to his honey. I knew now that as long as Doña was around, Geronimo wouldn't stray. He went from being a handcuffed hostage to a gallant steed.

I walked over to him and stroked his neck. He didn't shy from my affections, appearing content with his newfound freedom.

I couldn't help myself. I grabbed his cropped mane and swung myself onto his damp, bare back. Clutching the strong, thick hair with both hands, I said, "Take me for a ride, Geronimo."

As if he understood, he took off at a gallop, leaving my hat behind. He made a short arc in the meadow and then headed straight for the forested slope.

Moving at a good clip, he bounded up the incline through the thick forest, making the proper adjustments to avoid trees and fallen logs. I bent my body low and close to his back for protection and better balance. When we had climbed nearly fifty yards up the hill through the dense forest, he made a tight left turn, swinging around a tree.

Hold on, man!

Finding another pathway down the slope, Geronimo weaved this way and that, avoiding trees before returning to the meadow. He hopped the creek and navigated the lush ocean of tall grass and shrubs without slowing or missing a beat. A rainbow of colors flashed by.

My good horse made another arc around the meadow as I gripped his mane with my aching fingers, the air as sharp as a knife and as clean as polished silver. We galloped at high speed and in slow motion at the same time.

His hooves thundered and blasts of air burst through his nostrils. We had morphed into a man-beast locomotive charging through the universe. Yes! He was wild and free and jubilant and sure-footed. I felt his power, his freedom, his elation. I was vibrant and alive, without fear, as we moved as one.

Returning to our starting point, he slowed down—and headed straight for that mare's ass.

Oh no—not again!

I bailed, hitting the ground, angling away at a run. And just in time. Doña still wasn't interested in Geronimo's advances. Hooves and dirt flew.

I came to a stop without losing my balance and walked over to Mitch and the dogs, my heart racing. "That was some crazy shit!" I shouted, catching my breath. While admiring Geronimo with pride and affection, I worked my fingers to get the kinks out after my white-knuckled ride.

I cracked a smile. "Here's a good safety tip: never try to ride a horse that's trying to ride a horse." Mitch and I both laughed, and he handed me my hat as we walked back to camp.

That evening, we feasted on fried potatoes, onions, greens, fresh mountain trout, and toasted marshmallows. And we christened the meal with two cans of creek-chilled Coors I had purchased in Alamosa for a special occasion—more appreciated than many a glass of fine champagne.

Whoosh . . . Buzzzz . . . Zing . . . Whirrrr

We spent most of the evening in the lean-to, jawing, playing poker by flashlight, performing "Hog Fence" harmonica duets for our canine audience, and occasionally rolling a smoke.

Deep into the night, the acid buzz began to subside as images of my mind-boggling freedom ride continued to swoosh around in my head.

Thanks, Geronimo. That was some Independence Day!

43.

Over the Divide
July 1969

A sunny day and the birds celebrated with song. Feeling hungover, but lifted by my bond with Geronimo, I was motivated to do as little as possible.

In preparation for leaving the next day, we dried out our gear and washed our clothes. We spent all afternoon relaxing and hit the hay at dusk, the chilly air chasing me deep into my sleeping bag.

At first light, I pulled my head out and beheld another beautiful, clear morning. By now Mitch and I had been gone ten days. Fully rested, we were eager to move on.

After breakfast, we gathered the horses and our gear and headed down Bear Creek. The lower valley, just as green and enticing as the area where we had camped, had no trail, so we followed the narrow meadows bordering the creek. Sometimes we had to cross over to the opposite side to avoid steep inclines, boulders, or thick brush.

If there was no passage on either side, we'd mount up and ride in the creek bed. In a number of places, the impassable terrain forced us to take wide detours, making our progress slow. No matter the obstacles, the dogs bounced along behind us, their tails wagging and tongues lolling out of the sides of their mouths, happy to explore new sights and smells.

Five miles down, Bear Creek joined John's Creek, where we came upon a jeep trail. We stopped to snack on beef jerky, nuts, and—you guessed it—raisins.

Mitch glanced at the compass and studied the map. "I think our best bet for crossing the Continental Divide is through Cochetopa Pass. We can catch the headwaters of Cochetopa Creek and follow it to Gunnison." He held out the map, tracing the route with his finger. The creek stretched twenty-five miles north, longer and wider than the ones we'd been following.

We cleaned the mud and pebbles out of our horses' hooves and continued on. Now that Geronimo happily tagged along behind Doña, I let him loose while we walked, looping his reins on the saddle horn so they wouldn't trip him. Sometimes he would stop at a patch of clover to grab a few bites. He looked kind of cute, that great big worried eye of his watching our progress. If we went around a bend or got a little too far ahead, he'd come trotting up to us like a big puppy dog.

After we mounted up again, I reached for my tobacco. I was getting better at rolling a smoke while riding. The first time I tried it, the swinging movement of the horse tore my cigarette in two. With practice, I had it down.

I fired up my smoke, and when the match was cool enough to hold between my fingers, I stored it in a pocket for later disposal. Never leave a trace—that was our code. Before abandoning a campsite, we would dismantle the fire pit and shelter, drown and bury the fire and trash, and spread our mattress cuttings. Then we'd take a last look around to make sure we hadn't missed anything.

I watched the dogs chase after something high on the hillside. The rhythmic swaying of the horse and steady buzzing of insects had become as familiar as my own breathing. As I leaned back in the saddle and took in the passing scenery, I felt great admiration for nature and her gifts.

Out of the corner of my eye, I glimpsed something moving and looked down to see a gray-and-black-checkered butterfly land on my thigh. It stood still for a minute, then rubbed its forelegs together as if it was about to tell a dirty joke. But it changed its mind and fluttered away.

When the sun disappeared behind the mountains, we started searching for a suitable campsite. As usual, it took a while. We finally found a nice spot on Duckfoot Creek meeting all our requirements and set about doing our evening chores.

Mitch woke up beaming. "Today we should make it across the Continental Divide." Map in hand, he showed me where we were. "The way I figure it, we'll get through Cochetopa Pass by late afternoon if we don't dawdle. Let's go!"

I grinned, caught up in his excitement. "Okay! It looks like a long distance, but I'm game."

We hurried with our morning activities, then mounted up and headed north on a maze of trails. That day, like most days on our journey, the lazy creaking of saddle leather and the steady beat of hooves on earth, together with the beauty and serenity all around us, lulled me into a state of mindlessness. Daydreams emerged, usually concerning the fairer sex, fueled by famine from nearly two weeks in the wilderness.

I'd see images of Gina or Marna—or I'd fantasize about Rosehips, this new woman Mitch kept saying I should meet. But more times than not, I longed for Susanne, that mysterious Kansas City charmer, who had now risen in my mind to an exotic Indian princess. I imagined riding up to her on Geronimo at the Aspen love-in and scooping her up into my arms. Then we'd ride off to a wooded glen, where we would lose ourselves—

Just then, a few feet ahead, Doña shifted her tail up and to the left. Out of her rear end came the familiar sound—"p-p-p-p-p-p-u-u-u-u-u-u-t-t-t-t-t-t"—followed by ten cubic feet of noxious equine gas so thick I swear I could see it.

"Noooooooo!" I buried my nose in the soft sleeve of my leather jacket and held my breath as long as possible, but there's no way to escape the wrath of a horse fart. Somehow the reek lingered, penetrating every pore as I fought not to gag. Hell, it nearly knocked me to the ground.

When Mitch and I were on foot, we could walk side by side while one of us led Doña, Geronimo in line behind her. That way we could stay in front of the horses, giving us a much-appreciated reprieve from the gas warfare. But in the saddle, I had to repeatedly brace myself for Doña's life-threatening attacks.

Horse flatulence wasn't the only type we had to deal with. Since we'd chosen to use onions and raisins as our favored condiments, we discovered their dire side effects—they turned an anus into a lethal weapon. Mitch and I agreed that onion-raisin farts were the most foul-smelling human emissions. We had both "cut the cheese" in our bed-rolls, forcing us to hold our breath and fan our blankets for ventilation.

Most men can suffer their own farts. Truth be told, some might even admit enjoying them—just a little. But, trust me, and I speak from experience here, no normal man could handle the stench of an onion-raisin fart. In fact, it took a "real man" just to survive one.

The Continental Divide was close. West of the zigzagging line on the map, all waters flowed into the Pacific, and east of it, to the Atlantic. I had crossed the Divide several times by car via the highest paved road on Independence Pass—but today we would cross on horseback, as pioneers and mountain men did in the past.

In the early afternoon, we stopped above the tree line to eat lunch. Tundra surrounded us, stretching for miles, with a scattering of stubby flowering shrubs—rugged yet striking in its many textures and subtle colors. We had nothing to tie Doña to, but the low vegetation must have been tasty because the horses got busy nibbling at it while we munched on some leftover stick bread and beef jerky.

Without a tree for my back or a rock to sit on, I leaned against one of Geronimo's hind legs. He didn't seem to mind, so Mitch made use of his other leg. I didn't worry about him kicking us. We were family now.

Mitch pointed to the map. "That dry creek bed must have been Cantonment Creek. We shouldn't be too far from the top. According to the map, Cochetopa Pass is 10,032 feet high."

I smirked. "I'm feeling pretty high right now."

"Could be the altitude . . . or maybe just brain damage." He cracked a smile and nodded in the direction of the trail. "Let's keep moving.

We have to get to Corduroy Creek before we camp, and it's still a ways on the other side of the pass."

The summit was farther away than we thought, and we didn't reach it until close to six. By then, the sun had dipped in the sky, casting long shadows behind us. We dismounted next to a beautiful pale-red rock formation, checked out the view, and then, back to back, took a leak—Mitch into the Pacific and me into the Atlantic.

"Who'd have thought a stereophonic opposing oceanic urination could feel so good?"

Mitch the navigator chuckled. "Say good-bye to Rio Grande National Forest. This is where Gunnison National Forest starts. I had to study two maps this morning."

Though tired and hungry, we pushed on, needing to find a good campsite for the horses. As usual, the dogs were good sports, following behind without complaint.

After riding and walking downhill for another three hours, returning to the forest, we still hadn't found Corduroy Creek.

Mitch studied the map with a flashlight. "Christ, where the hell is it?"

We rode on.

My muscles ached with fatigue, and my stomach cried out for food. Of course, when you are totally exhausted and can't possibly do one more thing, something bad happens.

Focused on finding the creek, Mitch hadn't noticed Doña's saddle working loose. In a matter of seconds, he went from riding upright to hanging off to the side, one leg on her back and the other under her belly.

"Goddammit. Holy crap. Give me a fuckin' break."

Groaning, Mitch removed his duffel and saddlebags, hoisted his saddle upright, readjusted the cinch, and replaced his gear.

We trudged on in silence.

Finally, under a darkening sky with traces of pastel pink and brilliant orange to the west, we came to a creek—without the time or energy to admire the sunset. Was it possible to be too tired to be hungry and too hungry to be tired? After pitching camp in the dim light, we struggled to take care of the animals and ourselves.

Bone-weary, I fell into a sleep fit for a crypt.

Mitch studied the map in the morning light and figured out we were at Los Creek. Where was Corduroy Creek? Maybe an error on the map? Or maybe this high in the mountains the creek had dried up?

Whatever—it was a new day.

When I went to fetch Geronimo, I found him next to the creek feasting on a clump of tall grass. He lifted his head in my direction and held his jaw as if it had come unhinged. Holding his mouth in this comical manner, he bobbed his head up and down. A horselaugh! I had heard the term, and now I knew where it came from. Geronimo looked as if he were laughing at a private joke. He was probably trying to dislodge a chunk of grass caught behind his back teeth, but it still struck me as hilarious.

After traveling downhill all morning, we reached the lush headwaters of Cochetopa Creek, bordered by inviting green meadows loaded with vibrant wildflowers—purple larkspur, white yarrow, blue lupine, and orange paintbrush, along with tons of yellow dandelions. We followed the creek north and stopped at a shady grove for lunch.

Leaning back on my elbows in the thick grass, I watched the bugs skip on the water. "I think we should continue on until late afternoon and then look for a place where we can settle for a few days again."

"Good plan." Mitch took off his hat and ran his kerchief across his forehead. "It'll be nice to take it easy. I'm still pooped from yesterday."

"The horses could use a break too."

He nodded. "Yeah, if we find a good spot, we should do what we did before—stay for three days and on the middle day get ripped."

I turned to him and flashed a wide smile, surprised to find my serious partner so adventurous. "Right on! I'm easy."

We returned to the trail in the rugged, untouched country. Mitch pointed out Cochetopa Dome up ahead and Sawtooth Mountain to the northwest. After scoping out and nixing several possible campsites, we came to a place where another tributary joined the creek. The forest at the edge of the meadow offered plenty of firewood as well as shelter if a storm moved in.

"This looks as good as we'll find," Mitch said.

"It has everything we need. Let's call it home for a few days."

We slept under the stars, staking out our spots on opposite sides of the fire pit. In the evening, a chorus of crickets and frogs accompanied our harmonicas. Charlie lay close to the fire, gnawing on a branch. At the cry of coyotes, she perked up her ears. Shawn jumped to his feet but stood his ground.

So far we hadn't encountered as much wildlife as I had expected. We saw lots of signs—tracks and droppings of deer, elk, and rabbit, and a tree a bear had used to scrape its claws. There was also evidence of beavers, but we had seen only one, up on Bear Creek. It was rare to come across anything larger than a chipmunk or squirrel.

I guessed that the smell of the dogs and the clattering of the horses' hooves drove most critters away. Of course, who knew what lay ahead. But on this night, I was just looking forward to a few days' rest.

44.

Discovery
July 1969

"**H**ave you ever had a bad trip?" Mitch asked me.

It was our second morning in camp, and the weather was smiling on us, the perfect mix of sunshine and a gentle mountain breeze. After our usual breakfast of oatmeal, raisins, and stick bread, we sat around the fire and took another hit of acid, washing it down with the last of our coffee.

I thought of the night Susanna ditched me on the King River. "I haven't had a bad trip per se. I felt real lonely in Arkansas, and that was horrible enough. I've seen a couple of people on super bummers, though. LSD takes whatever's inside you and puts it under a microscope. If you have fear, you will visit it—and it won't be fun. Paranoia is worse. If you have sorrow, it can hit you like a school bus. Any negativity can eat you alive."

I pulled out my cigarette papers and bag of Bull Durham. "If you're not in balance, you shouldn't touch any drug. I've learned that the hard way with pot. Acid would have been worse. Have you ever seen people hallucinating out of their mind? Can you imagine what it feels like when they look straight into your eyes and let out a blood-curdling scream? It shakes your soul. That happened with a girl out at Brad's."

"Sounds bad."

"You have no idea. It was really shitty. Worse for the gal, I'm sure."

"So why do you take it?"

"For discovery, I guess. Acid is the great revealer—you just have to respect it and carefully assess your ability to handle it at any given time. You should choose a good environment like this"—I pointed to the meadow—"and be with people you can trust. I also make sure to have the necessary supplies, like food, water, and the proper clothing, to avoid hassles. My Boy Scout training, I suppose. You know—'Be prepared.'"

I poured tobacco on a paper and spread it around with my fingers. Grasping one string in my teeth, I drew the tobacco bag shut and dropped it in my shirt pocket.

"But there have been times when I made a spontaneous decision. That's when I just had to trust and enjoy the ride. I like adventure—another reason I trip—and LSD can be an exciting roller coaster, but it can also help you look deeper at things because your senses are amplified. If your heart feels love, it may explode in your chest. It's especially cool to share acid with a lover."

I finished rolling my smoke and ran the tip of my tongue over the paper to seal it, then struck a wooden match on my zipper and took a long, deep drag. "I promised myself I wouldn't take a strong drug more than four times a year, but I'm breaking that rule this summer. It just seems like perfect opportunities keep popping up. Discovery and adventure—that's what I live for. So I'm not thinking twice about touching the stars."

Mitch nodded as my head began to buzz. Tired of jawing, I wandered off with Charlie and sat in some tall grass with my back against a boulder. She lay next to me and anchored her butt against my thigh, staring off in her own direction. She was always present but never intrusive—a perfect partner.

Around noon I found Mitch out in the meadow sitting on a boulder the size of a car. I joined him watching the horses. Their massive jaws tore off tuffs of sweet clover and chewed and chewed and chewed. The dogs dug at a gopher hole near the feet of the horses, but the large animals paid them no mind.

Whoosh . . . Buzzzz . . . Zing . . . Whirrrr

Mitch and I tried panning for gold, but it was hard to tell if the sparkles were gold, pyrite, mica, or merely hallucinations, since so many things in and out of the pan were sparkly. We gave up and returned to the boulder and horse watching.

"So did you ever hear anything from your draft board?" Mitch asked.

"Nah, nothing yet. You?"

"No, but the war is starting to get more attention. Maybe they'll lighten up."

"It's encouraging, but I don't think the draft board is capable of compassion. Someone needs to put some weed in their oatmeal. The way I see things, even if it wasn't a moral decision, it's still practical to refuse to go."

"How do you mean?"

"Well, if you're in the military and stand up for what you believe, like refusing to pick up a gun, you'll get tried by a military court and get a long sentence in a military prison—or worse, they'll pack you off to the front lines in Vietnam like that guy at the air force base. Chances of getting out of a federal prison alive are better than those alternatives."

"Yeah, that's true. At least people are starting to get hip to the stupidity of the war. I don't mind fighting for justice, but devastating a country, killing and killing . . . what justice is there in that?"

I fiddled with the ends of my mustache. "You know what really gets me? People think we're against the soldiers. I respect the hell out of those guys. What they do takes guts. It's this damn war and the senseless carnage I can't stand."

"I'm with you. We have no idea how hard it is for them." He paused. "Hey, check that out."

I followed his gaze to a hummingbird flirting with a flower. Its wings moved a hundred miles an hour, and something inside my chest beat at the same speed. The tiny bird flitted around a few times and then zipped off.

Mitch turned back to me. "Do you ever worry about going to prison?"

"Hell, no. Sure, it's a possibility, but thinking about it can only lead to misery, so I shove it off in a corner, way back in my brain. I'll deal with it when I have to. Meanwhile, I have a life to live, and I plan to enjoy every sweet minute of it."

"I know what you mean. Love is the only thing that makes any sense." He swatted at a deer fly. "Whatever will be, will be. It just amazes me that mankind is so brutal."

All the talk of war and prison hung heavy in the air. "How about we change the subject?" I said. "It's too beautiful here to dwell on such things."

Whoosh . . . Buzzzz . . . Zing . . . Whirrrr

"I hear you." Mitch pointed over my shoulder to a pair of beavers swimming together, creating intricate patterns in the water. "It's like they're dancing," he whispered.

"It must be some type of mating ritual."

We watched the pair's ballet in silence until they disappeared. *What a gift! Nature is so cool.* I jumped off the boulder and romped with Charlie in the meadow. We played keep-away with a stick—a game she loved. She ran circles around me, darting in and out, teasing and daring me to grab the stick.

When I returned to camp, Mitch was on his knees, working on a fire. We were both accomplished fire makers, but he was meticulous about it and a pleasure to watch. He'd start with dry grass, and when it was burning, he'd gently stack on small, dry sticks. He'd repeat this process over and over again, working up to good-sized logs.

I, on the other hand, would use the same materials but get right to it, building the whole structure first, from grass to logs, and then lighting it. I always figured that the smaller elements burning below would help dry, if not ignite, the larger elements. I never mentioned this to Mitch because I could see he loved what he was doing. Besides, both our methods worked.

In the warm glow of a sunset, we ate our dinner, never tiring of the same simple meals of brown rice and packaged soup. Mitch turned in after dark, but my mind still buzzed, so I grabbed my flashlight, and Charlie and I paid the horses a visit.

The soothing sound of crickets and frogs filled the air, and the coyotes joined in, piercing the night with their high-pitched, distant screams. I listened for a while, feeling at home in this wild, remote wonderland. I even had a strong urge to howl back, but I didn't want to lure wild dogs into our camp.

Looking up, I marveled at the millions of bright stars. There seemed to be more stars than the spaces between them. Could it be there were many more stars in the sky than we normally thought? Maybe you just had to get this far away to actually see them.

"Or perhaps," I said out loud to Geronimo, "I'm just stoned."

I took an enormously long, satisfying pee, appreciating the freedom to unzip whenever and wherever I pleased. Then I patted my horse, and Charlie and I went off to bed.

45.

On Pins and Needles
July 1969

I woke to the delicious aroma of coffee, but I could hardly drag myself from my bedroll. Standing and struggling for balance, my brain fuzzy, I tried to shake off an angry acid hangover.

"Man, I guess we pay for our sins," I muttered to Mitch. "Where the hell did I leave my tin cup?"

He pointed to a rock behind the fire pit. "It's over there. Did you stay up late?"

"It took a long time for my mind to stop buzzing. I'll be okay after some coffee. We have a couple of potatoes left. How about I make hash browns?" I reached for the coffeepot.

"And I'll do the stick bread."

"Good thing we aren't too far from Gunnison. Our supplies are getting low."

"I'm looking forward to a cold beer myself."

"I've been dreaming of a cheeseburger."

"Mmmmm. That has my vote!"

After cleaning up the breakfast dishes and saying hello to the horses, I reached into my saddlebag and pulled out Herman Hesse's short novel *Journey to the East*. For whatever reason, it felt like the right time to start. I found a comfortable reading spot on a large log near the creek, and not too far away, Mitch settled down with his letter-writing paraphernalia and his Hesse novel, *Siddhartha*.

I read Hesse's first line: "It was my destiny to join in a great experience." Perfect. His writing pulled me in, and soon I embarked on a pilgrimage with the League, a secret society. Other than stopping to roll a smoke or two, I spent most of the afternoon reading, Charlie coming and going as she pleased.

As the sun dipped in the sky and my empty stomach complained, I tore myself away from the book to take inventory of our supplies and start a fire for dinner. We had enough rice, raisins, oatmeal, dry milk, and Bisquick for a handful of meals, along with half a week's worth of dog food and oats. I made a shopping list, even though we wouldn't reach Gunnison for at least two days.

Mitch and I hit the sack early, wanting to leave soon after daybreak. As much as I enjoyed the wilderness, I couldn't wait to gaze upon a pretty woman again. Who knew—I might get lucky.

We headed north, following the Cochetopa. The dogs ran ahead, searching for chipmunks and gopher holes. The horses, hungry as always, even after stuffing themselves for three days, had to stop and taste every sweet shrub within reach. Their persistence kept us alert. No dozing in the saddle.

Soon after mounting up, I noticed that the undersides of my toes hurt. Had I been gripping my boots with my toes? Perhaps the way I leaned in the saddle affected how I held my feet. I tried different positions, but that didn't help, so I ignored the discomfort. Come to think of it, my toes had been tender since we crossed the Continental Divide.

For days, Sawtooth Mountain had towered over the landscape like a matriarchal aunt. As we left it behind, dense brush and steep, rocky inclines near the creek forced us inland to the meadows and sparse woodlands. When the sun rose directly overhead, pounding us mercilessly, we entered a broad, grassy valley filled with Hereford cattle. An hour later, we were still riding through that colossal herd. At one point, we passed a large bull with a forehead of curly white locks— lucky for us, he glanced at us with disinterest.

I pointed to a lone sizable oak in the near distance. "Look, there's some shade. Let's stop for lunch."

"Suits me. I'm starving. Amazing, huh? How many head you figure?"

"Gotta be in the thousands."

"And we haven't seen the end of them."

We sat in a small, unspoiled circle, free of cow patties, and a soft breeze provided some relief from the scorching heat. My toe pain had nagged at me all morning, so I removed my boots and shook them upside down to see if rocks were to blame—nothing fell out. I was more comfortable barefoot, but I couldn't ride or walk the trail that way.

I stared at the herd of cattle stretching as far as I could see. "Doesn't it feel like we're in a scene out of *Rawhide*?"

"Sure does—loved that show. Did you see the bull back there?"

"Huge. But he had no grudge with us. Probably had a busy schedule taking care of all those cows."

He laughed. "They got him all tuckered out."

"Yeah, he has it rough."

Life was really like a western now, and no doubt we had started walking with a bit of a swagger. Sometimes it felt good to be macho. I'm not talking about the rednecks who hurt or degrade women. Or the idiots who always want to prove how tough or cool they are.

But it's nice to feel like a man. I suppose it's like when a woman enjoys feeling feminine. I loved being a cowboy—I felt strong, rugged, and free. A gentle cowboy, but not one to be reckoned with.

Before we got going again, I ran my hand along the inside toe area of my boots and felt a roughness at the tips. Applying downward pressure, I was surprised by several sharp pinpricks. "Shit. The soles have worn so thin the nails have pushed deeper into my boots—tiny, fucking sharp ones. No wonder it felt like needles stabbing my toes."

Mitch gave me a sympathetic look. "That's a pisser. Maybe there's a shoemaker in Gunnison. But that's a couple of days away."

I examined the soles, shaking my head. The nail heads weren't visible from the bottom so I couldn't pull them out. I tried pushing them back with a flat rock, but that didn't accomplish much.

I slipped on my boots, cringing with the pain, and we mounted up. It took another hour before we left the herd behind. We traveled until dusk and camped by the creek. My feet hurt like hell, so I took off my boots and went barefoot.

We sat up past dark, just talking. I rolled a cigarette and poked at the fire with a stick. When it was smoldering, I used it to light up.

"That was the end of our rice," Mitch said. "Good thing we're close to Gunnison."

"Do you think we'll make it there tomorrow?"

"I'd be surprised. We have to follow the creek until we come to a railroad grade. Then we follow that west to town. I think it will be more like a day and a half."

"Sorry to bitch, but it will be good to get these boots fixed. You know, I had a pair of Redwings for four years, wore them practically every day. I bought them when I got my motorcycle because they were like biker boots but not black and like cowboy boots but without the pointy toes or fancy-dancy stitching. They were even waterproof. I've had *this* pair six months, and they leak water and are already falling apart. They just don't make stuff like they used to."

"I heard that in the Old West, when a man turned eighteen, he got one pair of boots that lasted the rest of his life."

"They were made that good back then, huh? Man, it would be cool to learn how to make quality boots like that." I took a long drag off my cigarette and flicked the ash into the fire.

"The quality of a lot of things is going downhill. Cars are starting to all look the same. They aren't as classy as they used to be."

I shook my head. "You got that right."

One of our horses whinnied in the darkness. "Hey, something I was thinking about today. You know how the horses always want to be close together. What if one of us got injured? The other would have to ride for help. We should give them practice riding separately in case that happens."

"Seems reasonable," Mitch said. "Should we try it tomorrow?"

"Yeah, just to be safe."

He nodded but seemed somewhere else.

"What's up?" I reached to scratch Charlie behind the ears.

"Oh, just thinking about Jasmine. I sure miss that chick."

"Sounds like you found a good one. I wouldn't mind having a steady woman. Are you getting serious about her?" Shawn came over, wanting some attention too. I stroked his soft fur with my other hand.

"I could get serious. We groove together really well. What can I say—she's got my heart sewed up."

"You're not talking marriage here, are you?

"I've been thinking about it."

"Wow, really? Relationships and love are great. Just don't bet your whole bankroll on it. If there's one thing I've learned, it's that people change. Who you love today could be someone else tomorrow. That's why marriage isn't in my vocabulary."

"Well, I think this one's different. I can see spending the rest of my life with her."

"Best of luck, pal." I was sincere, but not convinced. There were too many sweets in the candy shop to do the forever thing. I got up and headed for my bedroll, Charlie at my feet.

46.

Walking Tall
July 1969

Our gear packed and the camp tidied up, I winced as I pulled on my boots, all ten toes swollen and shrieking with pain. Walking on nails might work for the Hindus, but they could have *that* shit. I took some comfort in knowing I'd get relief soon in Gunnison.

We mounted up and headed north on a dusty trail along the creek, keeping an eye out for a good place to separate Geronimo and Doña. After an hour or so, we came to a "Y" in the trail and split up. Not so fast. Both horses whinnied and jerked around, trying to get back together. But we toughed it out and finally maneuvered them to a distance where they couldn't see or hear each other.

Geronimo lasted mere seconds. He spun around and around, raising a fuss. When this didn't get him what he wanted, he reared up on his hind legs, pawing the air with his forelegs. I held on, except when he was vertical and my feet slipped from the stirrups. Then I stood on the ground behind him, reaching up with one hand on the reins and the other on the saddle horn.

"Easy, Geronimo, easy. C'mon, man, settle down."

When he came down on all fours, I used the leverage to plop myself back in the saddle from behind. I also tried twisting his ear the way Thomas said to do if a horse didn't listen. But that was like pouring gasoline on a flame. After ten intense minutes struggling with my stubborn companion, my gentle words devolving into ear-splitting curses, I rode back to see how Mitch had fared.

He had done better, but not by much. If one of us had to go for help, we'd just have to deal with it. I gave Geronimo a lot of strokes, hoping I hadn't injured our relationship.

We rode and walked, and I suffered sore feet for a second day. I couldn't wait to take off my boots, but I knew the closer we got to Gunnison, the sooner my torment would end.

On the banks of Tomichi Creek, we found an inviting place to camp, equipped with tons of firewood and ample foliage for the horses. As we tended to our evening chores, gorgeous reds, purples, and golds danced across the sky.

But it wasn't enough to distract me from my throbbing feet. Sitting by the fire massaging my toes, I told Mitch, "Let me tell you, when we get to Gunnison tomorrow, a cobbler is going to look better to me than a naked woman."

He just laughed.

On the morning of the nineteenth day, we pulled out our razors and tiny metal mirrors. Cold creek water made shaving mighty painful, and Mitch and I let a few expletives fly.

So now my face and feet were killing me.

For our trip into town, we had three parallel options: Tomichi Creek, the railroad grade, and Colorado Highway 50. We followed the creek for a short distance, switched to the railroad, and then rode the last couple of miles on the highway asphalt.

It had been two weeks since we'd stocked up on supplies, much less carried on a conversation with another human being. My body hummed with excitement as we headed down the quiet main street late in the afternoon. Small wood-framed homes and businesses lined both sides for several blocks.

We passed one lone pickup and then stopped to talk to a man standing with two young boys next to a corral.

"Could you tell us where we could find a shoemaker and a café around here?" I asked.

He took off his cowboy hat and pointed it up the street. "Two blocks down on the right. You can't miss 'em. But the shoemaker's closed by now. You'll have to catch him in the morning. Where are you boys heading?"

"We're on a ride from Taos to Aspen," Mitch said.

"Nice ride! If you need a place to overnight your horses, you're welcome to put them in here with mine," he said, nodding his head toward the corral.

"That would be great," I said. Noticing little foliage, I added, "We'd be glad to pay for a little hay for our horses."

"One night won't kill me. Don't worry about it. You can find a stream up the hill behind the corral if you need a place to camp."

"Thanks, we really appreciate it."

We dismounted and led the horses through the gate, unsaddled them, and prepared them for the night. Geronimo swung his head around and stretched his neck in the direction of the other horses, eager to make their acquaintance. We thanked the kind stranger again and carried our gear up the hill into the woods.

After setting up camp and feeding the dogs, we walked into town for supper, the dogs close behind us. The owner of the country café gave us menus, and I schooled him on how to make a tomato beer, something he had never heard of. He made my day when it appeared at the table. How something that sounds so weird can go down so smooth mystified me.

I don't believe there were two other people on the planet as pleased with their meal as we were that evening. It was clear the chef needed no instructions on how to make a delicious cheeseburger, crispy fries, and a lush green salad. We topped the meal off with apple pie à la mode. Stuffed beyond comfort but happy beyond belief, we left the restaurant with a couple of bones for our faithful, four-legged companions. The dogs jumped to their feet as we came out the door.

"Have we got a surprise for you," I said, but their keen sense of smell had already delivered the news.

Before heading back to camp, we found the shoemaker, post office, and grocery store for the next day and stopped to say good night to the horses. When Mitch handed the bones to the dogs, they pranced around for a few minutes, eyeing each other suspiciously, before settling down a safe distance apart to devour their treats.

A wonderful night on the town was had by all!

The next morning, after a hearty breakfast of bacon and eggs at the café, I limped off for the shoemaker while Mitch went to find oats for the horses and check for a general delivery love letter at the post office.

As I stepped into the narrow shop, I heard the whirling sound of a polishing machine shining leather and smelled the familiar aromas of shoe glue, polish, and boot oil, bringing back memories of a cobbler shop belonging to the father of a childhood friend. I'd always loved that smell.

Behind the counter, a husky, mustached man wearing a well-worn cowboy hat concentrated on a pair of ladies' shoes he was bringing to a perfect shine. He looked up. "What can I do for you, young fella?"

"I have nails coming through the soles of my boots. We're on a trail ride from Taos to Aspen, and I've been suffering something awful for days." I slipped off my boots and handed them over the counter.

The cobbler slipped his hand into one boot, turned it over, and examined it carefully. He repeated the process with the other. "I can take care of that. You should consider getting new heels too. These won't last long." He showed me how worn they were.

"I guess you're right. How much time do you need to repair everything?"

"I'd say an hour or so."

"Perfect. Okay if I hang out on your porch until they are done?"

"Help yourself. I'll get right on it."

I waited on the shop porch with Charlie, soaking in the warm morning sunshine. There was hardly anyone on the sidewalk, and not one car passed. Mitch showed up with a wide-assed smile, a bag of oats under one arm and a thick letter in his hand. He had already read it at least once, but he wanted to read it again. While he indulged, I reviewed our shopping list and added flashlight batteries.

When he finished, we headed for the grocery, Mitch bouncing along and me hobbling behind him in my tender bare feet. The little store was well stocked, and we soon had everything we needed.

Back on the shoemaker's porch, we didn't have to wait long for my boots. My socks slid in upon a new, slick, flat surface. The cobbler charged me only eight dollars—a steal when you took into account the relief I felt.

Good for another 10,000 miles! My new heels made me walk taller as I sauntered back to our campsite, ready to ride on.

Ahhh, that feels good.

47.

Bloodsuckers and Pincushions
July 1969

We packed our supplies, roped and saddled our horses, and secured our gear. Shortly after noon, we headed north out of Gunnison along the highway.

Still riding on asphalt when evening approached, we came to a marsh with brackish water. Against the background of the setting sun, the cattails, reeds, shrubs, ducks, mud hens, and pools offered brilliant shades of red and gold, blue and green. As beautiful as it was, we had to find a flowing stream with clear drinking water before we could camp.

I brushed off a mosquito or two as a mere nuisance, but several more took their place. So I grabbed my hat and whisked it back and forth around my head to keep the little critters at bay. Soon dozens and then hundreds of the bloodsuckers blanketed the sides of Geronimo's neck.

Likewise, ahead of me, Mitch waved his hat around to fend off the assault. "What the hell?" he yelled.

The horses' tails brushed back and forth, and their heads jerked around to shake off the pests. Within minutes, the hungry mob of mosquitoes had engulfed us, like something out of a Hitchcock horror film.

The horses bolted, and Mitch and I were too busy defending ourselves to object. I held on to the reins, flying through the air, brushing the insects away with my hat and off Geronimo's neck. They ran and ran, their hooves striking the asphalt in a deafening clatter. Adrenaline pounded through my veins. And the dogs raced behind, desperate to keep up with the pace. For a quarter of an hour, the horses galloped.

Finally, the endless marshland, along with the mosquitoes, disappeared behind us. We reined in the horses to a walk and caught our breath. Mitch looked over his shoulder. "Man, can you believe that?"

"I've never seen anything like it. Who'd have thought mosquitoes could make horses run like that?"

"We better check to see if they kept their shoes," he said.

Pulling the horses to a stop, we dismounted and found all eight shoes intact. Other than building up a lather of sweat on their necks and flanks, the horses looked fine.

"Whew!" I said. "We're lucky. One of them could have gone lame."

All of us needed to rest, but there was no time. We had to focus on the next challenge, the one we wrestled with every day on the trail: finding a suitable campsite. As the sun hugged the horizon, we trudged ahead, leading the horses. Fences lined both sides of the roadway, giving us no options, so we continued walking, tired and hungry, for more than an hour.

As the last vestiges of daylight lingered, we found an area where the fence sat back from the road. It wasn't ideal, but there was enough room to put Doña on a short rope. A narrow row of trees next to a small creek separated us from the roadway.

I gathered wood and made a fire, fed the dogs, and began dinner. Mitch tended to the horses and cut branches for under our bedrolls. We were famished when we sat down to our hot dogs and rice.

Once again, we were reminded of the harsh reality of life on the trail. Even so, a strange satisfaction came from being at the mercy of Mother Nature—and overcoming everything she threw at us.

The night sounds of crickets and frogs soothed my spent body. We had embarked on an adventure, and we sure hadn't been shortchanged on *that* commodity.

Sipping our morning coffee, Mitch and I talked about our route options for the day: following Ohio Creek or the road alongside it. We chose the creek because it was easier on the horses' hooves and a bit safer, though we seldom saw vehicles.

Our constant vigil to keep Doña and Geronimo moving forward had not changed. Our arms had grown stronger from steering our massive companions away from temptation. Life on the trail was relaxing, but most days we had to deal with at least one major adrenalized incident, making us more resilient and nudging up our threshold for excitement. A subtle transformation was taking place.

Mitch understood because he was living the same thing. And it said something to spend this much time with someone without an impatient word or a single disagreement. I couldn't have chosen a better partner.

As the hours passed, we spotted beaver houses, screeching hawks, and a million butterflies, along with more picturesque meadows and aspen groves. When we smelled skunk, we kept the dogs close. So far, the day was turning out pleasant and uneventful—but it was presumptuous to think it would stay that way.

Late in the afternoon, we heard aggressive barking in the distant brush, followed by high-pitched yelps. We whistled for the dogs, and Charlie and Shawn came running out of the rocky terrain. Shawn approached with his tail between his legs and porcupine quills sticking out of his nose and mouth. His face had turned into a pincushion. Somehow, Charlie had escaped unscathed.

We tied our horses, and I fetched the pliers from my saddlebag, brought along for this purpose. While I held Shawn, Mitch attempted to pull out the quills. Each one had to be firmly secured in the jaws of the pliers and dislodged with a strong, swift yank. Shawn was in too much pain to cooperate, nipping at Mitch several times. Frustrated, he led Shawn over to the stream by the collar and dipped his muzzle in the cold water. After a few dips, the icy water soothed his wounds, and we tried again.

Shawn was a strong, muscular dog, and frankly, I had my hands full holding his neck and head still as he recoiled in pain again and again. Charlie, concerned for her companion, stood by his side throughout the whole ordeal.

After the last quill had been removed, Shawn sought refuge under a bush. Mitch went over to him and gave him some soft words and kind strokes.

We had collected twenty-one of the colorful quills. Mitch and I admired their white shafts and dark brown-black tips with the potent barbs at the ends. Though nasty weapons, they were really quite beautiful.

I took the opportunity to water the horses, and we snacked on beef jerky. Pulling out his map, Mitch studied it and leaned toward me. "I was hoping we would reach Carbon Creek by nightfall, but it's still a ways north. We'll have to camp on Ohio Creek another night." He pointed to where he figured we were.

"Looks right. We should be able to travel maybe three more hours."

"Yeah. We'll reach Carbon Creek by late morning tomorrow.

I nodded and glanced over at the dogs. "Shawn seems to be feeling better."

"I hope he learned his lesson. I got bit about eight times," he said, inspecting his fingers.

"Don't expect any miracles. Dogs don't seem to learn that one very well. I'm surprised Charlie didn't get into it, but maybe it was because we called them right away."

We mounted up and headed north. As usual when we rode, Geronimo and I followed behind Doña and Mitch.

The rhythmic clopping and swishing of horses' feet and tails lulled me into my favorite daydream—Susanna. By now, she had become a sultry Indian goddess with beads and bangles, in a buckskin dress and beaded moccasins. I allowed the fantasy to grow in the silent hours on the trail: feeling her soft body rubbing against mine in the saddle, peeling off her clothes in a soft bed of clover, and engaging in lustful, sizzling sex.

It became a joyful obsession, a mental movie I loved to view and feel and believe possible. Was it the musings of a lonely cowpoke or the longings of a helpless romantic? Did it matter? My mind and heart treasured the fantasy, so I played it over and over in my imagination.

I never let setbacks in the field of love slow me down. Love is too delicious. Even the pain has merit—something to do with being able to feel. Shit, I guess I was as sappy as the country tunes I loved.

"This looks like a great place to settle for the night." Mitch's words shook me from my thoughts. An amazing, multicolored meadow lay before us, its tall green grass flooded with yellow, white, and purple wildflowers and quartz-bejeweled boulders painted with red, orange, black, and yellow lichens. It was dazzling. "Way cool!"

After pitching camp, Mitch checked Shawn's muzzle. He was tender, but he didn't have any trouble eating. When we finally sat down to supper, we met it with the same enthusiasm.

I was dog-tired, but a good dog-tired. "You know, I was thinking. We work like animals from dawn to dusk, and sure, there're the leftover aches and pains. But heavy labor makes you feel you've accomplished something, you've met a challenge, you've worked your muscles—and you feel strong, like a man. And when you're tired, you're proud to be tired. Doing this kind of work surrounded by nature, a trusted friend, your dog, and your horse is the best. It's as sweet as it gets."

"I can dig it," Mitch said. "Hope we've seen the last porcupine, though. I could go a lifetime without another nightmare like that."

The next two days, we followed Carbon Creek northeast, and by some miracle, we managed to escape wild rides, insect scourges, prickly rodents—and every other kind of heart-thumping calamity.

The first day, we passed through a picturesque valley dotted with horse ranches, each with small groups of Morgan horses. These handsome, powerful beasts have huge chests and look like they were born to pull a Roman chariot.

At the head of the valley, we reached a ranch where close to fifty of them grazed—some in the shade of trees, some standing in groups, and one rolling in the dust. Leaving us in awe, the picture-perfect scene would have warmed any horse-lover's heart.

Our second day along Carbon Creek took us back into the national forest, the fresh, delicious scent of pine filling the air. Blue jay sentinels shouted their alarms as we passed, while hummingbirds darted about at high speed and several huge jet-black ravens glided silently above the treetops.

It felt good to be back in the trees. I share a kinship with the woods.

My middle name, Sylvan, literally means "the woods." I used to think it was a corny name, but now I was wearing it with pride.

We continued riding until early evening, passing through a number of barbed-wire gates along the way. The tranquility was broken only by buzzing insects, fluttering aspen leaves, clopping hooves, and squeaking leather. A hawk surfing the upper wind currents stood still, surveying something that had caught his eye. His elegant stance made me pause.

After passing through still another gate, we found a perfect site overlooking Carbon Creek. Sprinkled with small groves of trees, it begged us to stay. And because the weather showed no threat, we pitched our camp in the open meadow.

"I'm glad we're back in the wilderness," I said. "I could stay here for a few days."

"Yeah, I'd say it's about time to relax and do a little mind expanding. I still have plenty of acid left." Mitch grinned.

"All right, Geronimo. It looks like we're home." I patted him on the neck. "I'll take care of the dogs and the horses."

"I'll do kitchen detail."

By the time the animals were set, Mitch had dinner cooking over a robust fire. We settled down and talked long into the night. The dogs curled up at our feet, near the warmth of the fading fire, as an owl hooted from across the creek.

48.

A Lotta Bull
July 1969

L ying on my side, I opened my eyes to see two small tree trunks inches from my face. As my vision cleared, I realized I was looking at the front hooves of a horse. I peered up at Geronimo's big head staring down on me.

"Morning, pal," I said.

He nodded, turned, and walked away. Just saying hello, I guess.

Geronimo and I had become close. How could I say good-bye to this sweet hunk of horseflesh?

I saw a difference between Mitch's animals and my own. Perhaps it had to do with our temperaments. My partner's industrous nature lent itself to hasty, fast-moving mannerisms—at least compared to mine. Simply put, someone once paid me a compliment when he said, "If Rich was any mellower, he'd be dead."

Our animals mirrored those traits. When Mitch fed his dog, Shawn would stand over Mitch's gold pan and gulp down his food. Doña would also stand and eat her oats in normal horse-like fashion from a feedbag. Charlie, on the other hand, would lie down with my gold pan between her outstretched front legs and take her time chewing each bite. I fed Geronimo his oats in the same gold pan. To my surprise, he took up the practice of lying down with the gold pan of oats tucked between his front knees. He would relax as Charlie did, munching away on his oats.

After oiling my saddle, I discovered a quiet place near the creek to read my book, and Charlie scratched a nest in the soft, cool dirt nearby. I read for several hours, caressed by a gentle breeze. When I returned to camp, Mitch was reading *Siddhartha*, and a thick, stamped letter addressed to Jasmine lay beside him.

In the evening, by the fire, I rolled a cigarette, and we talked about our Hesse books, waxing poetic about everything from love and nirvana to the soul and true consciousness.

Before turning in, we joined the horses and said good night. Geronimo looked handsome in the bright moonlight. He nuzzled my hand and as I stroked his broad forehead and soft muzzle.

I woke up excited about our plans for the day. It was July 20, our twenty-fifth day on the trail, making this our final three-day camp— and final acid trip.

After filling our stomachs, we sat near the creek and indulged. Mitch's blotter paper had gotten smaller and more irregular, but that had no bearing on its effectiveness. As the drug began to come on, we went for a walk, following the creek. Several hundred yards ahead, we came to an intersecting fence and turned right. After passing a crude gate, we continued until the fence intersected with yet another barbwire fence, forcing us to turn right once again.

A light bulb went on in my head. "Remember how a little before we found our campsite we passed through a gate?" I asked.

Mitch thought a moment. "Yeah, why?"

"Well, there could be fences on four sides of our camp. If we follow the fence around, we might find a complete rectangle." I traced the shape on my hand. "If that's the case, we're in the middle of a large corral. We could let both horses run free while we're here."

His face lit up. "Let's take a walk."

We headed south and soon found we had company—a dozen brown-and-white Hereford cattle grazed about twenty feet away in a small clearing on the other side of the fence.

Now, everyone has a calling, and though I often thought of myself as a man of many talents but a master of none, there was one exception:

I could imitate the bellowing of a cow like few others. I don't remember how I'd learned this artistry, but I could do a cow, a bull, or a calf with precision. Cattle would always stop and take notice. Sometimes, if I was in good form, they would bellow back at me.

Contrary to popular opinion, a cow doesn't say "moo." The sound they make is more like the marriage between a moan and a yearning roar. To imitate it, you need to drag it from deep in your chest and adjust your head to get in touch with your inner cow. The bellow must rise to a crescendo and then drop off in a short, abrupt note, fine-tuned with enhancements: high pitched innocence for a calf, a lower, concerned expression for a cow, and a deeper, booming tone for a bull.

Like I said, I'd mastered the art of cattle talk.

The acid was kicking in, and I felt spunky, unable to resist displaying my skills. So I took a big breath and let out a low, generous bullish bellow: "uu-uh-uo-oo-OR-RR-RR-rr!" We stared at the steers and cows, and they stared back at us.

After about thirty seconds, we heard a cracking of tree limbs and the slow clopping of hooves as a heavy animal approached, each crashing footstep accompanied by a low-pitched grunt. The crashing and grunting came closer, and a bull emerged from the forest. He, too, stood staring at us.

I looked him in the face, his forehead adorned with white curls. Pleased with myself, I let out another bellow—"uu-uh-uo-oo-OR-RR-RR-rr!"—this one slightly louder and deeper than the first. The bull just stood there like a statue.

Within seconds, we heard more crashing, grunting sounds, this time coming from farther away and louder than with the first bull. This new bull, slightly larger than the first, appeared from the woods and took his place next to the first one. Again, he just stood there, and the two of them stared at us, their tails whipping back and forth uneasily.

Really getting into it, I took a deep breath, concentrated, and let out an even louder bellow: "uu-uh-uo-oo-OR-RR-RR-rr!" And again, we heard the now familiar sounds of another bull coming our way, this one even louder and larger than the two before him. We were soon staring at three white curly-haired stoic faces.

Whoosh . . . Buzzzz . . . Zing . . . Whirrrr

Emboldened by the acid, I couldn't resist. From even deeper within my chest, I let out a more splendid bullish bellow, my head arching upward to produce the best effect: "uu-uh-UO-OO-OR-RR-RR-rr!" And again, the sounds escalated as the next bull came crashing through the forest, grunting louder and stomping heavier and breaking larger branches under his weight.

The bulls, representing some sort of herd hierarchy, now stood four abreast and stared at us like junkyard dogs. The fourth one had to be the granddaddy of all bulls. Made of solid muscle, he must have weighed a ton.

Like a fool, I dug deep into my arsenal of bellows one more time. With all I had, I let out the most ostentatious bovine scream anyone could ever muster: "uu-uh-UO-OO-OO-OR-OR-RR-RR-RR-rr-rr!" My vocal chords strained to their limits as my call shattered the serenity of the forest. A silence followed, as the four massive bulls stood and eyed us in expressionless wonder.

Proud of my accomplishment, I stared at them with a wide smile. Yes, another bull was coming. We heard the familiar stomping and grunting and cracking of dry branches. But the noise was amplified to a frightening, unthought-of level.

"What the fuck?" a hollow echo of a voice said. Was it mine?

This was not just another bull. When his feet hit the ground, the earth shook, and his roars thundered through the air. He had to be the King Kong of the bovine world.

My heart pounded—that barbed-wire fence was looking mighty flimsy. Mitch and I eyed each other nervously.

"Hey, man," Mitch whispered, pointing ahead of us, his body already in motion. I was quick on his heels, with no desire to stick around to face this new challenger. We summoned the dogs and beat feet along the fence line.

When we had reached a safe distance, we both started laughing. My pulse still racing, I said, "Who would have believed there could be another bull? He had to be a monster!"

"I'll say. That's one story nobody will ever believe."

"You're right. I barely believe it myself. You know what they're going to say?" My throat was sore from all the bellowing.

"What?"

"That's a whole lot of bull."

"I udder-ly agree," he said.

"I'd steak my life on it."

"Sounds like bullpucky to me."

I paused. "I guess we milked this one as much as we can."

Mitch burst out laughing again, and it was contagious. Our snorts and howls echoed throughout the forest, and the dogs tilted their heads, looking at us as if we were nuts. We laughed until it hurt.

When we recovered enough to move, we finished walking the perimeter. "It's just as I thought," I said. "We're in a huge corral. You can let Doña loose."

"Cool, man. I'll go release her."

I stretched out by the creek and lay back on my elbows, Charlie by my side. I thought about my relationship with her. At times she was like my kid, needing encouragement, instruction, or protection from danger. Other times, when I had to leave her for a few hours, she became a nagging wife, scolding me with high-pitched whines. And then, when my heart was heavy, Charlie was a mother to me, soothing me with her undisputed love and loyalty. Today, we were simply pals, enjoying the grace of nature.

Whoosh . . . Buzzzz . . . Zing . . . Whirrrr

As the day ended, I listened to the symphony of hundreds, maybe thousands, of crickets, and I realized they were harping in unison. They created a steady pulse that rocked me into a deep sleep.

Morning came with me again nursing an overworked brain. I was indulging more than I normally did, but it didn't worry me. I had seen enough dopey people who took too much acid. Their choice, but I preferred my brain cells intact. Once this summer was over, I'd cool it. But for now, I was hell-bent on living life to the max.

As I pulled myself out of my bedroll, Mitch sat up in his.

"Good morning," I said. "Did you get the license plate of the truck that hit me?"

He scratched his head. "Too busy getting hit by it myself."

"What's a few brain cells among friends?" I laughed. "That was quite a day."

"I was thinking about those bulls. Wondering what that last one looked like. Could there have been more after the one that drove us off?"

"We'll never know. I wasn't going to stick around to find out.

We spent the day reading. Once I finished *The Journey to the East*, I reread a few lines:

> *He who travels far will often see things far removed from what he believed was truth. When he talks about it in the fields of home, he is often accused of lying, for the obdurate people will not believe what they do not see and distinctly feel. Inexperience, I believe, will give little credence to my song.*

I thought about the five bulls. I knew folks would listen politely and even laugh at the story, but most would take it as a wild yarn. Only Mitch and I would know the beauty and absurdity of the experience we shared. In fact, that was true of this entire trip.

49.

A Dusty Gulch
July 1969

We woke at dawn, as we did every morning. By now, time in the traditional sense had lost all meaning. The sun had become our clock. When it was light, we got up, and when it was dark, we went to bed. It wasn't early or late. It just was—a simplicity I would sorely miss.

Another gorgeous Colorado blue sky greeted us. Anticipating we would make it to Crested Butte that day, I shaved, improvising a little ditty with a country-western twang:

> *Shaving with cold water really puts a smile on my kiss.*
> *It's better than a poke in the eye with a sharp stick.*
> *Here's hoping all this torture helps me charm a pretty miss.*

Mitch, my audience of one, shook his head and laughed.

We packed our gear and took off in search of the horses, ropes in hand, knowing it wouldn't be easy to get them to surrender their freedom. When we spotted them, I made a wide circle and came up behind them so they would move toward Mitch. While I distracted them, he got close enough to throw a lasso over Doña's neck.

Geronimo gave me more trouble. After my failed attempts to rope him, he kept his distance, so we led Doña back to camp and saddled her. As we expected, Geronimo sauntered along a little ways back.

I ignored him for a while, then picked a fistful of long grass, gave some to Doña, and approached Geronimo without my rope. He finally accepted my gift. While stroking his neck, I pulled off my belt and ran it around his neck. As smart as he was, I always got the poor fellow with that trick.

We took the trail out the north gate, following Carbon Creek. It felt good to be in the saddle again. I noticed more aspens scattered among the evergreens, along with several beaver dams. As the morning passed and the temperature rose, the horses readjusted to life on the trail, and we moved as a unit again. When the creek became a dwindling brook, we stopped for lunch.

Mitch pulled out his map. "It says Crested Butte is at 8,885 feet. There's no direct trail there, but Baxter Gulch heads in that direction. If we angle northeast, we should find it and be able to follow it to town."

"You're the map man. I trust your read. What exactly is a gulch, do you think?

"I don't know. I guess we'll find out."

Mounting up, we proceeded by compass. A couple of hours later, we came to a deep ravine, its steep sides extending down at least forty feet in some places. The narrow bottom was packed with boulders, trees, and underbrush—nothing like the arid, shallow arroyos of New Mexico.

"Crap," Mitch said. "This doesn't look good."

We blazed a trail through the dense woods along the western rim of the gulch, but the thick growth forced us to take wide detours, making progress painfully slow. At one point, we reached a stand of trees and brush that hemmed us in. There was no way to penetrate it. To our right, we faced a forty-foot, sixty-degree drop into the gulch and a climb almost as steep on the opposite side.

"We've got to get across," Mitch said.

"What a bitch. We'll have to slide down on our butts."

"It's our only option." Without skipping a beat, he slipped on his leather gloves, sat down, and went over the edge, letting out a loud whoop, a cloud of dust billowing up behind him.

The dogs ran after him, lost in another trail of dust. Just as Mitch reached the bottom, the horses followed without prodding, sliding down in half-sitting positions themselves. Mitch scurried to the side with the dogs to give the huge beasts plenty of room.

My turn. I plunged into the cloud of dust, flying down on the seat of my pants and using my gloved hands to control my descent. I was a little kid again, shooting down the grassy railroad levee by my house on a piece of cardboard.

We stood together at the bottom covered in dust. I wanted to laugh, but it would have left me choking. Still, the comical image of the horses sliding down—it was right out of a Saturday morning cartoon—combined with how unified we had become, left me giddy. Fortunately, the east side of the gulch was not as steep, allowing us to scramble up and continue our journey.

Later that afternoon, we rode out of the bush into a wide clearing and saw the back of a large log building in the distance. As we approached it, a middle-aged couple stepped onto the rear porch. The woman came toward us with a camera in her hand, her apprehensive husband trailing close behind.

"We're from Ohio," she said with a smile. "Would you mind if I took your picture?"

"If you want," I said, not seeing any harm in it.

As we stood there, I couldn't help think about how we must have looked. Sitting on our horses, duffel bags hanging over our saddle horns, bedrolls and saddlebags tied behind, the dogs standing at the horse's feet—I in my black misshapen cowboy hat, boots, jeans, and rawhide-fringe jacket, open in front, exposing my bare chest, and Mitch in his straw cowboy hat, more than a bit tattered by now, bandana around his neck, jeans, and boots—everything and everybody covered with a thick layer of dust. We must have been a sight.

As she snapped the picture, I thought about asking her if she could send a copy of the photo to my mother in California, just for a kick. I never got up the nerve to ask, and I began regretting it as soon as they disappeared into the building.

We circled the lodge and rode up a street to the center of Crested Butte, where we asked a few people about a place to put our horses for the night. One fellow offered his corral at the edge of town. Horse people seemed to be generous like that. He said we could camp there as well.

At the corral, we found adequate grazing for the horses—and a much-welcomed hand pump. Mitch and I took turns pumping while the other washed off layers of caked-on dust. Our plan was to eat out for dinner and breakfast, then take off for Aspen. As always, I hoped for a glimpse of a pretty woman.

A quaint little town, Crested Butte was even smaller than Gunnison, with a population of "about 423 folks," we were told. Walking down the main drag in search of a restaurant, we bumped into an amicable, well-tanned couple in their thirties, both dressed in ranch-worn western wear. When they heard about our month-long horse adventure, Kate, a baby-faced woman, said, "That means you probably haven't watched the news lately?"

Mitch and I shook our heads, and her face lit up.

"You missed the moon landing!" she cried out, clapping her hands. "They showed it on TV. Unbelievable. The astronaut—what was his name, Danny?—was almost floating down this ladder, and then he bounced across the surface of the moon. Somehow they televised the pictures all the way down here. Isn't that something?"

Mitch's eyes grew wide. "I would have loved to see that."

Kate nudged her husband. "The astronaut, Danny—what was his name?"

The fellow removed his cowboy hat and scratched the back of his head. "Uhh, let's see. Neil something. Neil Armstrong, I think. I still can't believe it."

"Yeah, he said something neat like 'a small step for man, a giant step for mankind.'"

"I've heard of Armstrong," Mitch said. "Man, what a trip!" He turned to me. "And we thought *we* traveled a long way!"

• • •

At the end of the street, we discovered a cozy café with rough wooden beams on the ceiling and wood planks on the walls and floors. Country music crackled on a radio. The soft, padded booth felt like a luxury.

It turned out that the bartender knew how to make a tomato beer, and I enjoyed it so much I ordered a second one with my cheeseburger. When we were ready to leave, we asked our waitress if they had any bones in the kitchen. She brought us a generous bag for our canine friends.

We found Charlie and Shawn hanging out on the front porch, and as soon as they saw us, they started wagging their tails and jumping. Mitch held the bag high, out of their reach. "Cool it, guys," he said. "There are too many dogs in town to give these to you here. We don't need any dog fights—far too pleasant an evening for that." Both of them kept pestering Mitch as we strolled around looking for a place to get supplies in the morning.

At the corral, we said hello to Geronimo and Doña, but they barely acknowledged us, far more interested in the other horses they were bunking with. Back at camp, the dogs danced around Mitch, almost knocking him over in their eagerness to get at the bag. We gave each one a small pile of bones, and they spent more than an hour meticulously polishing and gnawing at them.

I pulled a piece of paper and a pencil from my saddlebag, and Mitch and I compiled a shopping list, the last one of the trip. Then we turned in for the night.

As I lay in my bedroll, I thought about the other news Kate and Danny had told us, that Nixon was making good on his promise to start withdrawing troops from Vietnam. The first group of soldiers had come home. Had the protests helped? Could peace prevail?

Under the light of the rising full moon, I felt the first glimmer of hope that the world might be waking up—just a little.

On our way to breakfast the next morning, Mitch stopped at the post office to deliver another multi-page letter. I really liked Crested Butte. It was simple and rustic, and everyone was friendly. After eating and shopping for supplies, we passed Tony's Grocery, and a sign in the window caught my attention:

ICE CREAM CONES 5¢

"A nickel ice cream cone!" I said. "Can you believe it? They cost at least a quarter everywhere else. There's no way I'm passing that up. "Let's do it!"

We walked back to camp carrying bags of supplies under one arm while licking away at our cones. After rounding up the horses, we rode down the main street. It was a comfortable place, far enough from the highway to maintain its mountain-town personality. I'd make sure to return there someday.

As we traveled north and climbed in altitude, the road soon turned to dirt, and any trace of inhabitants disappeared behind us. The aspen leaves reflected the sunlight and whispered softly in the cool breeze. It was spectacular country, one impressive vista after another appearing before us.

The slight chill in the air signaled the rise in elevation. We came across several hillsides covered with fallen aspens, all their treetops pointing downhill. These stark slopes, sometimes three hundred feet across, demonstrated the power of avalanches—a testimony to the severity of the winters at this altitude. Our horses had no problem stepping over the fallen trees.

By early afternoon, our road had become a narrow trail. As we passed the eastern face of Snodgrass Mountain, we had to lead the horses along a treacherous shale incline. First Mitch slipped and Doña stepped on his leg, then I slipped and Geronimo stepped on mine.

"Shit! I can't believe how much I hate being stepped on by a horse." We'd both have bruises to nurse that night.

Of course, now that all of us were hot, tired, hungry, dusty, and thirsty, something bad was bound to happen. Sure enough, the dogs started barking in the brush, and minutes later, we heard the yelping. Back they ran, each with a beard of quills.

"Just what we need," I said. "Now they *both* look like pin cushions."

"Don't you guys ever learn?" Mitch shouted. "Man, I could have gone all day without that."

Because the horses were overheated, we couldn't let them drink, so we tied them to a dead tree. I fished in the saddlebags for the pliers and joined Mitch in the arduous task of de-quilling the dogs. While wrestling with them and getting numerous bites, we heard a loud "CRACK!"

Geronimo had pulled the dead tree over on Doña, and both horses were heading for the stream.

"Oh no!" we shouted.

I hurried to untangle Doña and then pulled the two of them away from the water. When they were secured again, we resumed our veterinary work. It took close to an hour to remove all the quills.

After watering the horses, Mitch and I fell back in the grass, too exhausted to move. I eventually got up to retrieve some candy bars and apples from my saddlebag to hold us for a while. Mitch took the opportunity to study the map.

"We should be close to Judd Falls on Copper Creek," he said, "which will lead us to Conundrum Pass. We won't get there today, though."

"Tomorrow, we soak in Conundrum Hot Springs. You'll love it. I walked seven miles in from the Aspen side with Hal. It has a great little pool, surrounded by beauty and nothing else."

"I could use that pool right now. My body is tired and sore. How's your leg?"

"A little tender, but I'll live—my thighs ache more from riding. You'd think we'd be bowlegged by now. How did the guys in the Old West manage?" I stood and stretched. "I guess we should get going if we want to make it by tomorrow."

We stayed on foot, still navigating the rugged terrain on the narrow trail. Although we should have come upon Judd Falls, we never found it and had to be content following Copper Creek. Light was diminishing faster than usual in the dark, cloud-filled sky, and it started to drizzle. We pulled out our ponchos and walked on, anxious to find a camp before a storm hit.

Trees were scarce at this altitude, limiting our choices. Finally, we found a quartet of stunted pines we could use to string up our plastic tarp, and the horses could graze in a nearby meadow.

The solid granite landscape descended down from three directions, forming a depression where the trees had taken root. We laid freshly cut pine boughs in the space and covered them with our second tarp, then layered our sleeping bags and gear on top. Because we had to squeeze everything into the equivalent of a long closet, we placed our sleeping bags side by side, but positioned them in opposite directions so we didn't have to sleep face-to-face. Truth be told, we were having enough trouble dealing with our own onion-raisin farts and didn't need to deal with someone else's.

Before long, we had a damp fire burning a few feet from our bedrolls. Mitch cooked dinner while I fed and cared for the dogs and horses. The drizzling had let up, but the air remained thick with moisture.

Huddled by the fire, we ate hot dogs, stick bread, and canned beans, water dripping from the brims of our trail-worn hats. It felt cold, even with our long johns on.

"Sure hope we have clear skies tomorrow," Mitch said. "Conundrum's at nearly thirteen thousand feet—it will be tough enough to climb in fair weather."

I took a long drag off my cigarette. "The good part is the hot springs isn't that far on the other side."

After eating, we sought refuge in the warmth of our bedrolls. The dogs were already curled up, and they snuggled close throughout the chilly night.

50.

Cliff-Hanger

July 1969

The morning light danced on my eyelids, coaxing me into consciousness. As I peeked out of my bedroll, all I could see was white.
Huh? I blinked my eyes, not understanding.

Lifting my head for a better look, I saw that we were packed in
marble-sized hailstones like fish in a butcher shop. Our sleeping bags
were covered except for a thin band running down the center.

"Hey, Mitch!"

He stirred, then sat up and stared, his mouth wide open. "What
the hell?"

"Apparently, all the hail bounced down into our trough. How did
we manage to sleep through the noise? Should have camped somewhere else."

"We didn't have a lot of options. Good it was hail and not rain."

Even though we were packed in ice, we'd been warm and snug
the entire night. We got up, dressed, and lay our bedrolls over some
branches to dry. Happily, the sky was nearly cloudless.

We started out riding on a narrow, well-defined trail, but after a
few hours, it turned into large, uneven granite sheets, making it difficult to discern, so we walked, leading the horses until early afternoon.
Ahead we could see Conundrum Pass, looking like a saddle perched
on top of the ridge.

The slope leading up was concave, a good mile across, and rose
many hundreds of feet. The massive incline, covered in shale, had a

faint, diagonal trail, angling to the top. We had traversed our share of shale fields, but nothing as immense as this. Far above the tree line, it barely had a shrub. We stopped to rest before embarking on the last few miles to the summit.

Once we began crossing the shale, iridescent blue, copper, yellow, and red-orange colors shimmered in the sunlight. Easy to identify, the trail was broken up by occasional narrow strips of loose dirt where erosion had flushed the shale away. The strips were only two to three feet wide, but they required extra care to secure a foothold.

We continued up the trail, the dogs in the lead, followed by me and then Mitch, who led Doña. Geronimo lagged a few feet behind. About halfway up the diagonal, we came to a swath of eroded soil, about six feet wide. I stepped across, followed by Mitch.

When Doña stepped onto the loose dirt, she lost her footing. Arching her front legs, she tried to dig her front hooves into the soft dirt but couldn't gain any ground. Eyes wide with panic, she made a series of jumping motions uphill with her front legs, jerking the reins out of Mitch's hand. After she took three jumps, I watched in horror as she started to fall over backward.

Acting on instinct, I grabbed her reins as they swung past my face. *Don't hold on to a horse going over a cliff!* Taking the advice of that silent, rational voice, I let go.

"Oh shit," was all I could say.

"OH NO! OH NO! FUCK! FUCK!" Mitch threw his arms in the air.

What happened next was like watching a bad movie in slow motion. First, a loud crunching, scraping noise, then down Doña went, rolling over and over on the steep incline for what seemed like forever. The dust flew as the duffel bag and saddlebags flopped this way and that before detaching from Doña's saddle and shooting out across the hillside. Horse legs reached for the sky in awkward directions and then curled underneath, only to reach for the sky once again.

NO! NO! NO! With every revolution, my stomach lurched. Just when I thought it would never end, Doña stopped, lying with her legs folded under her, seventy feet below.

Descending a steep slope of shale shards requires much angling and weaving and slipping and sliding, along with some swearing and stumbling. But there was no time for that. We ran straight down that treacherous incline, "we" being two men, two dogs, and a buckskin horse—moving as one toward Doña. We dodged the duffel and saddle-bags littering the slope as we made a rapid decent.

My heart raced with fear and exertion. If her leg was broken, we'd have to put her down . . . and all we had was a rock and an ax.

When we reached her, she was lying down with her head up and her tongue hanging out, gasping for air. Mitch made a slow approach and stroked her neck, helping her regain her composure. After ten minutes, she calmed down, and Mitch urged her to get up. She ended up standing east on the south-facing slope. Her right hind leg was up, balancing on the tip of her hoof, indicating an injury.

My chest tightened with dread. "She's not standing on that back right. Do you think it's broken?"

"I don't know," Mitch said, his face clouded with worry. "We'll have to wait and see. The direction she's facing, there's no way out, so I'll have to turn her around." His eyes swept the hillside. "It's not as steep that way"—he pointed over his shoulder—"and we can angle across to the trail. I'll give her a few minutes before I try."

"Why don't you take off her saddle to make her more comfortable?"

While Mitch unsaddled her, I climbed up the slope to retrieve the rest of his gear. When I returned, Doña's breathing was close to nor-mal, though she still had a frightened stare and a layer of sweat on her coat. Mitch took her reins and steered her around toward Geronimo standing behind her. When she was fully rotated, facing her compan-ion, she lifted the left hind leg in the same manner she had previously held the right one.

The tension drained out of me as I realized her leg wasn't injured.

Mitch released a long breath. "Look, man. She was just keeping her balance. She's going to be all right." He wiped his brow. "We are so lucky. Good going, Doña! Let's get you out of here."

Geronimo, seeing the face of his sweetheart, pivoted and led the way across the slope to where it intercepted the trail. Mitch hoisted his saddle and blanket upside down over his shoulder, while I threw the rest of his gear over mine, and we followed the horses.

I secured Mitch's saddlebags to Geronimo's saddle and continued carrying his duffel on my shoulder. Likewise, Mitch continued carrying his saddle as he took hold of Doña's reins and guided her across the wide area of erosion. Because we were both weighted down with a heavy load, we inched our way towards the mountain pass.

It was difficult enough carrying the gear uphill in the hot sun at that altitude, but then we bumped into yet another obstacle. Shaking our heads, we stared ahead at an eighty-foot field of snowpack, much too wide to circumnavigate. Oh man.

With each step, we crunched through the crust and sank to our thighs. The going was so strenuous we had to stop in the middle of the snowfield to catch our breath. Soaked in sweat, we sat in the snow, too winded to talk. I rubbed snow on my forehead and the back of my neck, summoning the will to continue over the summit. Meanwhile, the dogs lounged in the snow, chomping on large mouthfuls to satisfy their thirst.

Past the snow, we still needed several more rest stops before the top of the ridge. As we stood at thirteen thousand feet, a mixture of pride and relief filled my exhausted body. Sweat fell into my eyes as I gazed down at the valley on the north side of the pass.

"It's downhill from here," I said between breaths. "The hot springs can't be more than a couple of miles away."

"Far out!" Mitch panted like a dog. "I can use some downhill."

We sat there briefly to rest and savor the view while the horses stood quietly, waiting for us to continue. Small tributaries trickled down from patches of snow on the north-facing summit. Farther down, forest awaited us.

Standing and taking a few gulps of the thin air, we lifted the gear onto our shoulders and prepared to move on. Though Doña seemed fine, we wanted to give her plenty of time to recover.

We crept down the slippery, muddy trail, our legs shaky from the arduous climb. It was almost impossible to keep my knees from buckling. As we followed a small stream, the beauty of the landscape and the cheerful wildflowers eased our exhaustion. Carrying the heavy gear made me appreciate the work our horses had done for us.

Just as the sun dropped below the mountain ridge, we arrived at the hot springs. My insides beamed with gratitude. Another person was there, a young, bearded fellow soaking in the rock pool.

The stream separated and rejoined to form a narrow, thirty-yard-long, oval-shaped island, covered with tall, lush grass—a perfect spot for the horses. Mitch led Doña across the creek, and as I crossed with Geronimo, his saddle and all the gear attached slipped to the side, almost submerging in the water. "Jesus Christ—give me a break!"

I ditched Mitch's duffel bag on the bank and jumped into the creek. Grabbing the saddle with both hands and mustering my last ounce of energy, I fumbled to hold it above the stream. Geronimo just stood there.

"Mitch, help!"

He led Geronimo onto the island as I supported the dangling load. After tying both horses to a stump so they could cool down before drinking, we carried our gear across the other branch of the stream and deposited it close to an existing fire pit. My shoulders rejoiced.

Now that the horses could drink, Mitch tied Doña on her tether, both of us amazed she showed no sign of trauma. We made sure the dogs stayed close—no more wrestling matches with porcupines.

Our turn, at last. We stripped down and lowered ourselves into the rectangular pool, the size of four deep bathtubs. "Paradise!"

"This feels sooooo gooooood!" Mitch said.

"No shit. I told you this was a bitchin' place. My body's so tired the horses will have to pull me out of here."

"All I can say is we earned this bath."

"Damn straight."

The stranger introduced himself as Paul. "I've been living like a mountain man up here for the past three months," he said. "You can't beat this place."

He chatted with us briefly, then got out of the pool, dried off, and threw on jeans and a worn flannel shirt. Adjusting his dog-eared leather hat, he said, "Hey, would you guys like to come to my camp for dinner?" His hand sliced the air toward the west. "It's just a short hike over that way, about an eighth of a mile or so."

I looked at Mitch, who nodded. "Thanks, man. It'd be a pleasure. We have some serious soaking to do first, and we need to take care of our animals and set up camp."

"No sweat. Head over when you're ready. If you have mess kits, bring them along. I'm slim on plates and forks." He disappeared into the woods.

I didn't think my energy would ever return, but after soaking for a good while, I felt refreshed. Invigorated by the cold evening air, we tended to our chores, then grabbed apples and cheese to share and hiked off with a flashlight in search of Paul's campsite, the dogs behind us. It didn't take long to spot his fire through the trees.

Hey, Paul," I called.

Outside a lean-to shelter, he had a stew cooking with venison and several wild plants he had gathered. We took a seat on one of the logs arranged around the fire, and Paul pulled out a small pipe fashioned from a deer antler, packing it with weed. He lit it up, inhaled a deep toke, and passed it to Mitch, who took a hit and choked and sputtered as clouds of smoke shot from his mouth. When he handed it to me, I proceeded with caution. A few more times around, and I felt quite altered.

As the moon rose bright and full over the ridge, Paul dished up dinner. "Sorry I don't have any beaver tail to offer. You wouldn't believe how good it is."

I wasn't disappointed. Chewing on a tough chunk of venison, I asked him how long he planned to stay.

"Probably until mid-September. I'm not keen on getting snowed in for the winter."

We swapped stories for the next couple of hours. Mitch and I described our recent cliff-hanging experience, only to be outdone by Paul's wild, bone-chilling encounter with a mama bear and her cubs.

On our way back to camp, everything looked magical in the moonlight, enhanced tenfold by Paul's dope. We found the horses grazing on their lush island and leaped over the creek to bid them good night, the tall grass swishing against our boots as we approached them. Geronimo shone, as if surrounded by a golden aura, and Doña was bathed in a silver sheen.

The mare nibbled contentedly, but we remained concerned. I said to Geronimo, "Take good care of Doña, boy."

Nothing could have prepared us for what he did next. My equine friend, standing with his right shoulder next to Doña's left rear flank, picked up his left foreleg and pawed the air in a circular gesture that seemed to indicate mounting her—as if to say, "Yeah, man, I'll take care of her all right!" Then he turned his head toward us and arched his jaw in a lengthy horselaugh.

Mitch and I both fell into an uncontrollable, belly-splitting fit of laughter. Holding our sides in agony, we rolled in the grass, tears running down our cheeks. "Oh God, oh GodohGodohGod!"

"Ouch," I finally sputtered. "Damn. That didn't really happen, did it?"

Mitch caught his breath. "No one will ever believe us."

51.

Trail's End
July 1969

When I finally pulled my tired body out of bed the next morning, Mitch was already soaking in the pool. It didn't take me long to join him. What a luxury to have a hot springs just yards away from our bedside.

"Ahhhh," I said, slipping into the water. "I could get used to this."

"Yep, I'm still sore from yesterday."

If it hadn't been for the rock concert coming up soon and maybe some friends joining us, we most likely would have stayed there longer. It was July 25, our thirtieth day on the trail. And we were about to ride to Aspen, our final destination.

"It's only seven miles to the trailhead. From there it can't be more than another seven to my truck," I said. "It should be an easy ride."

"I wonder if the concert is still on," Mitch said. "Paul said he hadn't heard anything about it."

"Yeah, but he's been isolated, so he may not know. We'll find out soon enough. I wonder if any of our buddies made it. Or Susanna, the chick I told you about from KC." I sank deeper into the water until it reached my chin. "Man, don't you love this hot springs?"

"The best." Mitch wiggled his toes above the surface.

We soaked until our fingers were wrinkled, then climbed out and let the sun dry our naked bodies. Getting dressed, I noticed that my belt size had decreased by two notches in the past month—I had never been in such peak physical shape.

I looked over at Geronimo and Doña. They were more trim and muscular too. Their bellies used to hang a little, but now they were tight under their frames. We had all gained more than adventure from our travels.

After breakfast, we packed up and fetched the horses from their island paradise. Filled with lush grass, Doña seemed in top form. We mounted up for our last day of travel.

As we rode through thick groves of aspens, I thought about selling Geronimo. I had no alternative, but it would be gut-wrenching to say good-bye. It gave me some comfort that we had shared this wonderful time together and that Geronimo would likely spend the rest of his life in fairer pastures than those around Taos.

Before long, we approached a fast-flowing loop of Conundrum Creek and spotted hikers coming toward us on the other side. The trail took us to a fallen tree wide enough to cross on foot, but we continued ahead and turned the horses into the twenty-foot-wide stream. The dogs jumped in after us. Swimming vigorously, they got caught in the current and were whisked downstream.

The hikers shouted in alarm, waving their hands.

"Thanks, but they're fine," I called to them. "They're used to it."

We had navigated so many streams with Charlie and Shawn that we knew there was nothing to fear. Besides, we wouldn't have chosen a crossing near rapids. Sure enough, the dogs scrambled out thirty yards downstream, shook off the water, and made an energetic dash to rejoin us.

By early afternoon, we emerged from a succulent forest and found the trail intersecting an asphalt highway. "We have to take this road down a few miles to a church," I said, no longer needing a map. "And there we'll find the road to Maroon Bells."

We dismounted. It felt good to be on my feet. Despite all the riding we had done, my thighs still ached after a few hours in the saddle.

Because of the traffic, I kept Geronimo with me rather than letting him tag along behind. After a longer walk than I remembered, we came to the church and took the left fork to Maroon Bells. It was still another four or five miles to my truck.

About a half hour later, something caught my eye in the gravel next to the road—a shiny horseshoe—that age-old symbol of luck. I picked up the piece of cold, hard steel and pushed on, reflecting on our month-long adventure.

I had to marvel at our good fortune. For the six of us to have made it this far without suffering any serious injuries, especially with all the challenges thrown our way, was nothing short of a miracle. I clutched my newfound treasure, a perfect testament to our grand journey, now so close to completion.

It had been a long day, and my body had grown weary from the climb. Finally, at twilight, we descended into the dirt parking area where I had left my truck. There it sat, all by itself, just as I had parked it over a month ago. What a welcome sight—like reuniting with an old friend.

But as we approached, I noticed that the tailgate was down and the back door of the camper was slightly ajar. Someone had jimmied the padlock. I opened the door a few inches and caught a glimpse of my Mexican blanket torn up.

My heart plummeted.

I closed the door—I couldn't deal with distractions right now. I had horses, dogs, firewood, fire, camp, and food to tend to before the dwindling daylight disappeared. Placing the horseshoe on Evergreen's tailgate, I put the matter out of my mind.

Mitch came up beside me. "Everything okay?"

"Later."

We set up camp in an aspen grove next to my truck, below a string of campsites lining the road. When we sat down to eat, I looked across the fire at Mitch. "Well, partner, we did it."

"Can you believe it? He waved the smoke away from his face. "Enough to make a man proud."

My strength restored, I was ready to consider the condition of my truck. Hesse's book came to mind. "You know, *Journey to the East* is about a group of people who leave on a pilgrimage in search of consciousness. They take along a precious document that expresses their mission. At one point, it goes missing, and the entire group falls apart.

What I got from it was that matters of the heart are more important than material things. My home might have gotten messed up, but I won't let it ruin the beauty of what we've accomplished or the fun in store for us now that we've arrived. I told you I always read Hesse at the perfect time. This book was no exception."

I picked up my flashlight and wandered over to my truck. The horseshoe reflected in the beam. *Okay, lucky charm, help me out here.* Putting emotions aside, I opened the camper door and shined my light inside, again seeing the Mexican blanket I had tacked on the forward wall. Someone had tried to pull it off, but because I'd used so many carpet tacks to secure it, they managed to release only a corner of it, creating a ten-inch tear in the fabric.

Looking around, I saw that my Coleman stove and lantern were gone, along with a down vest, comforter, and three strings of beads I'd hung on the coat hook. When I pulled down the bed, I discovered a blanket had also been stolen.

I sat on the bed and took it all in.

The beads were all handmade gifts from different lady friends, and while I was sorry to have lost them, I could live without them. The missing stove and lantern only represented the inconvenience of having to replace them. And when I looked closely at the Mexican blanket, I realized I could tack it back up and the tear wouldn't show much. As for my thrift store down vest, I liked it but rarely wore it.

The only thing I would really miss was that cotton comforter. It wasn't fancy, just wonderfully soft and warm. I'd had it since I was a kid. You didn't find them like that anymore. Concluding it could have been far worse, I returned to camp relieved and refreshed. *Thanks, Mr. Hesse.*

The next morning, I went out to the truck and pushed open the driver's wind-wing window. Only I knew it didn't latch. Reaching through, I pulled on the inside handle, opened the door, and found my key under the dash, right where I always kept it.

I'd probably need a jump. After more than a month, it would be unusual if the battery still held a charge. I inserted the key, and to my surprise, Evergreen Carmen turned over, ever so slowly, over and over and over. And then she started up with a strong "Varooom! Varooom!"

"Thatta girl," I said, patting her on the steering wheel.

Mitch came running over. "It started right up!"

"Who dah thunk it? How about going to town for breakfast?"

"Perfect." He flashed a broad smile.

I left Evergreen idling to energize her battery while we made sure the horses were secure and the campfire was out. Then we grabbed a few things, loaded up the dogs, and headed into Aspen.

After a hearty breakfast of omelets, hash browns, toast, and coffee, Mitch wanted to check the post office for a letter. As we walked down the sidewalk, a police car crept by, the cop's eyes fixed on us.

"What's your problem?" I blurted out.

Shit. What the hell was I doing?

I prided myself on thinking before I spoke. The real me, the one with common sense, knew that provoking a cop was dangerous and stupid behavior. But after so many days fighting the elements and maintaining a dominant position with the horses, I had morphed into a no-nonsense shitkicker. Even though I was peace loving, if somebody confronted me right then, I was likely to deck them. This was strange for a guy who had lived twenty-three years with only one physical fight under his belt—a fight that consisted of a single punch from another fist.

Fortunately, the officer hadn't heard my remark.

At that moment I understood why cowboys would shoot up the town and raise hell after a long trail drive. And I also gained insight into Crazy Marvin's mentality. He was stuck in a reflex pattern that made him try to be Mr. Macho, even when he sensed he was stepping into trouble. It was amazing how easily reflexes could take over.

This couldn't lead to good things.

I made a pledge to exert control over these urges, but I could see it would take some work. For a month, Mitch and I needed a spirited attitude to complete our pursuit. Now I had to reverse my "fight or flight" programming and tame the beast—reclaim the pacifist within me, the guy who had stood up against the war. I could no longer remain at the mercy of my emotions. Besides, walking was damn uncomfortable with testicles the size of basketballs!

At the post office, Mitch ripped open yet another manuscript from his heartthrob. I had to wait until he read it twice before we walked to the market for supplies. We also purchased a bag of ice. Now that we had my ice chest (it hadn't been stolen), our limited menu could expand appreciably.

We returned to the truck and drove through the narrow streets of Aspen. Near the outskirts of town, we heard a shout and a loud "BANG" as the truck rocked violently. I looked to my left to see a smiling Russ clinging to my window frame, his boots planted on the running board.

"Hey, guys," he said in his familiar deep voice. "I was wondering how I was going to find you."

"All right!" I said, steering the truck to the curb. I got out and let Charlie mix with her friend Arlo. Shawn trotted over, and Arlo stiffened his posture as Shawn sniffed his acquaintance.

"When did you get here?" I asked.

"Three days ago. I've been staying up at Difficult Campground."

"Have you heard anything about the love-in?"

He shook his head. "It seems it's not happening. Nobody knows anything about it."

"Really? The flyer I saw had everyone on it—the Stones, the Beatles, Dylan, everyone. Maybe someone printed them so the bands would feel obligated to come. Good try! Oh well, Aspen is still a great place to be, right?"

"Yeah, I'm loving it." He turned away, and I followed his eyes across the street.

A tall, attractive brunette with long Joan Baez–style hair and sparkling, deep-brown eyes came sauntering across toward us. Russ put his arm around her waist and introduced us. "This is Kelly from New York. We met in the campground when I first got here, and we've been hanging out together ever since."

"Hop in the back," I said, "and we'll show you our camp."

Once back at Maroon Bells, we introduced them to the horses, now both of them tethered on fifty-foot ropes. It started to drizzle, so we climbed into my camper and swapped stories while I made cheese sandwiches. I opened the top of my Dutch door, giving us a gorgeous view of the woods.

Mitch offered Russ a bag of beef jerky. "Have you heard anything about your draft case? Someone in Crested Butte told us that Nixon had started pulling troops out of Nam."

Russ took out a piece and handed the package to Kelly "Haven't heard a damn thing. Maybe all our noise is finally getting to Tricky Dick." He tore off a large bite. "It'd be great if they all came home."

As the rain subsided, the forest lit up with an intense flash of light, then "BAM! BABOOM!" A powerful thunderbolt had struck nearby, shaking the camper. Mitch and I turned to each other and shouted, "The horses!"

I stuck my head out the open door and didn't see them in the meadow. They must have torn their ropes loose. Leaning out farther, I spotted them up on the highway, disappearing as soon as I caught a glimpse of them. Russ and Kelly looked worried.

"It's no big deal," I said to them. "Something like this happened all the time. We ran four miles before breakfast one morning chasing these horses down in New Mexico. Now we can use the truck." I dug in my pocket for the keys. "You two make yourselves comfortable here. This won't take long."

I walked around to the cab of the truck while Mitch grabbed the bridles and lead ropes and jumped in the other side. We caught up with Geronimo and Doña about two miles down the road. They were just ambling along, enjoying their freedom, the ropes dragging behind them. I parked ahead of them, and we had no trouble getting them under control. Mitch put a bridle on Doña, mounted up, and I handed him Geronimo's rope.

"See you soon," he said, starting up the road.

I reflected again on our temperaments as I drove back to camp. The ride from Taos had conditioned us to accept the unexpected with a cool nonchalance.

It would be almost impossible to return to an ordinary life.

52.

What Now?

July 1969

Crouched by the fire, Mitch prepared stick bread for breakfast, his face downcast. "It's going to be hard as hell saying good-bye to the horses. You've been close to Geronimo for a while now, but I didn't really bond with Doña until after she fell off that cliff."

"It's a bummer," I said. "But we knew we'd have to sell them."

"Doesn't make it any easier."

"No kidding. I was thinking of taking a bareback ride. Want to come along?"

"Let's do it. Some quality time with our mounts."

After putting bridles and saddle blankets on the horses, we rode through the woods, Mitch in the lead. Something on the ground caught my eye, so I turned Geronimo back. Lying there, folded and a little faded, was my childhood comforter.

Mitch called out, "What's up?"

"You know, after I checked out everything that had been stolen, I realized there was only one item I would really miss. And guess what? Here it is—my cozy cotton comforter. How cool is that? I guess the thieves dropped it."

"Out of sight!"

I hopped back on Geronimo and draped the comforter over his broad shoulders as we continued our ride.

Back at camp, I let him roam free. Around noon, I heard a commotion coming from the closest campsite. Several hippies at a picnic table were shouting and waving their arms wildly at Geronimo, who had invited himself to lunch, unaware it was rude to stick his monstrous nose in everyone's plate.

"Don't worry about him," I called out, walking over to retrieve my problem child. "He's just a big puppy dog."

Friendly folks, they had arrived late the night before in a big, rainbow-painted school bus. We got to talking, and they offered me wine from a gallon jug. We talked some more. When I mentioned I was feeling a buzz, they remembered to tell me we were drinking "electric Red Mountain wine."

The jug was laced with LSD, and I was a goner before I knew any better. Oh well. All I could do was flow with the river.

Whoosh . . . Buzzzz . . . Zing . . . Whirrrr

As I started peaking, I drifted off alone—well, not exactly alone—Charlie was always close by. We wandered downstream, where I looked for a decent skipping rock. This proved difficult because everything moved with a soft, rhythmic harmony.

Across the stream, the white trunks of an aspen grove had separated into legs, and they were performing a high-kicking can-can. *Wooooo!*

Relaxing my shoulders, I took in the show and chuckled out loud. "Shit, Charlie. I'm really fucked up here." I picked up a smooth, trapezoidal-shaped stone that fit exactly between the base of my thumb and my index finger, as though it were made to be there. I carried it for hours, before finally securing it in a pocket of my jeans. The roar of a dozen imaginary locomotives charged through my head.

The following day, Mitch and I planned to check out a rent-a-horse place near Aspen to inquire about selling our two charges. He was anxious to complete the task so he could head west to see his lady.

Before we left, I heard music coming from the woods behind me. It sounded like a harmonica . . . it *was* a harmonica. But wait. It wasn't playing just any old tune—it was playing "Hog Fence." I turned to see Albert, the mechanical wizard, walking among the aspens, blowing on his harp.

"Hey, you made it!" I said.

He gave me a sly smile. "I got up this morning and decided to sneak up on you and play 'Hog Fence' in your ear. I started driving, chose this canyon, and spotted Charlie by the road. You know the rest."

I laughed. "Too much! It looks like your psychic training paid off. Have a seat."

"I better move my truck before a ranger gives me grief." He went back up to the road.

After coming around to the parking area, Albert offered to drive us into Aspen, and we brought each other up to date on the way. The owner of the rental place, a man named Dusty, told us to bring the horses the next morning and he'd help us find buyers.

Then we left for Difficult Campground to see Russ and Kelly. We were one big, happy family, reunited in a mountain wonderland.

Riding Geronimo for the last time down to Dusty's, I reminisced with Mitch about our trip. "I'll never forget those bulls."

"Wasn't that nuts?"

Dusty told us to put our horses in a corral with a dozen rental horses and said he'd make some calls. While we were there, a horse got his foreleg tangled in its reins. A young hired hand freaked out, trying to control the beast. His actions agitated the horse, making him rear up and jump around.

I pulled the kid back by his shoulder and approached the horse, talking softly and stroking his chest. He responded to me, and when he settled down, I lifted his leg and removed the reins.

I turned to the kid. "You need to stay calm when working with horses. Otherwise you'll spook them, and it only makes things worse."

"Thanks." He shuffled his feet, embarrassed. "I'll remember that."

Albert drove us back to camp. "So what's next for you guys?" he asked.

No surprise what Mitch was going to do—Jasmine had set her

hooks deep. "As soon as we sell the horses and I get to my car," he said, "I'm going to drive straight through to Davis."

"Albert, the boy's a bit pussy-whipped. He's been missing his honey the whole ride something fierce."

Mitch laughed, taking the jab good-heartedly. Nothing could get him down now that he was this close to his long-anticipated reunion with Jasmine.

"What about you, Rich?" Albert asked.

"I'm not sure. I keep thinking of that old song 'How Ya Gonna Keep 'Em Down on the Farm (After They've Seen Paree)?' I can't imagine settling down to a normal life after this amazing adventure."

"Well, listen to this," Albert said. "I got a letter recently from Crazy Nina. She and Crazy Marvin moved up to Alaska, and he's building a cabin in the woods. Says it's on a lake they named Our Lake. Supposed to be nobody else around for miles."

"When did they go up there?"

"About mid-June. Marvin got busted at the border. They found some pot stashed in the motorcycle he had in the back of his truck."

"Shit! That sounds like something he'd do. What happened?"

"Not much. The border patrol put the fear of God in both of them. But in the end, all they did was confiscate his bike and charge him a fine."

"Boy, were they lucky."

"So you know what I was thinking?"

"What?"

"How about we mosey on up there, sneak up on Marvin, and play 'Hog Fence' in his ear? We could help him build his cabin."

"That would be so cool! Yes, let's do it. We'll blow his sick mind all to hell."

Albert laughed. We agreed that after the horses were sold, he'd follow us to Taos to pick up Mitch's station wagon. Then Albert and I would work our way back to California and on to Alaska.

Perfect!

· · ·

Now that the horses were boarded at Dusty's ranch, Mitch and I moved to Difficult Campground, where a small hippie community still gathered. It took four days for Dusty to find buyers, and by then, Mitch was beyond antsy to be with Jasmine. We received $125 each, making me even, but putting Mitch $25 in the hole.

Driving to say good-bye to the horses, Mitch and I fell silent, the mood solemn—you'd have thought someone had died. When I spotted Geronimo tied in the corral among a mass of saddled horses, a knot formed in my chest. I'd hoped the same person would have taken both of them. Knowing they would be separated made it even harder.

Please make their new owners kind.

I took my time with Geronimo, and Mitch did the same with Doña. "You're going to a new home, boy. At least you're in the land of sweet fresh grass. Thanks for taking me on the adventure of my life. I couldn't have had a better trail partner. I'll never forget you, buddy. If I'm back this way, I'll look you up. You're named after a warrior, so walk proud. I love you, man." I shuffled away with heavy feet and a heavier heart.

"That sucked," I said to Mitch.

"Of all the challenges we faced on our trip, that one was the hardest."

"I agree. At least they're in greener pastures."

We stopped at the youth hostel where Albert stayed to let him know we'd be leaving first thing in the morning. Back at the campgrounds, I wandered around, trying to get my mind off Susanna, who never showed up, and my buddy Geronimo.

Sitting alone at a picnic table playing a guitar, a young woman looked up as I passed and invited me to join her. Petite, but well-proportioned, Karen had a cute, cherub nose, curly brown hair, and an infectious smile. It was a good day to have a friend.

"I just got this guitar," she told me, "and I know only one line from a song but not all the words." She also knew only one chord. Over and over and over and over, she strummed the same chord and sang the same line.

Blackbird singing da da dum da dum
STRUM
Dum da dumda dum da dum dum dum
STRUM
All your life.
STRUM
Blackbird singing da da dum da dum
STRUM
Dum da dumda dum da dum dum dum
STRUM
All your life.
STRUM

Now I don't have anything against the Beatles. Quite the contrary. And she was a sweet girl. But she was driving me crazy with that one-line, lyric-deficient song—though I didn't have the heart to tell her. Who was I to curb her artistic enthusiasm? So I endured this torture for much of the afternoon.

My patience was rewarded when she invited me to her pup tent that night. It had been way too long since I'd gotten laid, so I felt like a kid in a candy store with a whole dollar to spend. I crawled into her snug lodgings, where things started out slow, then escalated to hot and heavy—that is, until she whispered, "I have a yeast infection, so I can't go all the way."

What?

I didn't know if she was being honest or it was a creative way to stop the music short of the finale. I didn't contest it. Being a gentleman sucked. We had fun anyway, though I had to wonder about my luck getting to home plate with the ladies.

We were finishing breakfast when Albert drove up. He wasn't alone. Sitting beside him was a stunning black woman named Serena—tall and slim, with a well-sculpted face and gorgeous skin the color of creamed coffee. I found myself staring, I have to admit. And she had a disposition true to her name. Albert told us he was giving Serena a ride to a Taos commune.

Karen and I stepped off into the woods to say good-bye. Her loving eyes stared up into mine. "Next month, there's going to be a huge love-in in Woodstock, New York," she said. "Why don't you meet me there?"

"I'd like that, but I already have plans to head for Alaska. Any other time, I would have taken you up on it."

She pouted. "Darn, I'm going to miss you."

"Me too. But the time we had has been real groovy." I brought my hands up under her shirt and squeezed the sides of her soft breasts. We shared a long, tender kiss. I liked this lady, but to be truthful, I wouldn't miss that darn "Blackbird" song.

We left for New Mexico, Albert and Serena taking the lead and Mitch riding with me. Charlie sat between us, and Shawn curled up on the floor. The farther south we traveled, the deeper blue the sky became, a transformation that never ceased to amaze me.

Stopping only for lunch and gas, we arrived in Taos just before dark. Not far from the highway, we dropped Serena off at the commune and proceeded to Thomas's saddle shop, now closed for the day. Mitch's station wagon was waiting for us, but unlike my truck, it needed a jump. Albert obliged. Following a café dinner, we camped where our journey began, near the Rio Grande Gorge.

As soon as it opened, we went by Taos County Tack and Saddle. Thomas jumped off his stool when he saw us enter the shop. "Hey, I was thinking about you guys yesterday. How'd it go?"

I grabbed his outstretched hand. "Sensational."

"Did you fellows make it all the way to Aspen?"

"We did. Had to get a lift from Tiny up to Del Norte, though. New Mexico nearly cooked us alive."

We went on for a good half hour, filling Thomas in on our wild adventure. As the minutes passed, Mitch started fidgeting with his keys, impatient to leave.

In the parking lot, he fired up his car and put it into gear. "I'm outta here. See you guys in Davis," he shouted, waving a hand out his window.

As he zoomed off, I joked, "Give her a squeeze for me."

"Give her a poke for me," Albert added. "That guy's whipped bad."

"That's for sure. He's been roped and tied."

As for me, I was free, no strings attached to anyone. Yeah, the dry spells could be painful and lonely. But hell, life was too damn sweet to let that get me down. Besides, after riding a horse for a month, I was more than ready to take on the world.

Charlie leaned up against my leg, her big brown eyes begging for attention. As I stroked her soft fur, I couldn't stop thinking about my next adventure. Johnny Horton's song "North to Alaska" kept playing in my head.

"What do you think, Charlie? Alaska. How cool will that be?"

The journey continues . . .

Did Rich and Albert make it to Alaska?
Did the government send Rich to prison?
Did he end up with Gina or Jasmine's sister, Rosehips?

Find out the answers to these questions
and more in Rich's new book:

TRIPPIN'
ROADS, RAILS & MOUNTAIN TRAILS

Packed with fun, romance, and adventure,
featuring Rich, Charlie, and their wacky friends

www.richisraelauthor.com

Coming fall 2017

Acknowledgments

My love and gratitude to my dear wife, Doris, for her years of patience and support while I focused on my book, and to my daughter, Danielle, who inspired me to record this history.

A very special thanks to my brilliant editor and publisher, Sandra Jonas, whose expertise, creative talent, and endless hours of dedicated persistence helped move this project toward completion.

Also, many thanks to my preliminary editor, Rivvy Neshama, for her keen eye and valuable help.

My sincere thanks to my longtime friend Bruce Brewer for providing the photo for the front cover, one of the few existing visual records of my journey through the '60s, as well as for feedback and support.

And my heartfelt appreciation to all those who offered encouragement and information: Linda Banks, Andrew Bunin, Daniel De Kay, Michael Gardner, Tom Havstad, Mary Hendrick, Peter Hentchel, Kim Kraul, Robin Lowry, Vicki Meadows, Angela Mergentime, Eileen Mergentime, Ken Mergentime, Jennie Nourse, Eric Reinemer, Michael Shurtz, Sally Vanmanen, Dana Wallack, Susan Wallack, Todd Wallack, and to all the wonderful friends and lovers (including some listed above) who shared these memorable adventures with me.

And my apologies to Crazy Marvin (not his real name) for telling his secret after keeping it to myself for nearly fifty years. I love you, buddy.

About the Author

Rich Israel was born in December 1945. The baby boomer generation officially began January 1, 1946, so Rich says, "I was sent ahead as a scout to prepare the way."

Raised in a middle-class Jewish household in Sacramento, he spent his college years at the University of California, Davis, campus, where he initially studied engineering, then transferred to biological sciences because of his love for nature. After graduation, he worked for the entomology department at the university for a year before dropping out and embarking on many of the adventures described in his writings.

In the early 1970s, Rich coauthored what appears to be the first back-to-the-land book for his generation—a self-published guide titled *Homesteader's Handbook*. He went on to study natural medicine and worked in the natural foods industry for a dozen years. In 1991, he authored *The Natural Pharmacy Product Guide*, which remained on the Nutri-Books "Top Ten List" of health books for four months.

Rich is currently working on *Trippin'*, the second book in his Hippie Adventurer Series. He lives with his wife, Doris, in Boulder, Colorado. For more information, visit his website: www.richisraelauthor.com.

Made in the USA
Charleston, SC
13 January 2017